CONTENTS

The Network Society

Social Aspects of New Media

Jan van Dijk

Translated by
Leontine Spoorenberg

SAGE Publications
London

First published 1991, *De Netwerkmaatschappij* © Bohn Staflen
Van Loghum, Houten, The Netherlands

SAGE Publications Ltd
6 Bonhill Street
London EC2A 4PU

SAGE Publications Inc
2455 Teller Road
Thousand Oaks, California 91320

SAGE Publications India Pvt Ltd
32, M-Block Market
Greater Kailash – I
New Delhi 110 048

British Library Cataloguing in Publication data

A catalogue record for this book is available
from the British Library

ISBN 0 7619 6281 6
ISBN 0 7619 6282 4 (pbk)

Library of Congress catalog card number available

Typeset by Mayhew Typesetting, Rhayader, Powys
Printed in Great Britain by The Cromwell Press Ltd,
Trowbridge, Wiltshire

INTRODUCTION

1

**New Roads of
Communication**

New roads are being built at tremendous speed and yet we hardly notice. After all, the countryside is not being cleared by bulldozers and covered with rails, canals or asphalt. These roads are for communication. Apparently they are part of an abstract, barely visible reality. We might see them as yet another cable running into our homes. We do not realize that they are making us dependent on yet another technology in our private lives and our workplaces. Soon, we will be tied not only to roads, electricity cables, water pipes, gas lines, sewers, post-boxes, telephone wires and cable television, but also to new communication networks. At present they still make use of existing telephone wires and television cables (such as **electronic mail**[1] and the **Internet**), but in the future they will make new connections: so-called information highways.

In large companies and organizations, automation through detached hardware is followed swiftly by computerization of the entire organization by connecting all this hardware in networks. In our homes, construction of these new communication roads does not happen so quickly. Yet, existing means of communication have undergone a major change in a short time. **Teletext** and cable TV information services have become sources of information for most families. Cable and satellite broadcasting have caused an explosive increase in the provision of television and radio programmes. Our telephones are equipped with all sorts of new gadgets that offer more opportunities to get in touch with other people. Furthermore, telephones, computers, televisions, VCRs and audio equipment are being increasingly integrated in new machines. Within 20 years home networks linking all kinds of household utilities will have appeared. In the meantime our homes are being connected to new networks from outside, like the Internet.

One cannot read a magazine about computers, telephones and audio-visual equipment without encountering the words 'network', 'new media' or 'multimedia' on almost every page. The shift in terminology is striking. In the 1980s, people talked about automation. Computerization and information technology (IT) largely replaced this term. Now the buzzwords have become information and communication technology (ICT) and multimedia.

1 Words in bold type in the text are explained in the Glossary, pp. 244–51.

The Age of Networks   With little exaggeration, we may call the twenty-first century the age of networks. Networks will be the nervous system of our future society, and we can expect this infrastructure to have more influence on our entire social and personal lives than did the construction of roads for the transportation of goods and people in the past. 'Information highway' thus is an appropriate term. We did not foresee what the consequences would be of choosing predominantly small-scale private transportation rather than large-scale public transport. But now we are only too well aware of the consequences of our decision. Traffic congestion and environmental degradation are all too evident. The potential consequences of choosing a certain kind of communication infrastructure and embedding this infrastructure in our social and personal lives may be less visible, but it will be much more severe. Continuing this line of argument, at stake here is not only the ecology of nature – that is, transportation of information and communication will partly replace transportation of goods and people – but also 'social ecology'. Hence, some people are talking about the 'pollution' of our social environment by the new media penetrating our private lives. According to them, the new media are reducing, diminishing and even destroying the quality of face-to-face communications and are making relationships at work more formal (Kubicek, 1988).

Values at Stake   This book demonstrates how the most fundamental values of our society are at issue when it comes to the development of new information and communication technologies, in which networks are already setting the tone.

Social equality is at stake, since certain categories of people participate more than others in the information society. Some profit from its advantages, while others are deprived. Technology allows for a better distribution of knowledge. Its complexity and costs, however, may serve to intensify existing social inequalities, or even create large groups of 'misfits' – people who do not fit in with the information society.

The fact that the new media enable well-informed citizens, employees and consumers to have more direct communication with and participation in institutions of decision-making should, in principle, strengthen *democracy*. On the other hand, because the technology is susceptible to control from above, democracy could be threatened. Some would argue that *freedom*, for example the freedom of choice for consumers, will increase because of the interactivity offered by this technology. Others paint a more pessimistic picture, and predict that freedom will be endangered by a decrease in privacy for the individual as a registered citizen, a 'transparent' employee and a consumer screened for every personal characteristic, and by the growing opportunities for central control.

For certain groups of people (disabled, sick and elderly people) as well as for society as a whole, *safety* can be improved by all kinds of registration and alarm systems. At the same time, safety seems to decrease because we have become dependent on yet another type of technology. And a very vulnerable technology at that.

The *quantity and quality of social relationships* might improve if communication technology enables us to get in touch easily with almost everybody, even over long distances. On the other hand, they might decrease because the possibility of chance contact (typical of traditional public environments) will slowly disappear, or because new media communication will become a substitute for face-to-face communication, causing the quality of communication to be diminished in certain respects.

The *richness of the human mind* may increase owing to the diversity of impressions we gather through these new media. On the other hand, it may also be reduced because these impressions are offered out of context in schematic, (pre-)programmed and fragmented frames. And because it is available in huge amounts, information can never be fully processed by the recipient.

Social Choices   All the issues mentioned, and many others, present us with choices. These choices will be made at different levels of generality with respect to the size of the social groups involved and the conditions that limit choices. For example, someone may have trouble believing that his or her grandparents made a deliberate choice for a system of private transportation and against a system of public transport. Yet definite economic and political forces and consumer groups did do so. The expansion of transportation in the nineteenth century commenced with an explosive growth of public transport. Then the switch to automobiles took place.

In designing and introducing information and communication networks, decisions have to be made at the same higher level: for public or for private networks, for large-scale or for small-scale networks (which could be linked), for more intelligence in network nodes and centres or in terminal devices, for centralized or decentralized networks, or even for or against networks as such. After all, in the 1990s, decentralized equipment, for instance all kinds of CD players, has competed with on-line connections in many applications.

Technology   At a lower level of generality and on a smaller social scale, the options
Assessment   will increase even more, though they remain within the limiting conditions of the general choices made. Usually discussions about options only start here. This is also where we find most examples of so-called technology assessment (TA)*.[2] The key question in TA is: *can technology be developed in socially sensitive ways?* The contents of this book are the result of some sort of TA. However, they deal not only with the consequences but also with the causes of the rise of the technology concerned. Furthermore, only general aspects of society are considered, such as the values mentioned earlier. Ordinary TA takes place only within the narrow boundaries of technologies that are already largely developed and are to be made profitable and socially accepted as soon as possible. Contrary to appearances, there is still little discussion in society about general options like those mentioned earlier.

The Start of a   In the first Dutch edition of this book (van Dijk, 1991), the author
Public Debate   championed a wide public debate about the outcome of ICT. This call has been partly heeded. Between 1994 and 1996, a huge boost was given to discussion of the possibilities of the Internet and the perspective of the

2 An asterisk indicates that the explanation of the term follows in the text itself.

electronic highway, a term introduced in the United States in 1993 as 'information superhighway'. In those years, much hype about the Internet was created. Hype is the exaggerated recommendation of a product that has yet to show its real value. However, the debate may be considered disappointing for the following three reasons.

Limitations   First, hype goes hand in hand with huge exaggeration and excessive speculation, even about short-term effects. Some people claimed that, before long, everyone would be on the Internet and that it would turn organizations, the market and even whole countries and democracies upside down. Talk was full of vague new terms like **cyberspace**, of which no one has given a clear definition.

Second, the discussion is mainly driven by the fear of falling behind in economic and technological competition between countries and companies. North America, Europe and Asia are fighting to gain control of the (future) market and employment in ICT. Companies and governments are afraid they will miss the boat if they do not buy new media and get on the Internet soon. This has resulted in excessive attention to short-term technical, economic and juridical aspects. Social, cultural and political aspects and long-term perspectives have been given less attention or have been merely the subject of speculation.

Third, this discussion, too broad (speculative) on the one hand and too narrow (economic and legal) on the other, does not pay enough attention to the fundamental causes and effects of the development of this technology. For example, everyone thinks it is normal that corporations build the new ICT infrastructure of our society and control the major part of the traffic and content of the future electronic highways. In the 1960s and 1970s, people would have made different choices. The choices that are made now determine what society will look like in the twenty-first century. Most probably they will result in public, cultural and educational services that are dominated by private economic interests (Brown, 1997). Another example is the absence of a discussion about the ethics of ICT. In contrast, such a discussion has been held about biotechnology, perhaps because the issues seem to be more concrete and tangible than the abstract and immaterial issues related to ICT. The quality of **information** and **communication**, and the privacy or autonomy of individuals, are still things that are hard to grasp for most people. Moreover, the most basic question has not been answered at all: that is, does ICT really improve the quality of our existence? The fact remains that there is a growing demand for this technology. This fact has to be explained in its historical context, and this will be attempted in the next section.

A SECOND COMMUNICATIONS REVOLUTION?

Growing Demand   Demand for mediated communication is growing. Even though 90 per cent
of Media   of Western households and almost every Western company have telephones,

demand for telephone lines still grows each year. Demand for mobile telephony is rocketing. The increase in demand for **data communication** is similarly explosive. In mass communications, however, supply appears to be greater than demand. The multiplication of broadcast channels with smaller audiences is a good example.

The increase in supply of and demand for mediated communications in general is accompanied by a huge expansion in the number of channels for transmission and in equipment for transmission and reception. This growth is based on new microelectronics, transmission techniques, transmission equipment and carriers of data. Figure 1.1 gives an outline of the historical development.

Media History

Even this extensive outline is not complete. For example, we have not been able to position a medium like teletext. Devices that do not use transmission (e.g. CD players and VCRs) are not included. The outline shows how telecommunications, data communications and mass communications have developed side by side in the past. However, it does not show how they have started to integrate in the present (we will return to this later). Another point of critique of this outline is that it suggests an evolutionary development. In reality, development has been more like two concentrations of innovations, of which the first can be placed roughly in the last decades of the nineteenth century and the early decades of the twentieth century, and the second is to be observed in the last decade(s) of the twentieth century and the first decades of the twenty-first century. James Beniger was the first to describe and analyse the first concentration and its background in his book *The Control Revolution* (1986); Frederick

Communications Revolution

Williams first identified the second concentration in his book *The Communications Revolution* (1982). We dare to speak here of the *first and second communications revolutions of the modern age*. 'Revolution' is a big word, all too readily referred to in the history of industry and technology, whether it is appropriate or not. Every so-called revolution in fact took decades to complete. For the major technological developments are seldom revolutionary; the technological process is usually much more evolutionary. Innovations are preceded by a long process of preparation. It would be misleading to suggest that new technologies arise suddenly. Rather they are a combination of techniques developed earlier. It would be wise to ask ourselves what exactly is new about the **new media** and why the term 'revolution' can be used here. In the same way we should keep questioning fashionable terms such as the 'information society' and the 'network society'. If there was merely a considerable quantitative acceleration of the arrival of innovations in the two concentrations mentioned before, we would not dare mention the word 'revolution'. *Structural changes* or *qualitative technical improvements* in mediated communications must take place in order for something to be called a revolution in communications.

Structural Communications Revolution

In the history of media, several communications revolutions have taken place. These can be divided into structural and technical communications revolutions*. In *structural* revolutions, fundamental changes take place in the coordinates of space and time. Media can be a form of communication

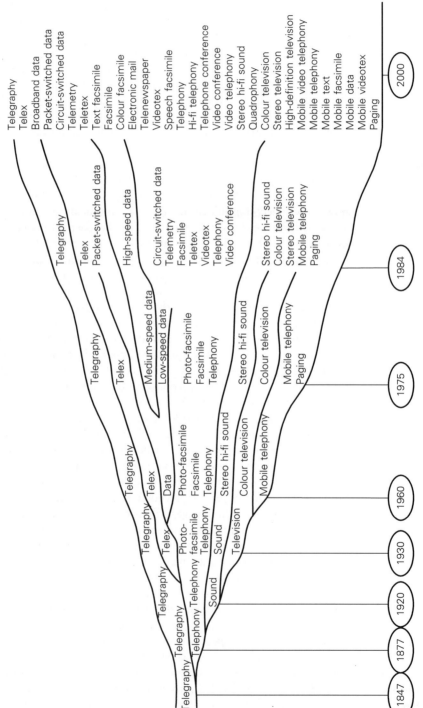

FIGURE 1.1 Innovations in transmission of tele-, data and mass communications
Source: Consortium of British Teleconsult, Detecon etc., with European Commission

fixed in space (in one place) or they may allow communications between different places. Furthermore, they can fix the moment of communication to a certain time or enable us to bridge time.

The switch from communication fixed in space and time to communication bridging space and time marks the two first communications revolutions in the (pre)history of man: sending smoke, drum and fire signals over long distances, and sending messengers in order to bridge places. Time was transcended by making illustrations on pottery and inside caves – signs which passed to future generations.

The next and presumably most important structural communications revolution was the development of writing, which enabled humans to overcome both space and time. The most recent communications revolution – the subject of this book – is primarily a structural revolution. It signals an end to the distinction between media that are fixed in space and time and media that bridge these dimensions. The new media, after all, can be used for both purposes. Even though the purpose of bridging time and space is predominant, the new media can also be used in off-line environments, for example in consulting a CD-ROM. The new media are a combination of on-line and off-line media (see Appendix 1). They are a combination of transmission links and artificial memories (filled with text, data, images and/or sounds) which can also be installed in separate devices. Therefore, the new media require a step outside the scheme of revolutions that bridge space and time which have described media history until now (see Figure 1.2). The combination of on-line and off-line applications of the new media, used both in traditional social environments fixed to a particular time and space and in on-line media environments bridging these dimensions, produces the structurally new characteristics of these media. In this book it will be demonstrated that this combination helps to realize perhaps the most promising social perspective of the new media, which is not a replacement of local face-to-face communication by on-line mediated communication but a potential fruitful interplay between them.

Technical Communications Revolution In a *technical* communications revolution, a fundamental change takes place in the structure of connections, artificial memories and/or the reproduction of their contents. The development of the printing press was a revolution in the reproduction of writing. In the second half of the nineteenth century a second revolution took place. It was mainly a technical revolution, based on the invention and construction of long-distance connections by cable and air, the introduction of new **analogue** artificial memories (photograph, film, gramophone record and audio recording tape) and new techniques for reproduction (the rotary press in particular). Qualitatively new was the development of media for a direct transfer of sound/speech, text/data and images by separate channels and over long distances. The *invention* of the telegraph and telephone date from a long time before the turn of the nineteenth to the twentieth century, and **telex**, radio and television from the years immediately after. Their *innovation**, meaning introduction in usable form, took place between 1890 and 1925. *Large-scale introduction* needed another 50 years. The most recent technical

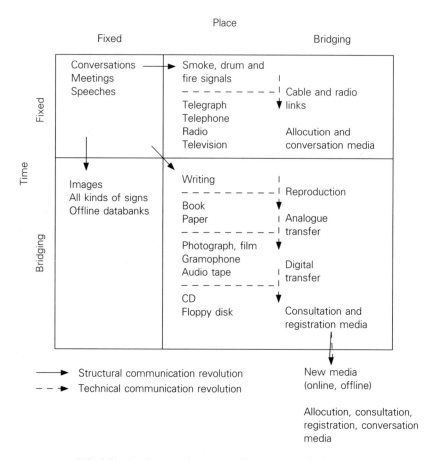

FIGURE 1.2   Communication revolutions in media history

communications revolution is characterized by the introduction of **digital** artificial memories, and digital transmission and reproduction. The term 'digital revolution' is appropriate in this context.

Developments in the current communications revolution follow the same pattern. The inventions took place during the past 50 years (the most important of these inventions are shown in the last two columns of Figure 1.1). We have now entered the phase of innovations through the introduction of networks, terminal equipment, programs and services. After the year 2000 these will be introduced on a large scale, a process that will probably continue until about 2040.

Current Communications Revolution   Now we are able to answer the key question: how has quality improved in the current structural and technical communications revolution? It is not because the crucial coordinates of space and time have been reduced to insignificant proportions, or because it is possible to communicate with everyone all over the world within seconds if you have access to the means to do so. In other words, it is not the fact that 'the world is turning into a village', to use a popular phrase. This would simply mean an evolutionary development along the axes of space and time, which had already taken place with the communications revolution of the nineteenth century. It would 'merely' be an acceleration of this evolution. No, the essence of the current revolution can be summarized in the terms **integration** and **interactivity**.

Integration   The most important structural change is *the **integration** of telecommunications, data communications and mass communications in a single medium*. It is the process of *convergence*. For this reason, new media are often called multimedia. Integration can take place at one of the following levels:

1   infrastructure – for example combining the different transmission links and equipment for telephone and computer (data) communications;
2   transportation – for example teletext and **Web TV** riding on cable and satellite television;
3   management – for example a cable company that exploits telephone lines and a telephone company that exploits cable television;
4   services – for example the combination of information and communication services on the Internet;
5   types of data – putting together sounds, data, text and images.

This integration leads to a gradual merging of telecommunications, data communications and mass communications; the separate meanings of these terms will probably even disappear. We are already looking for alternatives. A first invention was the word 'telematics'. Telecommunication and data communication have largely integrated. **ISDN** is one of the most important technical developments to accomplish this integration. In the meantime, through all kinds of **hybrid** constructions, developers work on the integration of mass communications, for example in two-way cable connections for television and other services, in **videotex** using both a TV set and a telephone, and in **broadband** 'local area **networks**'. This integration might be completed by large-scale, broadband networks in the beginning of the twenty-first century. Figure 1.3 shows the process of integration (Chapter 2 and the glossary in Appendix 2 offer more information on terminology). This process is enabled by two revolutionary techniques:

1   complete **digitalization** of transmittable information in equipment that works on micro-electronics;
2   *broadband transmission* through *fibre-optic cables*, satellites with **microwave** *transmission* and new optical techniques, including lasers.

While the first technique enables a complete integration of telecommunications and data communications, the second is more relevant for the integration of mass communications in the process of convergence.

Interactivity   The second structural change produced by the current communications revolution is the breakthrough of *mediated interactive communication*.

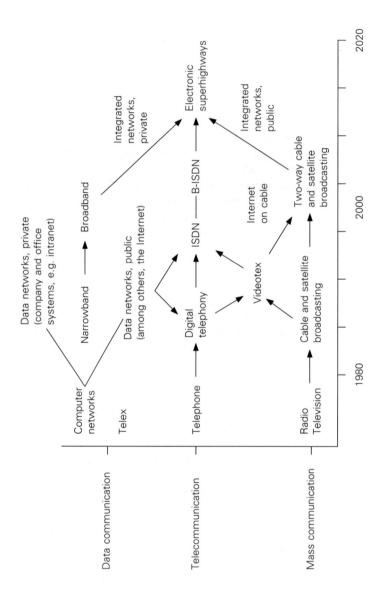

FIGURE 1.3 The integration of transmission in communications

Another term often used instead of 'new media' is 'interactive media'. The media of the first communications revolution of the modern age were suited to one-sided communication (the modern press, audio, radio, television) or to two-sided communication which was of poor quality in terms of technical and communicative capabilities (telegraph and telephone). The new media give rise to a fundamental *shift to technically advanced forms of two-sided and even multilateral communication, itself potentially multiform and rich in content because of the integration of sound, text, numbers and images.* As mentioned, an alternative for the term 'new media' could be 'interactive media', but the word 'interactive' is often used in a superficial or even an incorrect sense. This book distinguishes between different *levels of interactivity**. They apply to interactivity between human beings, between human beings and media or machines, between human beings by means of media, and even between media or between machines (technical interactivity). They indicate the quality of interactivity.

The first and most elementary level is the possibility of establishing *two-sided* or *multilateral* communication. This is the space dimension. People who interact need to be connected in one way or another, in proximate space or by transmission link, in order to be able to act and react (reactivity). The system of electronic mail is a good example of a new medium as it enables connections from different places.

The second level of interactivity is the degree of *synchronicity*. This, of course, is the dimension of time. An uninterrupted sequence of action and reaction usually improves the quality of the interaction. This is the case when working with a fast computer. Some interactive media, like electronic mail and other messaging systems based on the principle of the answering machine, are used mainly for their lack of synchronicity. They are available at any time and place and the user is given time to think about a reaction. However, they lack the possibilities of reacting immediately, and of sending different signals simultaneously, which are characteristic of face-to-face human communication.

The third level is *the extent of control* exercised by the interactors. The extent of control is determined by the ability of the sender and the recipient to switch at any given moment. Furthermore, it is about control over the contents of the interaction. This third level is achieved in a telephone conversation. However, complete control from both sides still leaves a lot to be desired in this medium (Chapter 8).

In mentioning the word 'contents' we have introduced the fourth and highest level of interactivity: actions and reactions with an *understanding of context and meaning*. This level of interaction has not been reached in the interaction between human beings and machines or media. And according to the analysis in Chapter 8 it will remain this way for a long time to come. This level of interactivity is reserved for the interaction between human beings and animals with consciousness.

These four levels are cumulative (see Figure 1.4). The highest level of interactivity is not possible without two-way communication and without control over this communication by the interactors concerned.

Level of interactivity	Space (multiway)	Time (synchronicity)	Control (of interaction)	Content (understanding)
1	X			
2	X	X		
3	X	X	X	
4	X	X	X	X

FIGURE 1.4 Levels of interactivity

Information Traffic Patterns

As stated, the first level of interactivity is two-sided or multilateral communication. Bordewijk and Van Kaam (1982) had this concept in mind when they designed their typology of the four *information traffic patterns* of allocution, consultation, registration and conversation. They have proved very useful in social and communication science, as will be shown in this book. They illuminate the structures of communication and the aspects of power these structures contain.

Allocution

In the twentieth century, the pattern of *allocution* has gained most importance in communication media. Radio, television and other mediated performances have come to the fore in this century of scale extension and massification. They perform important coordinating functions in society, because they are based on a pattern of allocution*: *the simultaneous distribution of information to an audience of local units by a centre which serves as the source of, and decision agency for, the information (in respect of its subject matter, time and speed)* (Figure 1.5a). The new media do not enhance this pattern. The only exceptions are where 'old' broadcasting media offer more opportunities of choice for viewers and listeners, such as by means of **pay-per-view** and home-video programming with feedback channels at freely chosen times. Here, within the limits and menus offered, the local unit is able to co-decide about the information to be received – the subject, the time the information is consumed, and the agenda of future broadcasting – by reactions to current programmes and by answers to questions posed. However, these innovations do more to damage the pattern of allocution than to enhance it. Therefore this pattern transforms into the next one in the new media environment.

Consultation

The pattern of *consultation* is enhanced by the new media. Consultation* is *the selection of information by (primarily) local units, which decide upon the subject matter, time and speed, at a centre which remains its source* (Figure 1.5b). Old consultative media are books, newspapers, magazines, audio and video. New consultative media are teletext, videotex (including databases), **audiotex** (e.g. free and pay telephone numbers), cable TV information services and interactive TV. Because they add new routes, these media are to be viewed as a basic improvement to the pattern of consultation. Often they are on-line connections enabling more consultation at the centre than the old media. Moreover, they are working at the expense of allocutive media, like audio and video equipment did with radio and television in the past.

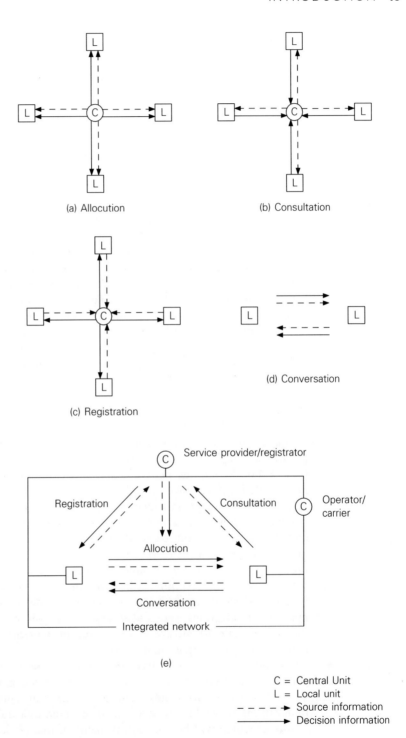

FIGURE 1.5 **The integration of information traffic patterns in networks**

Registration   The opportunities for *registration* also grow in the new media. Registration* is the *collection of information by a centre which determines the
subject matter, time and speed of information sent by a number of local
units, who are the sources of the information and sometimes take the
initiative for this collection themselves (to realize a transaction or reservation)* (Figure 1.5c). In old media and data collection instruments, often
the centre not only decides but also takes the initiative and requests the
transfer of information. Examples of these media and instruments are
enquiries, elections, examinations, archives and visual observation by
cameras. To a large extent, these activities were already performed by old
media. The new media offer even more opportunities. And the number
of them grows with the diffusion of the new media: this certainly goes
for cable enquiries and cable referenda. The new media, however, also
offer more chances of registration by the centre at the initiative of the
local units, for example in electronic reservations, teleshopping and telebanking. A more serious problem arises when the reverse is the case –
when the registration initiative is taken by the centre, without the agreement of the local units. This might be the case with telemetry, electronic
surveillance from a distance (such as electronic house arrest) or the
observation of personal data without the individual concerned knowing or
wanting it.

Conversation   The most fundamental change takes place in the pattern of *conversation*.
Conversation* is an *exchange of information by two or more local units,
addressing a shared medium instead of a centre and determining the
subject matter, time and speed of information and communication themselves* (Figure 1.5d). The existing channels for conversation not only are
enlarged, but can also contain more kinds of data. The old media (telegraph and telephone) only offered room for speech and a limited amount
of data. Local computer networks and data communication over telephone
lines caused an explosive growth in the capabilities for transporting data
and text. The new media added a substantial new quality: the possibility to
combine speech, data and text *in one message*. Then pictures could be
added, and now we can even add moving images to these messages. This
qualitative enlargement of the range of options for conversation requires
broadband facilities, which until recently were available only in public
networks of mass communications. From the 1990s onwards integrated
broadband networks for telecommunications, data communications and
mass communications were added, first at the level of the organization and
the larger scale of advanced or intelligent networks for research and
defence institutions (see Figure 1.3).

Integration of   The birth of integrated networks implies a combination of allocution,
Patterns   consultation, registration and conversation in a single medium (Figure
1.5e). This would make such a medium important enough in social communications to enable us to speak of a communications revolution, the
results of which will be the central theme of this book.

    The evolution of the four information traffic patterns involves a clear shift
of patterns towards local units. The new media cause a shift from allocution

towards consultation, registration and conversation. (Refer to the list of new media in Appendix 1, pp. 242–3.) The initiative and selection by local units and the interactivity between these local units and the centre and between these local units themselves, have increased the opportunities in communications. But this does not mean that these opportunities will be taken up. That depends on the content and the context of the communication taking place. Opportunities for users can be enlarged by the combination of speech, text, data and images and by a firmer grip on the dimensions of space and time. On the other hand, they can be limited by new media management and supply. One-sided supply, limited access and increased possibilities for central control, manipulation and registration threatening privacy may just as easily result. One certainty is that these opportunities, and what is actually done with them, will cause a revolution in mediated communications, and perhaps even in all communications in our society. *For the first time in history, the new media will enable us to make a deliberate choice between mediated and face-to-face communication in a large number of social activities.* The implications of this choice will form a prime focus of this book.

COMMUNICATION CAPACITIES OF THE NEW MEDIA

Aproaches to Mediated Communication

In the last 25 years a lot of research has been done on the opportunities and limitations of mediated communication as compared with face-to-face communication. In social-psychological experiments among small groups using different media, the modes of communication and the accomplishment of tasks have been investigated systematically. Two approaches are prevalent. The first takes the *objective* characteristics of media and channels as a point of departure. The second emphasizes the *(inter)subjective* characteristics of the use of them, mainly as a reaction to the first approach. In this book an *integrated* (objective and subjective) approach is taken to develop the concept of communication capacities. This concept is developed to answer the question of what can be done with the new media. What are their special characteristics compared with the old media? The general properties of integration and interactivity have been described in the previous section. Nine so-called communication capacities of the new media will now be introduced. First, the origin of the concept of communications capacities has to be briefly explained.

Objective Characteristics First

The oldest social-psychological approach in this area mainly stresses the limitations of all media and channels as compared with face-to-face communication. Short et al. (1976) introduced the influential concept of *social presence*. It emphasizes the sociability, warmth, personal information and sensitivity of face-to-face communication which media are only able to transmit in a limited way. By means of these characteristics, presumed to be objective, all media and face-to-face communications produce a different experience of presence among communication partners. For example, the videophone offers more social presence than the audiophone.

An almost identical approach is the one that refers to the so-called *reduced social context cues* of the media of telecommunications and network computing (Kiesler et al., 1984; Sproull and Kiesler, 1986, 1991; Kiesler and Sproull, 1992). According to the psychologists concerned, media more or less lack the space for crucial non-verbal and contextual signs. In the somewhat further elaborated concept of *information richness*, Daft and Lengel (1984) have distinguished the following four objective characteristics of media: feedback capacity (immediate, fast, slow), channel used (audio, visual), nature of the source (personal, impersonal) and language richness (spoken, written and/or body language).

In the second half of the 1980s this kind of classical social-psychological research was increasingly criticized. A large number of phenomena could not be explained using its objective approach. It appeared that media which are lacking in social presence and information richness, e.g. electronic mail and videotex, are frequently used for social-emotional and even erotic communications. The same phenomenon arose with phone sex and phone helplines. After a period of habituation, the quantity of informal and intimate communications in computer networks increases (Rice and Love, 1987; Walther, 1992). Eventually there arises a (sub)culture of electronic communication with new norms, language and behaviour.

(Inter)subjective Characteristics In reaction to the social-psychological approaches just described, largely confining social reality to communication that is interpersonal and tied to place, a more social-cultural or sociological approach emphasizing (inter)-subjective social construction processes has appeared. Fulk et al. (1987) were the first to develop a *social information processing model*. They wanted to know how the media are really used in daily practice and how humans shape them (inter)subjectively in their social information processing. This is supposed to be conditioned by the opinions about and attitudes towards media of people themselves and of others in their immediate social environment, most often colleagues at work, in the early phase of computer-mediated communications (CMC). See Fulk and Steinfield (1990) for a summary of this view.

Walther (1992; 1996) has presented a comparable approach. In his *relational perspective* the media are used differently in relation to particular functions (tasks, goals) and contexts. According to the results of his experiments, after some period the quality of CMC approaches that of face-to-face communications. This conclusion is diametrically opposed to the claims of the social presence and reduced social context cues approaches.

The experiments of Spears and Lea (1992) support Walther's conclusion. According to their *social identity theory* the reason for the approximate equivalence of mediated and face-to-face communication is that people take their whole social, cultural and personal identity with them as baggage into computer network communications. The smallest cue is then sufficient, to compensate for the limitations of the medium, using the mental construction and imaginative power derived from this identity.

Integrated
Approach

The author of this book has proposed an integrated approach, one that is both objective and (inter)subjective (van Dijk, 1993b). According to this view it remains important to start the analysis with the structural, more or less objective properties of the media, old and new. Their (inter)subjective interpretation and their use in practice differ too much to allow any kind of generalization. Besides, the suggestion that media have no objective characteristics is incorrect. One event in an American computer discussion of women about intimate female affairs should be convincing enough (see Stone, 1991: 82ff.). When it transpired, after some time, that a male psychiatrist using the pseudonym 'Julie' had been taking part, the women were extremely shocked and insulted. In most other media this event just could not have happened.

So, media do have particular potentialities and limitations which cannot be removed (inter)subjectively. In this book they are called communication capacities, a concept which carries the connotation of both defining (objective) and enabling (subjective) features. Using the following nine communication capacities we are able to compare old and new media in a systematic way: speed, reach, storage capacity, accuracy, selectivity, interactivity, stimuli richness, complexity and privacy protection. A short introduction to these capacities follows. Old and new media are compared in Table 1.1 in terms of these capacities.

Nine
Communication
Capacities

The *speed* of bridging large distances in communication is one of the strongest capacities of the new media. In this respect they look like the telephone and broadcasting. Using the Internet and electronic mail one is able to send a message to the other side of the world within one minute. Face-to-face communication and print media are only able to connect quickly to proximate others.

The potential geographical and demographic *reach* of the new media is very large. The whole world might be connected to the converging networks of telecommunications, computer networks and broadcasting in the future. At present, every country and almost every region of the world is already linked to them, first via the telephone and the Internet. However, demographic reach lags behind as only about half the world population has ever used a telephone and only a small minority has access to the Internet.

Potential ISO
Capacity

Another strong quality of the new media is their huge *storage potential*. This potential is low in face-to-face communication, which depends on inadequate human memory. It was also low in telephony before the invention of answering devices. In digital media one can store much more than in printed media and analogue broadcast media.

The *accuracy* or exactness of the information transmitted is an important advantage of the new media as compared with the telephone and face-to-face communication. Signals in the latter media are often ambiguous. Historically, accuracy has also been an advantage of print media. The new media add the exactness of data or numbers and the informativeness of images. Both the storage capacity and the accuracy of the new media enable governments, politicians and managers to control the rising complexity of

TABLE 1.1 Communication capacities of old and new media

Communication capacity	Old Media				New media	
	Face-to-face	Print	Broadcasting	Telephone	Computer networks	Multimedia
Speed	Low	Low/medium	High	High	High	High
Reach (geographical)	Low	Medium	High[1]	High[1]	High[1]	Low
Reach (social)	Low	Medium	High[1]	High[1]	Low	Low
Storage capacity	Low	Medium	Medium	Low	High	High
Accuracy	Low	High	Low/medium	Low	High	High
Selectivity	Low	Low	Low	High	High	High
Interactivity	High	Low	Low	Medium	Medium	Medium
Stimuli richness	High	Low	Medium	Low	Low	Medium
Complexity	High	High	Medium	Medium	Low	Medium
Privacy protection	High	Medium	High	Medium	Low	Medium

[1] In developed countries only.

society and organizations. Without ICT many processes would become out of control and bogged down in paperwork and bureaucracy (see Chapters 3 and 4).

The *selectivity* of messages and addresses is another strong capacity of the new media. This capacity is rather low in the face-to-face communication of groups and other collectives. Here individuals have to make appointments and separate themselves from each other. Much of the communication using print media is not addressed, except for personal letters of course. The same goes for broadcasting. The telephone was the first fully selective medium used to address people. The new media advance this capacity by enabling us to systematically select (parts of) groups using electronic mailing lists and the like. In this way one can address very specific target groups. This is a capacity which is already used frequently in the corporate world (telemarketing) and American politics.

One refers to the new media as interactive, but actually their *interactivity* does not reach the high level which can be attained in face-to-face communication. The new media's general characteristic of interactivity described earlier has to be specified in terms of the concrete levels and types of interactive capacities to be observed in old and new media. Some new media do not offer anything more than two-way traffic and a central store-and-forward agency serving as some kind of answering device. Clearly this goes for electronic mail. In other new media like the interactive press and broadcasting, or digital information services, the user has very little control over content. The user does not (inter)act much; rather, (s)he chooses from menus and reacts. Moreover, fully fledged conversation in the new media is lacking. One is not able to exchange all the signals (often) desired. Even video conferences, which partly enable the participants to see each other, have their limitations. So-called kinaesthesis (the sense of movement) is largely absent and the sense of distance between conferencees is still present.

In terms of *stimuli richness*, no other medium is able to beat face-to-face communication. The reason is clear: all current new media are sensory poor. This is especially so for computer networks transmitting only lines of text and data. Multimedia offer a greater richness of stimuli, perhaps even an overload, in all kinds of combinations: images, sounds, data and text. However, the combination of these stimuli is not natural but artificial. Some stimuli can be strengthened while others recede, but there is still a clear lack of the movement and body language provided by someone who is close. So the most advanced kind of teleshopping will remain different from going to shop in town for a day.

As a consequence of the last two capacities described, the *complexity* that one is able to achieve collectively by using them is not high. Research indicates that one is able to make contacts, ask questions, exchange information and make appointments very well using computer networks, but it appears to be difficult to negotiate, decide, explain difficult issues and really get to know someone (see Rice, 1998).

A minus of the present design of the new media is the low capacity for *privacy protection* that they offer. Face-to-face communication can be secluded to a large degree. Current broadcasting and the press can be received anonymously. This does not apply for the new interactive broadcasting and electronic press media. In fact all usage, and often the personal characteristics of users, are registered in the new media. This is certainly the case for computer networks. For stand-alone computers and multimedia it is less so, because they are under the control of the user, but these media have internal memories which can be accessed. The countervailing use of so-called privacy-enhancing technologies, like encryption, in the new media themselves is still in its infancy. Often, these technologies are blocked by the authorities and other vested interests.

NEW MEDIA AND MODERNIZATION

In this book the rise of the new media is not explained simply by the opportunities offered by their strong communication capacities. A specific theory is used which is largely based on the works of Beniger in *The Control Revolution* (1986) and of Giddens in *The Consequences of Modernity* (1991a) and *Modernity and Self-Identity* (1991b) (see van Dijk, 1993b). Beniger's book is a more concrete analysis of the historic and economic aspects concerned, whereas Giddens's book is more abstract and deals with sociological and cultural-psychological aspects. Several abstract and concrete aspects of modernization clearly associated with the use of information and communication technologies can be gathered from their work.

Modernization: Abstract Characteristics

We will start by listing three abstract characteristics. Giddens defines modernization as the appearance of 'modes of social life or organization which emerged in Europe from the about the seventeenth century onwards and which subsequently became more or less world-wide in their influence' (1991a: 1). Its most important characteristic is the process of *time–space*

Time–Space Distantiation

distantiation. Traditional society is based on direct interaction between people living close to each other. Modern societies stretch further and further across time and space. Barriers of time are broken by the spread of customs or traditions. Information is stored to be used later or to be passed on to future generations. Barriers of space are broken by the increasing reach of communication and transportation. In the most recent phase of modernization, which Giddens calls 'late or high modernity', the process of time–space distantiation goes faster and faster. The process of expansion, however, turns into its opposite: time and space are shrinking within those ever expanding borders. Harvey (1989) talks about *time–space compression*; Brunn and Leinbach (1991) refer to *collapsing time and space*; and McLuhan (1966) spoke of a *global village* many years ago. Time and space seem to be losing relevance. This book challenges this popular view. In a way, differences in time and space become more important, because they are approached more selectively or critically. We are dealing with a radicalization of the meaning of time and space, made possible by the improvement of means of transportation, information and communication.

Disembedding Mechanisms

Connected to the first is Giddens's second characteristic of modernization: the development of a series of *disembedding mechanisms*, withdrawing people from traditional relations and environments. These are the means that help us to abstract special, physical activities that are tied to a particular place. This abstraction is also referred to using the popular concept 'virtual'. Giddens claims there are two types of disembedding mechanisms: symbolic means and expert systems. A symbolic means is, for example, money, which gets more and more abstract in the development from coins to money in bank accounts and to electronic money. Other examples are accepted languages, such as a country's official national language and English as an international language, and universal symbols of culture, like every child's friend Mickey Mouse. In this context digital language can certainly be added to the list. Expert systems consist of several technical means (hardware and software) and professional expertise. This book concentrates on information and communication technologies. It describes how the new media supply expert systems and symbolic means which help modern people to withdraw from traditional relationships and environments that are tied to a particular place.

Reflexivity

Giddens's third abstract characteristic of modernization is *increasing reflexivity*. A continuous review of nearly all social action as a result of new knowledge and experience has become a structural characteristic of modern humankind and society. This goes for society as a whole, as science, technology and media are prominent in it. The same applies to the modern individual, who is increasingly able to decide on his own course and style of living, his partner(s) and the environment he wants to live in. Reflexivity is not only based on knowledge and information. Lash and Urry (1994) drew attention to the growing importance of perception and style (aesthetics) in modern society. The importance of products of culture to the economy grows. Also more and more time is spent on designing and advertising material products. It goes without saying that information and communication technology plays a leading role in the increasing reflexivity of modern society.

Modernization: Concrete Characteristics

Several concrete characteristics of modernization can be observed alongside the abstract characteristics mentioned above. One notices them mainly in historical research. They are important additions to the developments outlined earlier. A broad analysis like the one by Giddens cannot explain why there are peaks, such as communication revolutions, and dips in the development of media. From historical-sociological and economic research the following concrete features of modernization can be derived.

Industrialization

The first concrete feature is *industrialization*. Beniger explained why the aftermath of the industrial revolution produced a revolution in the means of information, communication and organization. In this book, this historical analysis is continued. The needs of the present-day economy gave rise to the current communications revolution. Furthermore, the industrial production of material goods is accompanied by the post-industrial production of information, culture and intangible services. ICT in general, and new media in particular, support this development.

Capitalism   A second feature is the rise of *capitalism* as a principle of economic organization. Time and time again, changes in the system of capitalism have resulted in the development of new means of communication (Garnham, 1990). Developing countries, which are partly pre-capitalist, and (former) communist countries lag behind. This book tries to show how modern capitalism, with its globalization, centralization of capital and decision-making combined with decentralization of production, its growing number of financial transactions, and its emphasis on flexibility and logistics, has created the need for new means of communication.

Organization   A third feature is the tremendous increase of the power of *organization, coordination and control* in modern society. This has become so complex that it would go out of control without the use of ICT. Governments, companies and other large organizations increasingly need the new media in order to function.

These abstract and concrete features of modernization come together in the central thesis of this book. This thesis is about the combination of scale extension and scale reduction to be observed on every level and in every sphere of present-day society. A process of simultaneous extension and contraction of time was referred to earlier. The means of abstraction mentioned above enable an increase in scale. On the other hand, increased reflexivity lends understanding and meaning to these abstract matters at the relatively small scale of a single individual, an organization or a particular society. Industrialization, capitalism and the complexity of organizations will lead not only to scale extension, but also to scale reduction. The last movement can be explained as a direct individual response to intangible and incomprehensible forms of large-scale association. But it is also a response from within the organization to uncontrollable large-scale structures.

Scale Extension   These general statements can be specified for all spheres and levels of
and Reduction   present-day society. The following offers a few examples to illustrate how
Combined   this will be done in this book.

On the one hand, economic organization is expanding globally through international trade and transnational corporations. On the other hand, average company size has fallen over the past 50 years. In the past 10 to 20 years other forms of scale reduction and decentralization have appeared: subcontracting and contracting out business activities and privatizing public or state activities.

For governments and public administrations, international cooperation has gradually become more important. At the same time, strong movements for national and regional self-determination have arisen. On a national scale, decentralization of political decision-making (such as 'lump sum' financing) and deregulation are often accompanied by increasingly tight central determination of preconditions for local policy (for example in the case of cutbacks).

The law and the judiciary demand better national and international legislation and greater means for the enforcement of law, order and safety in order to tackle the growing problems of the globalization of and techno-logical support for crime and of the political and legal inability to control increasingly complex social processes. On the other hand, a growing number of people plead for self-regulation as a counterweight to the growing number of laws, regulations and cases in court which mark a society that seems to be disintegrating and to be no longer able to solve its own problems.

In the social infrastructure of society, we can see individuals participate in increasingly extensive and heterogeneous social networks. On the other hand the same individuals withdraw into shrinking private spheres (smaller families, domestic privatization as a cultural phenomenon). In culture, an unprecedented diffusion of mass media and cultural expressions from all over the world is accompanied by movements supporting small-scale reduction and motivated by a desperate search for self-identity in cultural expressions.

At the level of the human mind we can observe an extending scale of perception in the growth and differentiation of impressions from an expanding environment. On the other hand, perception appears to be reduced because the individual is thrown back upon his own mental resources in trying to process and combine these numerous and diverse impressions from media that are increasingly used alone.

So scale extension and scale reduction are strongly interrelated. In this book it is claimed that modern social and media networks make this inter-relationship possible. So, one of the most important theses of this book is as follows. Modern social networks and new media networks of information and communication technology are necessary conditions for the combina-tion of scale extension and scale reduction that currently characterizes all spheres of society. The existence of these networks provides this com-bination with its social and technological infrastructure.

FROM MASS SOCIETY TO NETWORK SOCIETY

Rough Typologies This interrelationship of processes and the growing role of media networks gives rise to a new type of society. The best name for this new type is 'network society'. In the course of the twentieth century, it has replaced another type of society that has been called 'mass society'. We are talking about rough typologies which explain nothing in themselves, although they cover many phenomena. They are descriptive terms summarizing an overall historical development.

Mass Society *Mass society* is a term used for the type of society that developed during the industrial revolution when large concentrations of people came together in industrial towns and trading centres. Typical of these concentrations was that the traditional communities already existing in neighbourhoods and villages were largely maintained when they were combined on a larger scale in cities and nations.

The basic elements of mass society are large households and extended families in the rather tight communities of a village or a city neighbourhood. In large companies, we see other mass associations in closely cooperating shifts and departments. These basic elements are marked by the physical co-presence of their members. Face-to-face communications and dense social networks are still dominant, but nowadays more and more (mass) media are required to maintain association and coordination in the complex post-industrial economy and society we have created. After all, interpersonal media (such as letters and the telephone) and mass media (such as the press and broadcasting) are used for communication within and between these basic elements. Every community has access to only one or perhaps a few of each type of mass media, such as one radio channel, one television channel and one newspaper. This simplified typology is referred to in the present tense because most developing countries are still mass societies and developed countries are partly so. Figure 1.6 illustrates the social and communicative infrastructure of mass society.

Network Society
In the course of the twentieth century, traditional communities have faded away. This has been caused by simultaneous scale extension (nationalization and internationalization) and scale reduction (smaller living and working environments). Other kinds of communities arise, consisting of people who on the one hand continue to live and work in their own families, neighbourhoods and organizations, but on the other hand frequently move around in large-scale social networks which are much more diffuse than the traditional ones. Daily living and working environments are getting smaller and more heterogeneous, while the range of the division of labour, interpersonal communications and mass media extends. The extension of both social and media networks is necessary to shape this type of community. However, the basic elements of the *network society* are not so much networks themselves but individuals, households, groups and organizations *linked by these networks*. Increasingly they shape the *form* or the *organization*, rather than the *content* of modern society. For we do not want to go as far as Manuel Castells (1996; 1997; 1998), who claims in his trilogy about the information age that networks themselves have become the basic units of society. The growing importance of networks for modern society is expressed in the spread of both social and media networks supporting each other (see the thesis above). Face-to-face communication is replaced or supplemented by mediated communication. A multiplicity of interpersonal and mass communication media is used for this purpose. The rise of ICT gives a new impulse to this multiplicity. For instance, forms of communication between interpersonal and mass communications arise, leading to so-called virtual communities. The extremely complex social and communicative infrastructure resulting is represented in Figure 1.7.

Here we can see how modern communities combine organic communities* and virtual communities*. The former are composed of the remaining direct relationships between individuals, shrinking households and other associations of living and working using mainly face-to-face communication in conditions of co-presence. The latter are called virtual because here

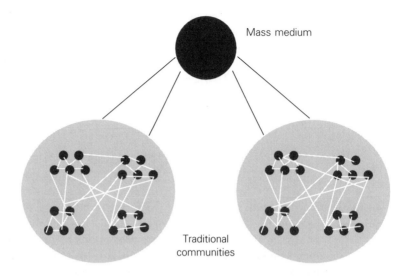

FIGURE 1.6   The structure of mass society

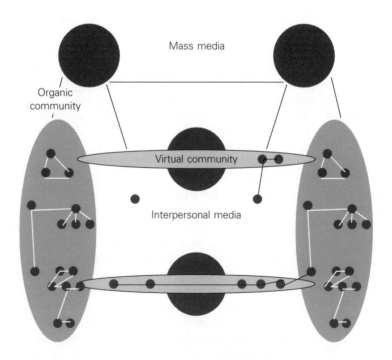

FIGURE 1.7   The structure of network society

associations between people are not tied to the same particular time, place and other physical conditions.

The infrastructure of network society is discussed in detail in Chapter 6. Other chapters will also demonstrate how networks increasingly create the organization and structure of activities in sectors like the economy and politics.

THE NATURE AND THE DESIGN OF THIS BOOK

Analytical Framework

So, this book is not simply a descriptive inventory of social aspects of the new media. Such an inventory is made, but is subsequently placed in an analytical framework. Concrete predictions of future new media developments and effects are not attempted, for this type of technology assessment has led to scenarios and prognoses that have often proved to be wrong. The predicted times of large-scale new media introduction have consistently proved to be ahead of real time by 10 to 20 years. The lure of technological progress leads to distorted views about social reality, which often evolves much more slowly than and differently from the developments foreseen. Often the most essential social needs and processes are disregarded, and existing trends in the design and introduction of new techniques are simply expected to continue.

The account is *analytical in nature*. An attempt is made to put forward not only the effects but also the causes of new media development. Both are located against the background of the broader social transformations sketched out earlier. If this attempt is successful, the contents of this book, dealing with a subject that undergoes rapid technological change, will not be outdated within a few years. We will focus on matters that will not be solved within one or two decades. These matters will be dealt with as options for our society over many years to come, or as choices with long-term effects that have already been made.

Stressing Social Values and Choices

In addition, the analyses are carried out against the background of *explicit social values* that can be *determined* to be at stake. The most important were summarized at the beginning of this chapter: material and spiritual welfare, social equality, democracy, freedom in general and information and communication freedom in particular, safety, the quantity and quality of social relationships, and the richness of the human mind. The explanation that these values are at stake in new media development enables us to draw up balances of pros and cons and to create general perspectives for policy-makers in the closing chapter of this book.

The emphasis on options for society certainly does not imply technological pessimism, but neither does it entail technological optimism. Most analyses of the subject matter concerned can be ascribed to one of these attitudes. At one extreme we encounter observers who consider the information society to be a heaven on earth for producers and consumers, enabling economic prosperity and efficiency, an increase in information and communication freedom and in equality, and a multitude of options. Furthermore, they consider the information society to be a political utopia allowing every citizen to take part in decision-making by means of tele-democracy, or to be a cultural paradise marked by an abundance of leisure time and opportunities for personal expression. At the other extreme we find observers who consider the information society to be the perfection of control by the state and big business, pushing large parts of the population towards the margins of society and imposing total surveillance, registration, screening or tracking of citizens, employees and consumers. Furthermore, these pessimists say it will result in a culture blunted by manipulative and addictive computer games and other virtual reality software and stupefying programmes of interactive TV, or by teleshopping dictated by the design of producers and resulting in the impoverishment of social and spiritual life.

It is not a coincidence that technological optimists, such as Alvin Toffler, John Naisbitt and Nicholas Negroponte, emphasize the processes of scale reduction, decentralization and the individualization of social space, whereas technological pessimists, such as Theodore Roszak, Jacques Ellul and Oscar Gandy, stress processes of scale extension, centralization and the socialization of individual space. In this book we try to avoid one-sidedness by bringing to the fore the *interplay* between these processes and the options they enable.

Interdisciplinarity   The design of this book is entirely determined by an interdisciplinary social-scientific approach. The economic, political, legal, social-structural, cultural and psychological aspects will be dealt with successively. They will be preceded by a relatively simple exposition of the most important technical features of the new media. The purpose of this exposition is to provide an introduction to the new media dealt with in this book and to explain the technical terms that will inevitably appear in it. The aspects mentioned are analysed on a macro-, meso- and micro-level – usually in that order. For understandable reasons, the emphasis will shift to a micro-level in the chapters on cultural and psychological aspects. So, we will try to link an interdisciplinary theoretical analysis to an approach oriented by general policies and explicit values.

TECHNOLOGY

2

Definition of a Network

A network is a connection between at least three elements, points or units. (A connection between two elements is called a relation.) This is the most abstract definition possible. It can be used for physical networks, social networks and media networks. The terms 'connection' and 'element' can be interpreted in several ways. The same goes for media networks: they consist of several sorts of connections by cable or through the atmosphere ('by air'). These connections can be developed either for distribution, that is a point-to-multipoint connection such as a cable television network; or for a circuit between all individual elements of the network, that is a point-to-point connection such as a telephone network. Thus, we can distinguish between **distribution networks** and *circuit-switching networks*. A network can have the physical appearance of a star, a mesh, a ring, a bus or a tree. On the basis of this typology we will also distinguish between several kinds of (media) networks. The most important technical terms used in this chapter and their meanings are listed in Table 2.1.

The first media networks were the cable connections of the *telegraph*, first used in the United States in 1845, and the *telephone* (1876). Two decades later, the first radio links were realized by wireless telegraphy using radio frequencies in the atmosphere, a technique copied in *radio broadcasting* soon afterwards. These were the first networks for telecommunication and mass communication. Networks were not yet used for data communication, with the minor exception of the telex network, a medium for relatively short coded messages. The first mediated data communication of some importance followed the introduction of the computer halfway through the twentieth century. At first, computer communication did not take place through networks, but via transportation of magnetic tapes and punch cards. It was not until much later that large computer centres and powerful computers (mainframes) and their terminals were connected by cables. Increasing use was made of telephone lines for data communication when computers became widely distributed and were reduced in size. This was the first indication of an integration of communication types and the beginning of the second communications revolution (see Chapter 1). The

Technical Foundations

technical foundations for this communications revolution were laid by four revolutionary developments.

TABLE 2.1   Technical concepts

Network structure	Distribution networks (point–multipoint) Switching networks (point–point) Switching techniques: circuit switching, packet switching, cell switching
Network typology	Star Mesh Ring Bus (tree)
Transmission lines	Cable connections: copper/coaxial (electricity), fibre-optic (light) Atmospheric connections: radio frequencies (electromagnetic)
Transmission capacities	Narrowband: < 2 million bit/s Broadband: ≥ 2 million bit/s
Transmission kind	Analogue Digital
Network size	Local area network (LAN) ≤ 10 km Wide area network (WAN) > 10 km
Communication and data type	Telecommunication: sound, text Data communication: text, data Mass communication: sound, text, video

Micro-electronics   First, the *revolution in micro-electronics* led to four generations of computers in 30 years. This revolution was characterized mainly by a miniaturization of components. The most important breakthrough was the invention of the integrated semiconductor, a chip consisting of hundreds of thousands of connections on a plate with a surface of just a few square millimetres. With these chips, microprocessors were developed for several different purposes: operating systems, artificial memories and processes linked to these purposes. The capacity of chips increased exponentially – it doubled on average every two years – and the multifunctionality of micro-processors has enabled the computerization of central telephone exchanges and micro-electronic updates in other nodes and switches of the telephone network. At the same time they caused a drastic decentralization of computer processing, turning data communication into an important phenomenon. Eventually, chips and processors were also used in audiovisual equipment for transmission and reception on a large scale. Thus, the foundation was laid for a uniform micro-electronic technology for telecommunications, data communications and mass communications. This technology has multiplied the capacity and the speed of mediated communications.

Digitalization   Second, this foundation would not have become so important as it is today without a uniform binding structure. This uniformity is a gradual *digitalization of all data streams* between every piece of hardware used in tele-, data and mass communications. Telecommunications and mass communications have always used natural analogue signals for sound and images. Before transmission these signals are converted into electrical signals. At the receiving end, they are converted back to analogue signals.

Although analogue signals are realistic, they are also open to flaws and misinterpretations. Therefore switching is relatively slow and transmission causes some interference. Digitalization means that these signals are chopped into little pieces, called bits, consisting of nothing but ones and zeros. With the aid of micro-electronics these bits can be transported and connected fast and without interference. The best result is achieved when the entire link, from transmitter to receiver, consists of digital signals. Yet, this technical superiority is not the primary cause of the swift digitalization of mediated communications. It is the need to assimilate the explosive growth of entirely digitized data communications into the complete infra-structure of communications. The main boost for digitalization came from acute problems of data communication in transporting data via modems and analogue telephone lines with a limited capacity.

New Connections – by Cable and by Air
The third fundamental technical development concerns lines of trans-mission, transmission capacity and transmission and reception techniques. Micro-electronic and digital signals cannot engender real changes until the connections used are adapted to transport large amounts of these signals. This is achieved by *new connections by cable and by air*. Copper wires and coaxial cables – made of copper wires twisted into a bundle – will be replaced by *fibre-optic or plastic wires**. These are extremely thin wires made out of glass or new plastics, transporting light signals instead of electric signals. Opening and closing transistors are replaced by flashes of light sent by **diodes** (LEDs) or semiconductor lasers. The capacity of fibre-optic wires can be increased up to four or five times the capacity of a six-wire coaxial cable and many times the capacity of an ordinary copper wire. And fibre-optic wires have many other advantages. They do not cause interference or noise, though they can break. They are easy to secure; the wires themselves cannot be tapped off. Signals have to be reinforced only every 20 to 30 kilometres, instead of every 2.5 to 4.5 kilometres as is the case with coaxial cable. Finally, they weigh less than copper wires and need only modest maintenance.

Fibre-optic wires are used for *techniques of optical transmission and reception* developed in laser technology. In the future, they will be con-nected to optical computers that also work using flashes of light. Currently, optical techniques are primarily used in satellite connections transmitting any kind of data through the atmosphere: telephone conversations, com-puter data, radio sounds and television images. The rise of *satellite tech-nology* and *radio telephony* increasingly extends and even replaces connections by cable.

Software Programming
The fourth innovative technical development is the growth of *software programming* in tele-, data and mass communications. It offers increasing control over communication flows. After digitalization, telephone exchanges and switchboards in telecommunications will be controlled completely by software, to be called 'stored program control'. In the next phase, more and more software will be installed in terminal equipment. Increasingly, networks for data communication are controlled centrally and secured with complex software – often so complex they actually are small

networks in themselves: value-added networks. In mass communications, more and more programs are coded centrally and transmitted to buyers and subscribers.

Convergence   These four trends in communication and information technologies have created the conditions for the two crucial features of the second communications revolution: the advancing integration of sound, text, data and images in a single medium, and the increasing interactivity in on-line connections. This will become clear when we describe how tele-, data and mass communications, symbolized respectively by the telephone, the computer, and the complex of television, video and audio, have integrated and are integrating further. Usually this process is called *convergence*.

TELECOMMUNICATION NETWORKS

Definition of   In this book, telecommunication is defined as *a type of communication*
Telecommunication   *using technical media to exchange sound – in the form of speech – and text over (long) distances.* The telephone network forms the backbone of existing telecommunications infrastructure. This network has surpassed and largely incorporated the old *telegraph* and *telex* networks. The telegraph is still used for telegrams, and so is telex for short messages sent by companies and media. In the larger part of their transmission, these text-based networks have been connected to the (international) telephone network. They will be made redundant by large-scale integrated networks (see later in this chapter).

Fixed Telephony   The telephone, telegraph and telex consist of networks that use circuit switching*. This means that in principle a permanent connection exists between all points connected to the network. This is realized by a large-scale point-to-point network transmitting signals both by cable and through by air. The heart of this network has the physical appearance of a mesh: all central exchanges and several, sometimes even all, nodes are connected to one another. At the edges of the network are local switchboards where all terminals (with subscribers using them) are connected to the centre. These connections have the shape of a star. Here terminals are only able to communicate through the local switchboard.

Mobile Telephony   Figure 2.1 is a simplified picture of a telephone network. In the 1980s, networks of mobile telephony were added to the periphery of this giant machine. They mainly used connections by air. These connections had been in use for some time for long-distance communications in navigation and aviation and in radio transmissions. For these communications, signals are sent in all directions at a low frequency. Mobile or cellular telephony needs higher frequencies and bandwidths. So, intermediate stations have to be installed connecting so-called cells of cellular telephony.

The oldest mobile telephone is the radio telephone which is part of a private network with a central radio control room. The radio telephone

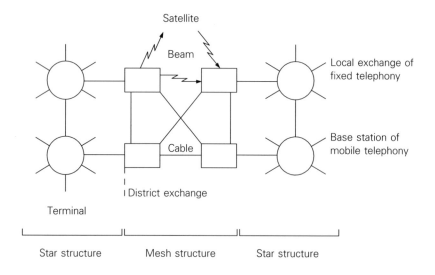

FIGURE 2.1 Simplified structure of a telephone network

offers only limited interactivity because communication is not synchronous: it is not possible to listen and speak at the same time. It is used by the police, fire brigades, ambulances, taxis and transport companies. A semaphone (also known as a 'beeper' or pager) offers no interactivity at all: the owner can only receive messages. A car telephone, on the other hand, offers the same possibilities as a fixed or mobile telephone.

During the 1990s the completely digital mobile telephony network of **GSM** (Global System for Mobile communications) was introduced on an international scale, first of all in Europe. (America has a number of other systems and standards.) The GSM network has better protection against 'eavesdropping', a major problem in mobile telephony. The rapid development of mobile and cordless telephony has made the special car telephone partly superfluous. The cordless telephone was originally meant for use at home. This is not the case with the cordless telephone for outdoors, the mobile pocket telephone. Like the car telephone, the pocket telephone is tied to intermediate stations, so-called telepoints. Step by step, all networks for mobile telephony are being integrated into single systems, like the Personal Communications Network (PCN and the (future) Universal Mobile Telephone System (UMTS) in Europe. UMTS can be placed alongside ISDN in Figure 1.3.

Mobile telephony made a breakthrough in places with high communication density like companies, offices and cities, and in places with few fixed lines such as rural areas and developing countries. Here it became an immediate rival to fixed telephony. However, an important obstacle to the development of mobile telephony is the 'battle' over the scarce available frequencies. These have to be shared with the broadcasting corporations which also use the 'ether' and need a lot of room there.

Automatic
Exchange

Traditional circuit switching, formerly requiring switching by hand, has been carried out without operators for a long time now. Over the past seven decades, three types of automatic telephone exchange have been introduced. First, rotary switching made physical connections mechanically; then electro-mechanical **relays** were introduced. In the third type of automatic exchange, switching was realized by entirely different techniques, namely computers and software. This third step in the evolution of switching has been accompanied by a digitalization of the entire infrastructure, leading to a higher capacity and increasing the speed of the connections made. It is no longer a matter of maintaining a permanent physical connection between communicators as in traditional circuit switching. Now the hardware and software in the exchanges ensure the best possible division of frequencies and units of time to allow many people to use the telephone lines at the same time.

Digital Telephony

Computer-controlled automatic exchanges and a digitalized telephone network are relatively cheap to maintain because single components can easily be replaced or switched. Yet it is not efficiency that will have the greatest social effects, but the facilities offered by completely digitalized telephone networks. These are known as *digital telephony*. They were introduced in the United States in 1989 by AT&T and the regional Bell companies. When a line is occupied, 'automatic call-back' repeats the operation when the line is free again. With the system of 'calling line identi-fication', the telephone number of the caller appears in a display. With 'distinctive ringing', the person called can hear who is calling before answering the telephone. With 'selective call rejection', a list of telephone numbers to be refused can be entered Then there is 'customer originated trace' to identify unwelcome, e.g. obscene, callers. Finally, there are a number of facilities offering further refinement in answering equipment. The most important of these is the so-called 'voice mailbox'*. This is a sort of spoken mail in which the sender enters one or more numbers and leaves a message. After entering the access code, the receiver is able to listen to this message on any telephone. Large-scale introduction of these facilities will complete the digitalization of the telephone network.

Computers and
Video Enter
Telephony

With digitalization the computer enters the telephone network on a large scale. Nowadays, the biggest concentrations of computer equipment are to be found not in computer centres, but in modern telephone exchanges. Here the innumerable switches of the digital telephone network are controlled by a huge number of microprocessors. The same goes for terminals (telephones and computers). Increasingly, all communications are controlled by soft-ware, from simple switches to extremely complex network services. The whole telephone network is adapted for carrying sources of information other than speech and text: data and images. In the next section we will see how the telephone network was put to use for data communication. The further increase in the capacity of the telephone network enables the intro-duction of the videophone and video or audio conferencing. In this way, the telephone is connected not only to the computer but also to audiovisual media. The contribution to the process of convergence sketched in this section is summarized in Figure 2.2.

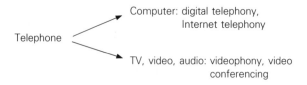

FIGURE 2.2 Convergence from telecommunications

DATA COMMUNICATION NETWORKS

Definition of Data Communication

Data communication can be defined as *a type of communication using technical media to exchange data and text in the form of computer language*. From connections within and between large computer centres, networks for data communication have changed mainly into connections between computers working on their own (personal computers) or in local units (workstations or terminals and network computers). In this way networks of varying scales were constructed, from international data networks to house information systems.

Kinds of Data Networks

International data networks are private, public or semi-public. Private networks are used by transnational companies and military or security organizations operating internationally. Public networks are used by companies dispatching large amounts of numerical data, for example by rental lines, and by companies and consumers transforming relatively small amounts of data, mainly text and images. Here the public network of networks, the Internet, is used along commercial networks like America Online, Compuserve and Prodigy. Semi-public international data networks serve only specialized purposes. They are used in systems of transport by land, sea or air and by banks and other financial institutions. Having access to these networks is only useful for corporations working in the particular business involved and prepared to accept the particular technical standards.

On a *national* scale, the same division into public and private data networks can be seen. Public networks are the special data networks used by national telephone companies, and those used for local communication over the Internet. Semi-public networks are those for harbours and airports. Private networks are the internal networks of banks and public administrations and, in general, intranets (see below).

Network Topology

Large-scale (inter)national networks are called *wide area networks* (WANs)*. They span a distance of at least 10 kilometres. A WAN can either stand alone or connect several *local area networks* (LANs)*. A LAN does not have a central exchange; it is controlled by servers and software. It is a small-scale network bridging a maximum of 10 kilometres, but usually it spans less than 100 metres, directly linking all terminals or stations that are part of it. At the beginning of the 1990s, LANs became the most important networks in data communication for companies and

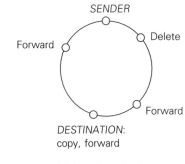

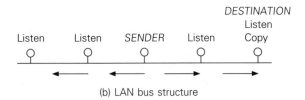

FIGURE 2.3 Two LAN structures

institutions. These networks consist of PCs, **net PCs**, workstations and **network computers (NCs)**, or any combination of these terminals. A LAN has a decentralized structure: it has neither a centralized star structure nor a mesh structure (a mesh network does have central exchanges and nodes). There are two ways in which data flow through the PCs or workstations (Figure 2.3).

In a **ring structure*** data circulate through the entire network (Figure 2.3a). The destination station copies the data and sends them back to the sender, which deletes them or sends them on to another address. In a **bus structure*** all stations continuously 'listen' to what is being sent (Figure 2.3b). Only the destination station copies the data. So the data no longer have to be deleted from the network. When a bus structure is expanded by putting more branches on the stem, it is called a **tree (structure)**. These network topologies are discussed in detail here to allow later explanation of the consequences for the balance of power in organizations using them (Chapter 4).

Switching Data communication uses switching networks, either by cable or by
Techniques satellite. The switching techniques used are circuit, packet and cell switching. Circuit switching, originating from telecommunications, is usually impracticable because the capacity of the existing lines is inadequate to maintain a permanent link for the transmission of data and text. For this reason, a series of ingenious packet-switching techniques* has been developed. Small 'parcels' of data are given address tags and are sent when the connection has sufficient free space. After all, most data communication

does not have to occur immediately and interactively since it usually involves bulk transport or transactions that can wait a while. The latest switching technique is cell switching*. Data are sent not in parcels of varying size, but in very small cells of 53 bytes containing a message and an address. This makes switching even more flexible as the network can be divided into constantly changing subnetworks joined by bridges. The small cells are divided over the subnetworks as efficiently as possible. These subnetworks are only used when they are needed. The result is a total network enabling many to communicate at the same time, as in a network using circuit switching. Furthermore, broadband links can be made with this technique. This is the main reason for the introduction of **asynchronous transfer mode (ATM)**, the latest type of cell switching, by the telephone companies. With this technique they hope to offer a broadband alternative to the Internet protocol (**TCP/IP**), which is known for its flexibility and decentralized nature. By introducing ATM they are trying to recover the ground they lost to the Internet. The Internet used their connections but gained too much independence and became a competitor, for instance in offering Internet telephony. See Steinberg (1996) for the struggle behind the scenes between ATM and TCP/IP and the corporate interests backing them.

Standardization   ATM and TCP/IP are so-called protocols. They serve as means for the standardization of network communications. Networks have to be constructed in the same way to enable internal and external communications. The leading standard is the **open system interconnection (OSI)** model. By means of this standard, seven layers of a network are defined. The bottom two layers determine which hardware and which system software should be used to be able to communicate within the network. The next four layers determine the communication protocols (like ATM and TCP/IP). And the seventh and topmost layer defines what the whole thing is about: applications. The problem with these seven standard layers is that they are filled in differently by existing networks. Different switching techniques are used, to name just one of the problems. Therefore, the call for standardization of networks in so-called open systems has grown. In an open system, network operators are able to connect to and use all layers of a network, except for the layer of application, no matter who manufactured it.

Capacity   A narrowband network is sufficient for transmission of speech, and usually for data communications. However, network users have quickly reached the limits of the analogue telephone network. With the aid of modems converting digital signals to analogue ones and back, a speed of only 14 000 to 56 000 bit/s (**bits** per second) can be achieved. A completely digitalized telephone network allows the use of more capacity. People connected do not need a modem. With the aid of complicated and expensive **compression** techniques the capacity has been increased considerably, for both analogue and digital networks. The digital service ISDN (see later in this chapter) began with a basic narrowband capacity of twice 64 000 bit/s (in both directions) and a signalling channel of 16 000 bit/s. This is still insufficient for the transportation of large databases: it would take four hours to transmit a 100-megabyte database. In this case compression techniques or broadband networks are better solutions.

Telephony and Video Enter Data Networks

For the lack of other infrastructures in data communication, the computer had to be connected to the telephone network. As this network is being digitalized rapidly, there is still room for growth. The computer is able to 'help' the telephone with certain programs which automatically call back, put conversations and data through to another telephone/monitor, and offer the opportunity for callers to temporarily break the conversation and consult someone at another telephone. The keys of a digital telephone can be used to collect data for computer processing, for instance when taking orders over the telephone. Telephone and computer have been fully integrated in systems for buying and selling on the stock market a long time ago.

The limits of narrowband networks are fully exposed when it comes to transferring moving images. The most elementary video images need a speed of 700 000 bit/s. Broadband LANs (see later in this chapter) cannot be linked through the existing narrowband infrastructure, including ISDN.

Videotex is a growing application that connects computers to televisions and audio or video equipment. It is moving into business and consumer on-line services, mainly using the Internet. The term 'videotex' was common in the 1980s but will probably disappear. A closely related application is data broadcasting* or 'datacasting'. A central exchange distributes data via television, teletext and radio among owners of decoders that are addressed by senders. In this way companies can send data to specific groups of customers on a regular basis.

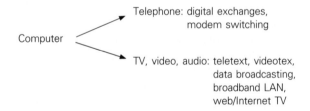

FIGURE 2.4   Convergence from data communications

Figure 2.4 summarizes the developments described in this section.

NETWORKS FOR MASS COMMUNICATION

Definition of Mass Communications

Mass communication can be defined as *a type of communication using media to distribute sound, text and images among an audience*. Until recently, most networks used for this purpose were connections by air. It is obvious, though not essential, that radio broadcasting uses radio communication in the 'ether'. However, FM radio and television need broader frequencies than ordinary radio. Recently, cable networks for broadcasting have been constructed in densely populated Western countries, for the main problem with the capacity of allocutive networks of mass communications is not the number of bits per second that can be sent through a cable, but the limited number of frequencies in the 'ether'. This applies to both terrestrial transmission and satellite transmission. Space is becoming

Terrestrial and full of equipment used for tele-, data and mass communications. The
Atmospheric limited number of frequencies has always been a reason for governments to
Transmission keep firm control over broadcasting. Broadcasting using cable is a solution to these frequency problems. Yet the deregulation of broadcasting, the technical possibilities offered by direct broadcasting through powerful satellites and small dish antennas, and the limited infrastructure in large, poor and sparsely populated countries, have paradoxically led to a revival of connections by air as the leading global transmission media. A vast number of local and global atmospheric networks for mobile tele-, data and mass communications are being rapidly constructed. Some of them use satellites in geostationary orbits much lower than traditional ones.

Almost every network of mass communications is still a distribution network. The structure of these networks is like a tree. A broadcasting corporation (the root) uses a transmitter (the trunk) to send sounds, images and text through carriers with ever smaller branches until they reach the recipient.

Erosion of In Western countries, these centralized broadcasting networks are reach-
Centralized ing their limits. This can be observed in five developments. First, broad-
Distribution casting needs ever increasing capacity. Over the 1990s, even the capacity offered by coaxial cable, about 30 channels, turned out to be insufficient. Compression techniques and fibreglass cables solved the problem. And since these cables are also used for the transmission of tele- and data communications, they are no longer pure networks for distribution.

Second, distribution of television programmes is accompanied by parallel flows of information, such as teletext and videotex (the hybrid version, partly using television). This means a transition from allocution to consultation as the need for two-way communication increases – which brings us to the third development. Subscription TV and pay TV have a significant advantage over traditional one-way distribution programmes. These two-way cable TV links also give consumers the opportunity to respond to programmes and other messages, if they have the right equipment. This also goes for **interactive teletext** and for Internet via cable and satellite, sometimes called web TV.

A fourth development is the gradual digitalization of audiovisual mass communications. Digital audio definitely took the lead here. In the meantime, satellites for sound, data and images have been digitalized. The introduction of high-definition television (HDTV)* will be one of the next steps. Digital sound and high-resolution images giving cinema quality are characteristic of this technique. If the (extremely costly) step of introducing HDTV on a mass scale is taken at all, it will be well after the turn of the century. The entire chain of production and distribution of once completely analogue audiovisual mass communications will have to be digitalized. However, this requires a transmission capacity of fibreglass or other connections of 10 million to 100 million bit/s achieved by compression. A precursor of this technique appears in the broadband LANs of the business world. Television images, sound, text and data are transmitted by connections with a capacity of 2 million, 5 million, 10 million, 16 million and even several hundred million bit/s. Corporate TV, videotex, videophone and video conferencing are among the current possibilities. These local activities used for organizational and interpersonal communication are revolutionizing the traditional structure of centralized national and international distribution in mass communications.

Computer and Telephony Enter Video and Audio   Digitalization of audiovisual mass communications enables the development of links between the world of television and that of computers. In a broadband LAN, television, video, audio and computer become a single medium. This is less true for Internet on television, because the **set-top box** and terminal required are digital devices, but are not computer equipment. It certainly is true for so-called **multimedia PCs** (see next section). Finally, the introduction of the videophone, video conferencing, videotex and audiotex complements the ultimate individual speech/conversation medium, the telephone. From now on, groups can have a conversation and exchange images and texts simultaneously.

These developments are summarized in Figure 2.5.

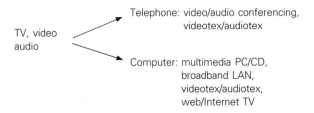

FIGURE 2.5   Convergence from mass communications

INTEGRATED NETWORKS

In the preceding sections we have seen how, starting in their own spheres, tele-, data and mass communications have moved towards each other. This process has been a *spontaneous* technical development based on the four trends discussed in the introduction to this chapter. The process has been controlled by technical innovations and new social and economic needs in the fields of tele-, data and mass communications themselves. This has opened the way for an integration of tele-, data and mass communications as a matter of *deliberate* design. The result is **integrated networks**, designed from the start to exchange several communication and information facilities, traffic patterns and types of data simultaneously. These networks vary in scale from a micro-level up to a macro-level, and will be described in that order.

Micro-networks: multimedia PCs and house systems

Media Integration at Home and at Work

The smallest possible integrated network is the multimedia PC*. In a bus structure, a PC with a high-resolution monitor and video and audio cards can be connected to a VCR, a video camera, a CD-ROM or a videodisk player and an audio installation. A telephone/fax, a modem or a TV receiver takes care of potential links to the outside world. Special cards in the PC control internal and external communications, and special software helps to control the applications.

A bigger micro-network is a house system*, also called 'smart house' or 'intelligent home'. Futuristic designs were put forward for this integrated network decades ago, but consumers have not yet shown much interest. It is to be expected that house systems will be introduced in our homes gradually and in clusters. The first cluster consists of audiovisual and computer equipment. The second will probably be house power supply in general and the regulation of central heating systems, kitchen equipment and water supply in particular. The third cluster might consist of security equipment: burglar alarms and special devices for the sick, the elderly and disabled people. Telephone, cable and satellite will link these clusters to the outside world and to macro-networks. However, it will be a long time before all microprocessor-controlled equipment in our homes is connected to a macro-network and can be controlled and monitored from single panels in a house.

Meso-networks: broadband LANs, telephone and computer systems and intranets

Media Integration in the Organization

At present, the introduction of integrated networks is proceeding fastest at the company or organization level. New LANs and other local systems are being rapidly introduced, integrating corporate telecommunications into data communication, audiovisual services and archiving (see Figure 2.6). The first equipment to be connected or integrated is corporate telephone installations and computer systems. Then the capacity of the local network is increased to transport not only pictures and numerical data, but moving images as well. Thus, a document archiving service, a system for video surveillance, a closed video circuit and files of interactive video courses can all be connected to a LAN. For the latter applications, broadband LANs with a capacity up to 500 million bit/s are available.

Since 1996, so-called *intranets* have been installed in the computer systems of companies and public institutions. Intranets are private branches of

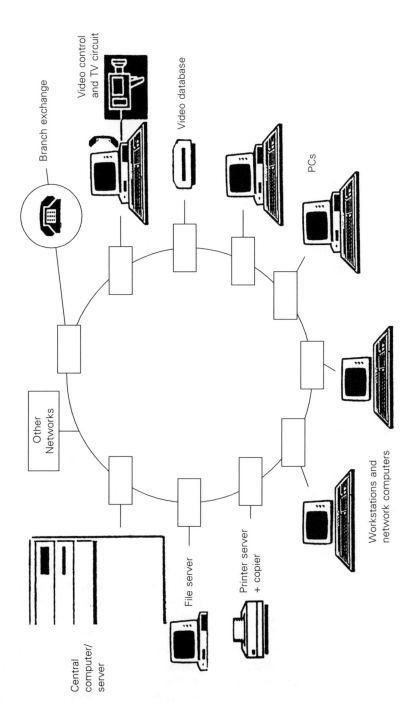

FIGURE 2.6 An integrated broadband LAN

the public Internet. They use the same protocols and browsers and they are especially suited for the transmission of texts and images within an organization. The Internet can be used for communication with the world outside. An intranet usually cannot incorporate all the internal networks of the organization. Central administration systems and databases usually use much more advanced techniques and require better data protection than an intranet can offer.

Macro-networks: Internet, ISDN, B-ISDN, IBCN

Integration of Large-scale Media   Large companies increasingly want to link the LANs of all their offices and outlets. This is done by means of special network bridges. In this way wide area networks (WANs) are constructed. However, most public networks have a small broadband capacity. The complete digitalization of their infrastructure cost the public telephone operators enormous effort and investment in the 1980s and 1990s. Broadband capacities come second. The most difficult and expensive part of the infrastructure is the so-called local loop, the innumerable terminal connections to the home. Here new techniques such as the asymmetric digital subscriber line (**ADSL**) are used to digitalize the last part of the public network.

ISDN   A prototype of a completely digitalized public network is the integrated services digital network (ISDN), which was being introduced on a large scale by the end of the 1990s. ISDN is also a narrowband network to start with, as it has to use cable with less capacity in links to homes and workplaces. So when organizations want to transmit video images, graphics requiring high-resolution screens and large amounts of data, they still have to use private broadband facilities (for instance satellites). Or they have to resort to all kinds of hybrid constructions, such as broadband cable TV networks, or to facilities that can stretch the capacity of a narrowband infrastructure (for instance by using compression techniques or both directions of ISDN simultaneously). A last resort is the isolation of high-speed intelligent networks, like the so-called Internet-2, for quick and safe connections, to be used by the government, universities, research institutions and large corporations.

The introduction of ISDN has not happened quite so fast as had been expected in the 1980s. ISDN is nothing more than a continuation of the digitalization of the telephone network combined with a public service of data communication. The most important communication need that ISDN will serve is a simultaneous transfer of conversations and text or data. This exceeds the existing combination of telephone and fax. Direct access to a file can be of great importance, for example when taking orders or selling and in making a diagnosis at a distance. Other services provided by ISDN are the facilities of digital telephony described earlier, sending faxes at 20 times the old speed, and 'surfing' on the Internet at five times the speed of an analogue modem.

Broadband
Infrastructures

A broadband public infrastructure will offer many more opportunities. It is known variously as the information superhighway, broadband ISDN (B-ISDN) and the integrated broadband communications network (**IBCN**). In the future, this infrastructure will swiftly send both large quantities of data and moving images of high quality at the same time. Current separate connections of the audiovisual sector will be integrated by this infrastructure to shape a single network. In this way the average consumer of broadcasting, video, audio and the telephone will be accommodated for the first time. In the meantime, the perspective of a single public broadband network, which still prevailed in the 1980s, has long gone. For this reason a division into public and private broadband infrastructures was shown in Figure 1.3.

The current communications revolution will be completed by the large-scale introduction of integrated broadband networks. Fully mediated, rich and pluriform interactive communication will be available at all levels of social living and between them. Figure 2.7 is one of many possible outlines of this development.

INTEGRATED EQUIPMENT: MULTIMEDIA

On-line or Off-line
Integration?

It remains to be seen to what extent the situation shown in Figure 2.7 will be realized, in which every household and company is connected to some kind of information superhighway. In the preceding discussion some doubts were cast on the prospect of a single public broadband network for all mediated communications. In the next chapter, these doubts will be intensified by the economic prospect that several information superhighways will be available. There are also doubts from a technical point of view. Perhaps many of the future information and communication services will be offered *off-line* instead of on-line. The two main characteristics of the new media, integration and interactivity, can also be realized in stand-alone equipment, which brings us to the exceptionally swift rise of so-called multimedia.

Definition of
Multimedia

Multimedia* are links between *several* devices in one interactive medium, or links between several media in *one* interactive device. Applications with sound, text, data and images can be integrated in a combination of several devices or in a single device. The main characteristics of multimedia are *integration of several types of data* and *high-level interactivity* caused by the relatively high control the user has over the interaction. The last characteristic is clearly perceivable in three other properties of the use of multimedia. The first is the *stratification* of information. Users can find more information about a fact retrieved in the shape of explanations, figures, illustrations, photographs, videos, animations, sounds and so on. So, the same information can be portrayed in several ways. The second characteristic is *modularity*: an information database is composed of pieces to be retrieved separately and combined in the way a user wants. The final

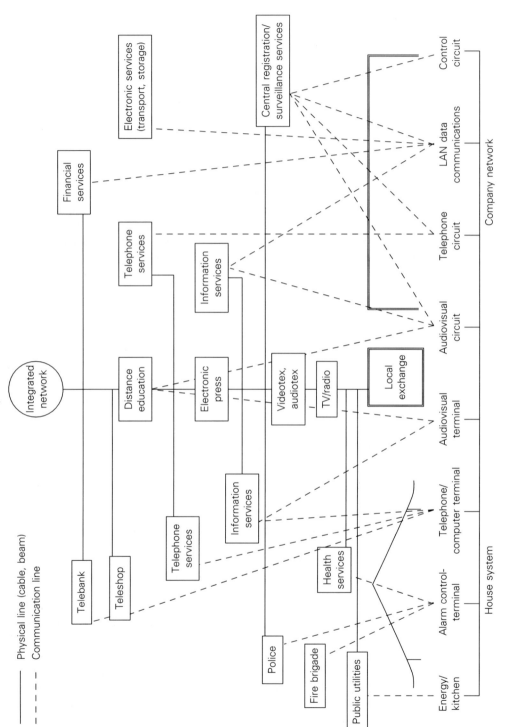

FIGURE 2.7 Public integrated broadband network in households and companies

characteristic is the *manipulability* of information in multimedia, enabling the user to 'cut and paste' pieces of digital information.

Kinds of Multimedia   The multimedia PC, the multimedia CD and the multimedia network will now be described, in a way similar to the earlier description of the difference between multimedia as a link within a device and as a link between devices (see Appendix 1, pp. 242–3, for an overview).

Multimedia PC

The multimedia PC is a result of developments in PC technology. PCs have become steadily faster since the introduction of new microchips. With the aid of add-on cards, colour monitors, speakers and special software, they can process sounds and images as well as data and texts. Before 1995, these machines were still very expensive and were primarily used for business and specialist applications: design, graphical representations, visualization, publishing and recording of images and sounds. In 1995 the multimedia PC made a breakthrough on the consumer market. Most PCs sold nowadays are multimedia PCs. This is made possible by more powerful and cheaper microchips and by a further miniaturizing of audio and video connections and built-in CD players. The built-in **CD(-ROM)** player, mainly used for entertainment and education, makes the multimedia PC especially interesting for the general public. Since 1995 more advanced features have been introduced, for instance the possibility to edit video images and audio clips and to connect a microphone to make phone calls over the Internet.

Multimedia CD

Unlike the multimedia PC, the multimedia CD is primarily based not on powerful microchips and special software but on disk and laser technology. Its primary application is storage and reproduction by a player, reproduction equipment and disks. One of the first types of multimedia CD was the detached CD-ROM player. It was primarily used for archiving and as work of reference by libraries, shops and companies. A CD-ROM player is connected to or installed in a PC. Other types of CD players for multimedia are connected to a TV. One of the first designs was the **CD-I** player, developed by Philips. It had no success. After some years it was replaced by the CD-ROM and the digital video disk (**DVD**). Perhaps the CD-I came too early, but there are other reasons for its failure. The CD-I was designed for the masses to be able to use simple computer applications displayed on a TV screen. This is a most doubtful concept. Technically speaking, the television and the computer are certainly integrating. However, there are great differences in the social context of the two media that will not disappear easily. The TV is primarily a medium for entertainment, consumed collectively and at some distance from the screen displaying moving images and the speakers emitting sound. A PC is primarily a medium for study and work, used individually, with the user close to a monitor displaying text, graphics and data, and working with an expanded keyboard to enter them. Moreover, the TV is usually located in the living room, with the kitchen and the bedroom for the second and third set, while the study is the typical place for a PC. These differences also cast doubt on designs for so-called web TV: the attempt to distribute Internet services on a TV screen using cable and/or telephone as a common carrier.

The CD in all its manifestations is likely to become the most important medium of multimedia storage and reproduction for the masses. Increasingly it will be used in all computers and audiovisual equipment. Among the advantages of these off-line multimedia are the autonomy and flexibility of using them, their relatively low cost and their suitability for a large public. However, there are three major disadvantages. First, the storage and processing capacities are rather limited. If one wants to consult large databases, one has to get on-line. The same goes for access to recent information. This may be realized on the Internet. Increasingly CD players are linked to Internet connections to add the latest information. In fact, a multimedia network is constructed in this way (see below). A third deficiency is that stand-alone multimedia PCs or CDs do not allow communication with others to ask questions and to give replies.

Multimedia networks

Multimedia networks are constructed to solve the problems just mentioned. Most multimedia networks consist of broadband connections by cable. The smallest multimedia network is the *house system* of audiovisual and computer equipment mentioned earlier. A house system can solve some of the problems through an on-line connection to the outside world, but not all. A larger multimedia network is constructed by linking a *workstation to a broadband LAN or WAN*. For professional applications such as the visualization of scientific data, a medical diagnosis at a distance, and video telephony with texts and still images in parallel, one needs much higher capacities for transmission and processing. The most advanced and large-scale type of multimedia network as a link between devices is an intelligent network or high-speed network, like the one offered under the label Internet-2. Here is the clearest indication that multimedia networks are combinations of on-line and off-line new media as they connect powerful multimedia PCs or workstations and high-speed transmission lines.

Even higher capacities of numerous computers linked in parallel are needed to realize the applications of ***virtual reality***. This most advanced of all multimedia, primarily designed for small-scale settings, surrounds the human body with several input and output media, enabling the person to see, hear, feel and move all at the same time. This all-embracing and mentally immersive technology is made for interaction with simulated and programmed environments and used for training (in aviation and surgery), design (architecture), research (visualization of complex data), film animation and games (perhaps the most important entertainment of the future).

Only small capacities are needed for the *personal communicator*, the *personal digital assistant* and the *palmtop computer*, that is small portable computers used for agendas, small files or simple programs and able to send and receive e-mails, radiophone messages or faxes. It is a multimedium in a nutshell, to be used both on-line and off-line.

The Nature of Convergence

This chapter has described how the networks and other media of tele-, data and mass communications are converging *technically*. In the meantime the idea of diverse technologies and media coming together seems to be commonplace. In the last 20 years many observers have developed the perspective of a single medium or infrastructure for all types of communication, for instance one line coming into our houses. To prove their case they have referred to the growing number of mergers between telephone and cable companies, mass media corporations and computer manufacturers. However, this far-reaching perspective of convergence has not yet become a reality in *economic, social and cultural* terms. For the time being convergence primarily means the development of new technologies serving as cross-links between tele-, data and mass communications. Clear examples are ISDN (tele- and data communications), web TV (tele- and mass communications), videotex or audiotex (tele- and mass communications) and high-speed multimedia networks to connect all three kinds of communication. A more realistic perspective is that they will contribute to a multiplication of media and networks: an extreme diversity of future media is to be expected. These will be more or less interconnected as a patchwork of links and devices dictated by economic and regulatory policy. Yet, *separate* economic and usage functions of tele-, data and mass communications will be seen in a totality of on-line and off-line media primarily integrating in technical terms. For instance, we will get or keep interactive broadcasting, advanced mobile digital telephony and high-speed multimedia networks of data communication. The reasons for this extreme diversity and the remaining divisions within the process of convergence are economic and cultural in kind. It is to the economy of network society that we will now turn.

ECONOMY

THE CURRENT COMMUNICATIONS REVOLUTION

The importance of networks for our economy can be viewed at several levels. The most common level is a description of the interaction of network producers, consumers and operators in the market. But such a description cannot sufficiently explain why the new media have advanced so quickly in the last two decades. An explanation of the growing need for information and communication media in our information society will not suffice either. We have to explain the sudden increase in the demand for tele-, data and mass communications in the past two or three decades and the current need for integrated networks in certain fields. This will be the subject of the first two sections of this chapter. Next, the supply side of the 'network market' (manufacturers, carriers, network operators, service providers) will be discussed. Finally, the consumers (those who use networks) will be discussed in the last section of this chapter.

Accelerating
Communication
Demand
In *telecommunications*, the number of telephone lines in Western countries grew 10 per cent every year in the 1960s and 1970s. In the 1980s and 1990s, growth decreased. However, the growth percentage is still high, considering the saturated demand for first telephone connections in ordinary households. The highest increase is observed in long-distance and international calls. In the meantime, demand for mobile telephony is increasing much faster than demand for fixed lines.

If we separate *data communications* from telecommunications, we will see not an acceleration but a virtual explosion. The demand for data communications has appeared to exceed supply on many occasions. This has regularly caused problems in corporate tele- and data communications.

A strong increase in the supply of media, channels and broadcasters is to be observed in *mass communications*. Over the past few years, many technical, political and legal issues obstructing supply have been removed. In most Western countries, one is able to choose from dozens of new channels, programmes and subscription services. At first sight, supply seems to exceed demand. This observation would be correct, but it would not acknowledge the lack of choice opportunities available over the past decades, the strongly increasing needs for cultural differentiation and social individualization and the lack of specific channels for companies to advertise on. And demand is still growing. The total money spent by households on media continues to rise, partly because the new media do not replace the old media but are added to them (Wood and O'Hare, 1991).

General Background

The acceleration, in some cases even the explosion, in demand for communication media over the past two or three decades cannot be explained simply by looking at *general* tendencies in society, economy and culture or at the availability of new technologies (van Dijk, 1993b). Saunders and Warford (1983) and Metcalfe (1986) were among the first to identify the following factors governing the increasing need for information and communication media in developed economies:

1 a scale extension in production processes;
2 an increase in the division of labour and the complexity of organization;
3 a rise in standards of living;
4 information production gaining its own dynamics.

This list is not entirely correct (in this book, scale reduction is stressed in addition to scale extension) and it is not complete either, because it is mainly based on economic aspects. For example, it omits the social-cultural aspects of individualization and the reduction of household size, which have a direct influence on the need for communication media. However, the most important objections to an explanation using these factors are the lack of historical specification – even from an economic point of view – and the assumption of linear evolution. Contrary to this, we will describe a combination of several background factors that produce their effects with varying speed and strength in the long, medium and short term. The American scientist James Beniger initiated such a description in a detailed, historic-economic analysis of technological developments in the United States in the nineteenth and early twentieth centuries (*The Control Revolution*, 1986). And since we want to apply his argument to the current state of affairs, it is important to briefly repeat his account.

First Communications Revolution

Beniger demonstrates that, during the period just mentioned, a veritable information and communications revolution took place. He considers it to have been a reaction to the faltering industrial revolution owing to its poor infrastructure. Many points of friction arose halfway through the nineteenth century. Together they produced a *control crisis*. This term describes a period in which the organizational and communication means of control lagged behind the size, speed and complexity of physical production, energy extraction and transportation. Beniger describes the control crisis in the industrial revolution as follows: 'Suddenly – owing to the harnessing of steam power – goods could be moved at the full speed of industrial production, night and day and under virtually any conditions, not only from town to town but across entire continents and around the world' (1986: 12). The crisis was visible in numerous frictions: problems of coordination in factories, in mass transportation (trains colliding, mistakes made in freight transfers, missing vehicles, divergent timetables) and in the distribution and sale of bulk goods in department stores. In the second half of the nineteenth century the crisis was solved by a *control revolution* marked by the following three series of innovations:

1 *bureaucratic organization*: the rise of bureaucratic functions, sharp task divisions and hierarchies, rationalization by formal procedures, preparations (for example paper forms) and time synchronization;
2 *a new infrastructure* of transportation and communication (paved roads, trains, telegraph, telephone and so forth) to handle the explosive growth in mass transportation of goods and people;
3 *mass communication and mass research* (national press, film, radio, advertising, market research, opinion polls) as ways to reach and map an elusive new mass of consumers.

Beniger describes the rapid development, within a lifetime, of a whole series of new communication means still controlling everyday life. He lists: photography and telegraphy (1830–40), the rotary press (1840–50), the typewriter (1860–70), the transatlantic cable (1866), the telephone (1876), film (1894), wireless telegraphy (1895), magnetic tape recording (1899), radio (1906) and, somewhat later, television (1923). Beniger considers them to be the means of a (very broadly defined) control revolution. Considering the list supplied, we prefer to speak of the *first communications revolution* of the modern age. For the innovations of the control revolution are much more than simply new means or media: they also contain basic techniques of organization and programming.

All the means mentioned were invented, developed and introduced on a small scale in the period indicated. In the decades between 1920 and 1970, they were diffused on a large scale as the main technologies of an economic age characterized by mass production and mass consumption.

A similar, but shorter, period of invention, development and innovation, with the computer as its central medium, resulted from World War II and the race in arms and in space that followed. With a staggering speed of development, computers are already in their fifth generation since 1950. With their miniaturization and chip technology, the third and fourth generations (from 1965 onwards) were the most important. They paved the way for large-scale digitalization and integration of communication media.

According to Beniger, the computer has replaced bureaucracy as the most important instrument of control since World War II. He considers the introduction of the computer, the revolution in micro-electronics and the information society in general to be only a new – albeit much faster – phase in the control revolution of modern times (1986: 427). To us this is an underestimation of the meaning of current innovations. However, it is productive to apply Beniger's analysis to the present situation, defending the thesis that we are now going through a *second* control crisis which is partly being solved using the media of a *second communications revolution*. For we can see that the three series of innovations, which Beniger considers to be the solution to the control revolution, have run their course. They have even become impediments to present development. This applies to certain bureaucratic modes of organization, to the congesting and polluting system of the transportation of goods and people, to the fragmented types of mass communication and to the growing problems for mass research and marketing in an individualizing and differentiating society. New media networks can be important *means* to solve these problems. They are able to support the flexibility, efficiency and productivity of organizations, to improve all kinds of logistic processes, to replace transportation of goods and people by transportation of information, and to reach effectively a segmented public of communicating consumers.

The question arises as to whether this technology is not just as much a reaction to the frictions and congestions in processes of production, distribution and consumption as nineteenth-century technology was to the control revolution of those days.

A FLOW ECONOMY

Specific Background

An increasing need for communication is visible in the relationships within and between companies and other organizations. This increase cannot be sufficiently explained by simple reference to a steady increase in economic activity – after all, demand increases in years of economic recession – or to an increasing share of information processing among all activities. Much more far-reaching historic-economic developments in modes of production and divisions of labour over the past decades have to be taken into consideration.

Decentralization of production and centralization of capital and control

In the United States, the turning point in the scale extension of production processes had already been reached before World War II (Jerome, 1934). Up to that time, production had been concentrated in ever larger units. Since World War II companies have slowly started decreasing in size, not only in the United States, but also in other Western countries. This should not overshadow a second process that has been going on simultaneously: the centralization of capital and strategic control over production processes (Harrison, 1994; Castells, 1996). These trends appear in the growth of international corporations and conglomerates of financial capital, and in the tendencies towards business monopolization or oligopolization, which are dealt with in this chapter. A present-day example of the convergence of both trends is the concentration of media in the hands of tycoons like Murdoch, Berlusconi, Kirch and Bertelsmann. These people have no wish

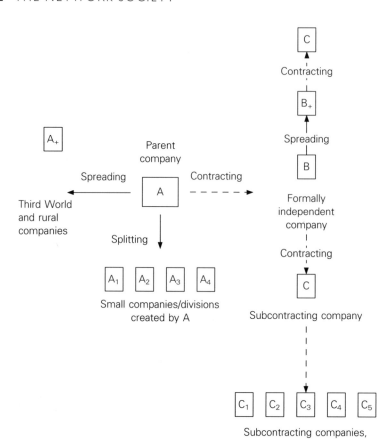

FIGURE 3.1   Network structure between companies (inspired by Murray, 1983)

to merge the media they appropriate: on the contrary, more often they are diversifying them in order to gain a larger share of a growth market.

If the all-embracing parent company of the past is taken as a starting point, the decentralization of production can be portrayed as in Figure 3.1. **Network Structure** The first phase of this process was the spread of Western transnational **between** corporations over the rest of the world. Subsequently, a division in depth **Corporations** took place in the Western countries themselves: a split in formally independent and regional departments first and in subcontracting business activities afterwards. In Japan, this process took place simultaneously and even partly in the reverse order. For it is now widely known that former Japanese economic successes were largely attributable to a very flexible hierarchical network of subcontractors and assembly plants. With their poor conditions of employment and very disciplined personnel, the large number of these subcontractors serve as a source for added value and as a shock absorber for the large, mainly exporting assembly plants in times of declining (inter)national demand.

Over the past 15 years, decentralization of executive power has also taken place inside Western governments and public administrations, by means of a regional spread of activities, privatization and subcontracting. In contrast to this, the commercial service sector has always been marked by small-scale organizations. In recent times the emphasis has shifted to scale extension. For example, cleaning agencies, IT companies and other service organizations are getting bigger. However, activities are still performed locally.

Behind these trends of predominant decentralization are specific *economic* motives which become more urgent in times of economic recession: rationalization and redistribution of added value towards the place(s) where all the money is concentrated (see below). A more general reason is the necessity to *control* the extending scale and organization of large corporations. This is also related to increasing *geographical restraints*. Formerly centralization of production led to high costs of establishment, traffic congestion and other problems with regard to transportation.

Decentralized economic organization was a reaction to all these organizational and financial problems. However, the result was a huge increase in the need for communications, and thus capacity problems in existing infrastructures (Palvia et al., 1992). The lack of capacity and flexibility in public networks is the most important reason for large companies to construct their own (inter)national networks and to install advanced private branch exchanges, for which they are willing to make large investments. This comes as no surprise if one realizes how many *strategic opportunities of choice* are created by this technology. Companies are able to choose the best place for all their specific activities of production, distribution, information, management, support and maintenance. So, production can take place in regions/countries with the best trained and most reliable personnel available. Subsequently, assembly is located in low-wage countries or near markets; distribution is based on the best infrastructure; and information is concentrated in centres of high technology. The preferred place for management, which requires high-quality internal communication and support services, is a metropolitan area close to financial centres. Thus, a spread of activities can be combined with extreme centralization and specialization (Castells, 1989; 1994; 1996; Nicol, 1985; Harrison, 1994). The spatial proximity of business activities appears to have lost its importance. A geography of places is replaced by a geography of flows (Martin, 1978; Castells, 1989; 1996). The conclusion is obvious: this corporate network structure, representing both scale extension and scale reduction, can exist only with the help of advanced communication networks.

Flexible automation of production: reorganization of labour processes

---

Network Structure within Corporations The conclusion reached in the previous paragraph will be underlined by trends *within* separate corporate departments, that is production processes. Within companies, a network structure of functions, tasks and activities also

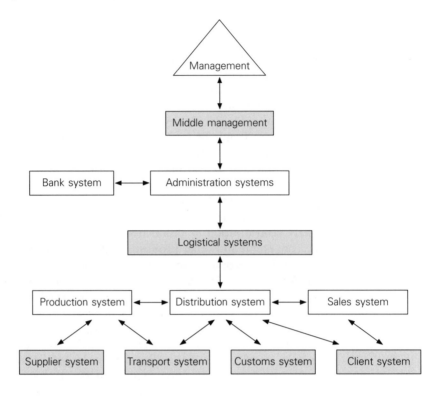

FIGURE 3.2   Network structure inside companies

arises (Figure 3.2). This is a fundamental transformation described variously as a movement 'from just-in-case to just-in-time production' (Sayer, 1986), 'from the separation of a hierarchical line structure and functional staff structure to a combined structure of production flows (De Sitter, 1994), 'from mass production to flexible specialization' (Piore and Sabel, 1984) and 'from **Fordism** to post-Fordism' (Aglietta, 1979). The first part of these distinctions refers to the modern industrial production process based on **Taylorism** and the system of assembly lines that was predominant in industrialized countries until recently. Here the goal is to achieve the highest production at the greatest speed. Machines have to work for as long as possible on a single (part of a) mass product. A high level of specialization between and within divisions is prevalent. Assembly lines and other systems of transportation take care of transit. Parts, components and personnel have to be kept in store ('just-in-case') to keep production going during break-downs. However this system, so devoted to the speed of continuous mass production, in fact suffers delay in almost every link (De Sitter, 1994). The linear structure has too many phases and links working at different speeds. So, numerous **logistical** problems arise. The structure is vulnerable to the smallest malfunction. Vulnerability is enhanced by a functional department structure with many specialized divisions which usually have a lot of work on their hands. An extensive hierarchical line structure is needed to coordinate all the processes and divisions. The more complicated the end product, the longer and more complicated the route between all the divisions. The results are long and unreliable delivery times. Only two decades ago a (part of a) product was processed only 5 per cent of the time it spent in the factory; 30 per cent of production costs were used for storage, coordination and transportation inside the factory (Balance and Sinclair, 1983: 148). To summarize: this type of production process is characterized by optimizing *partial aspects*, to allow separate machines and workers to work faster. The advancing complexity of products and differentiation of demand slowed this process and reduced the growth of productivity in the 1960s. However, it took the economic crisis of the 1970s and the model of the Japanese economic system to make manufacturers face the facts.

The alternative, developed in large Japanese assembly companies, optimizes the production process *as a whole*. The process is not split into stations, tasks and activities but runs in parallel streams in which entire products and components, all similar to each other, are produced. Of course, the phases in these streams are divided into segments too, but these segments are homogeneous and they are supported by production groups working relatively independently. These production groups are multi-functional; they constantly improve their work and they are charged with quality control of their own products. Hence the name 'quality circles'. The number of segments is limited and they can be coordinated by a small staff 'recruited' from the quality circles themselves. In order to make this system succeed, the work done in the segments has to fit closely ('just-in-time'). In production streams, quantity may differ by only 10 per cent (Sayer, 1986: 55). Waiting periods are unacceptable. Information always has to be where it is needed. Therefore, direct communication between production groups is vital.

Direct communication does not have to be realized by means of advanced technology. The Japanese have shown this with their famous *kanban* – a system in which communication takes place simply by holding up signs with questions and directions. So, this is a case of organization preceding technology. However, in the meantime production processes have become so complicated, and distances have increased so much, that media networks have become indispensable. However, flexibility is an organizational and not a technological characteristic (Hirschkorn, 1984; Wood, 1987). Technology's revolutionary characteristic in this respect is integration. Through communication networks, computer-aided design and computer-aided manufacturing are integrated in one cybernetic system: computer-integrated manufacturing. In turn, this system can be connected to distribution and supply systems, office systems, personnel information systems and management information systems (see Figure 3.2).

Networks for Flexible and Taylorist Modes of Production

Over the past 15 years, this mode of production has had a great impact in Western Europe and the United States. However, there has been no general adoption of it, certainly not in sectors outside industry (Wood, 1987). Often mixtures arise of classical, mostly Tayloristic, modes of production and more flexible modes of production adapted to local circumstances. We should not forget either that countless supply companies in Japan still work according to classical, Tayloristic production methods (Kamata, 1986). And in this respect it is very important to note that network technology can be used to support Tayloristic production systems as well. It can even help to refine these systems to the smallest detail. It is possible to integrate the standardization and automation inherent in every computer technology in order to form a coherent system that is still based on hierarchy and a strict division of labour. This will be discussed in detail in the next chapter. Here we simply wish to state that network technology can solve problems occurring in both modes of organizing production processes, and in their mixtures.

Streamlined offices

Even though it is hard to measure and compare differences in productivity in factories and offices, it is well known that, during the twentieth century, productivity in factories has increased far more than productivity in offices (for data see Gershuny and Miles, 1983). The difference was experienced as a growing economic problem: whereas the costs per single product gradually decreased, the share of administration and management in the total costs kept increasing both in absolute and in relative figures. The reasons are obvious: office work is, and always has been, highly informal, unstructured and little mechanized or automated. But this is about to change. Now traditional office work is being automated, in fits and starts, and with many organizational problems. According to computer manufacturer Carlo de Benedetti, the direction of this process is clear: 'Essentially, information technology is a technology of control and coordination of workers – in particular white-collar workers – not yet reached by Taylorism' (cited in Rada, 1980: 106). A more Tayloristic, or even a factory-like, organization could be created for office work when an office is **The Office as an** viewed as a *system of information processing* passing through stages of **Information** generating, producing, collecting, processing, multiplying, distributing, **Processing System** storing, retrieving and interpreting data (see Hawryskiewicz, 1996).

Such a concept of office work is necessary in order to first structure and then formalize and standardize this particular type of work. This will enable automation as soon as the necessary techniques are available. High-grade technology for offices is still a pretty new phenomenon. Take for example the copier: this piece of office equipment, indispensable today, was introduced only 30 years ago. Clearly, several separate phases of the above-mentioned process have been automated through information and communication technology in the past 10 to 20 years. But in the average office, this has not yet produced an increase in productivity. The changes seem to have been too basic and introduced too swiftly for personnel and organization to respond to them adequately. Therefore the 'paperless office' will continue to be a utopia for some time.

The really fundamental changes will be brought about by network technology. One should not expect major changes in the productivity, efficiency and structure of office work until either integrated office systems are introduced or all existing equipment and software are connected in networks. The first step in this process will be to connect activities such as word processing and graphical design to databases and documentary systems or electronic supply management. The next step is very aptly called *workflow automation*. The entire administrative procedure of an office is divided into separate tasks to be performed successively by the departments/workers in the network. A list of tasks for the day is displayed in a window on the monitor. All tasks performed are marked and passed on to the next station in the network. The process of office streamlining will not be completed until it is extended to the office environment of suppliers and customers by means of **The Office** integrated tele- and data communication networks. The network will be the **Assembly Line** assembly line of the office, an assembly line not stopping at the door but continuing outside to be connected to other lines. Therefore, the effects of networks in offices will be even greater than the effects that assembly lines had in factories.

Of course this does not mean that networks will lead to the same standardization and division of tasks that occurred in factories. It will still be possible to work in teams and on all-round sets of activities. Special programs have been developed for *groupware* or *computer-supported cooperative work* emphasizing cooperation (see Greiff, 1988; Hawryskie-wicz, 1996). Furthermore, activities like generating, producing, collecting and, above all, interpreting office information are difficult to formalize. Therefore, the network as the assembly line of the office can have different consequences for various groups of office employees: those who keep managing and communicating informally and those whose tasks are formalized in a factory-like way.

Virtual organizations?

Different Meanings Networking within and between organizations raises the prospect of the so-called virtual organization (Davidow and Malone, 1992; Mowshowitz, 1994; 1997). Unfortunately, this is a loose concept with several meanings. Most often, it is a mixture of the following organizational and technological principles.

In the first place it refers to the *internal network organization* described above. Here the growing importance of teamwork in so-called business redesign is stressed. Autonomously working and often shifting multidisciplinary groups cross the old divisions and departments of organizations.

The concept is also used to depict the growth of the *external network organization*. In this case it emphasizes the modern practice of splitting and cutting off parts of the (mother) organization by privatization, subcontracting and a search for partnerships, while keeping these parts together by networking.

A common third interpretation is the *flexible organization* of the labour process and labour conditions. In this way old limits of time, place and other conditions of labour are transcended as well.

Definition of Virtual Organization

A fourth interpretation emphasizes the decisive *role of ICT* in the virtual organization. This interpretation is favoured in this book. Here the virtual organization is defined as *an association which is predominantly based on ICT and tries to work relatively independent of the constraints of time, place and physical conditions*. In the words of a popular AT&T commercial in the 1990s: it is an organization which works anytime, anywhere and anyhow. It should be stressed that the first three meanings of the virtual organization concept described above may be realized without any use of ICT; they are just new principles of organization. Of course, the adoption of ICT substantially helps them, as was explained above. However, the core of the term 'virtual' is the possibility of doing things without the constraints of time, place and physical conditions. It means an increase in the opportunities for choice by continually switching the organizational means one uses to reach the goals, where both means and goals are defined in the most abstract way (Mowshowitz, 1997).

The virtual organization is the most abstract type of association we know. The ideal type of it is a web organization. This might be a temporary network of experts working together on a particular job at a distance using the Internet, perhaps not knowing each other but reaching a potential world market. Most organizations making significant use of ICT are not predominantly virtual organizations. Doing telework or telestudy for a couple of days a week does not make an organization virtual. The backbone of the organization still rests on time, place and physical conditions. A few aspects of virtuality, like more choice and opportunities for switching, are just added.

Viability

The big question is whether a virtual organization, in the sense of the fourth meaning given, is able to survive. It is not only an abstract type of association, it is extremely volatile as well. It runs the risk of a short life or perpetual splitting. The latest experience of using ICT in teleworking and offices without fixed working places proves that it can work as long as virtual ways of working are *added* to the traditional or organic ones. When virtual methods *replace* traditional methods completely, we get an ideal type of virtual organization which will not last for long and is not actually able to work according to this ideal. After all, a greater choice among time and place constraints does not mean that they do not exist anymore. On the contrary, as will be explained in Chapter 6, the application of ICT radicalizes the importance of time and place in all our activities as it helps to increase our needs. Finally, even a web organization is still tied to many physical conditions, for example the hardware and software of communication systems, using the international telephone system (the largest machine in history), and the minds and bodies of its own employees or independent professionals.

Process innovation as a crisis solution

According to the classical view, long periods of economic prosperity result from *product* innovations. Products mentioned in this regard are steam engines, electricity and cars. The computer is held to be the crucial product in the current innovation era. However, a closer examination of the information and communication technologies integrated in networks reveals that, for the time being, process innovation turns out to be much more important than product innovation. All elements of the 'flow economy' discussed here confirm this statement. Product innovation is not the cause but the result of process innovation. This is the concept of the reversed technological life-cycle. Initially, in traditional industrial technologies there was a large variety of product designs; then a process was started with scale extension, standardization, cost savings and a reduction in the number of manufacturers, the so-called industrial 'shake-out', as the core activities. It is best illustrated by the car industry at the beginning of the twentieth century and the chemical industry after the Second World War. However, information technology forces companies to invest in a very costly process of computerization first. Product innovations are not possible without these investments. Nowadays, shortening the life-cycle of products and increasing their variety are first and foremost aspects of process innovation. This usually applies to those products built in components and revealing only slight variations. Producing them faster and more reliably requires continuous process innovation.

Process Innovation Precedes Product Innovation

Keeping Beniger's analysis in mind, it may be considered that, compared with product innovation, process innovation has always been underestimated. As for the current information and communication technology, we can hardly avoid the conclusion that the market effect of its new products – a variety of new hardware and software – is less important for the partial economic recovery currently taking place in Western countries after the crisis of the 1970s and 1980s than its effects of reducing the costs of all relevant factors in production and raising its efficiency. Hence, economic recovery involves a shortage of jobs in those countries that have done least to cut back on labour costs and other production factors. The recovery of purchasing power and the introduction of new profitable products (goods and services) are less significant for the solution of the latest economic crisis than a whole series of rationalizations appearing in all parts of the economic and political process. Many economists will agree with this statement, as current economic language is full of terms related to it: flexibility, quality, market orientation, decentralization, deregulation and so on. In fact, process technologies based on ICT can solve an impressive list of problems (see Van Tulder and Junne, 1988):

1   *Direct cutbacks in the costs of production factors*
    (a)   Labour saving by network computerization exceeding that by computerization with detached equipment.
    (b)   Decreasing capital costs through optimizing the use of equipment by flexible automation and a potential extension of company hours up to 24 hours a day.
    (c)   Reduced and more efficient use of raw materials through: better coordination; reduction of supplies; and partial replacement of transportation of goods and people by data transportation.
2   *Improvements in the efficiency and effectiveness of production*
    (a)   Improvements in all kinds of logistics.
    (b)   Best possible use of labour and means of production.
    (c)   Higher availability of information in the right places.
    (d)   Shorter production and delivery times and direct communication with customers.
    (e)   Direct quality control.
3   *Strategic control over the economic and political system*
    Combined centralization of capital and control and decentralization of production, giving:
    (a)   better and more direct opportunities for information and control by management;
    (b)   more strategic options in the choice of production sites and task divisions;
    (c)   central control of flexibility and decentralization.

The most obvious *conclusion* would be that process innovation, summarized here by the term 'flow economy', is the central mechanism for a gradual solution of the economic crisis appearing as decreasing productivity growth in the 1960s and declining profits in the 1970s – a recovery not yet completed at the time of writing (see Brenner, 1998). In the 1980s direct cutbacks in production costs had the highest priority (point 1); in the 1990s the emphasis shifted towards the aspects named under points 2 and 3. This could very well be the foundation for a boom in future product innovations. The flow economy is the main explanation for the second communications revolution. It certainly explains the fact that business enterprise and some parts of governments and public administration have taken the lead in the steeply rising demand for tele-, data and mass communication and in the introduction of computers and networks.

On a more general level the current communications revolution will *help* clear some of the bottlenecks produced by the solutions of the previous control crisis: bureaucracy; the clogged traditional infrastructures of transportation and communication; and finally, media for and research into a rather undifferentiated mass of consumers. We will return to this subject several times below.

THE PRODUCERS: PRIVATIZATION, CONCENTRATION AND REREGULATION

This section discusses how the 'communication branch' of the economy takes advantage of the technological and economic developments discussed earlier. Since activities in this sector are extremely divergent, it is important to make a clear distinction between the five parties engaged in networks. They are the manufacturers of infrastructure; those who construct and maintain the infrastructure; the carriers and managers of both public and private networks; the service providers; and the consumers of networks. The last of these parties is discussed in the next section. We will start by describing the other four, the producers of networks, paying particular attention to the following trends and characteristics:

1 concentration and integration versus decentralization and differentiation;
2 globalization versus localization;
3 public ownership versus privatization and commercialization;
4 regulation versus deregulation;
5 nature and size of investments and returns;
6 employment.

Kinds and Functions of Network Producers In order to understand what is going on in the media sector in general and in the production of networks in particular, it is necessary to make a distinction between the vertical columns of the various networks – of telephone, computer and broadcasting – and the horizontal layers of the functions performed by them. This distinction is made in Figure 3.3. This figure displays the structure for the following description.

Manufacturers of infrastructure

These days the highest turnover of capital takes place at the level of material infrastructure. Total turnovers in tele-, data and mass communication equipment world-wide range between 50 billion and 100 billion dollars a year. Clearly there are strong links with the micro-electronics industry, particularly in components and terminal equipment. The largest sums are spent on nodes and exchanges: telephone exchanges, powerful mainframes and servers in data communication and recording, and transmission and receiving devices in mass communications. Sales of cables, switches and transmitters flourish every time a new network is constructed. Then a shift takes place toward terminal equipment – from single devices to complete company and house systems.

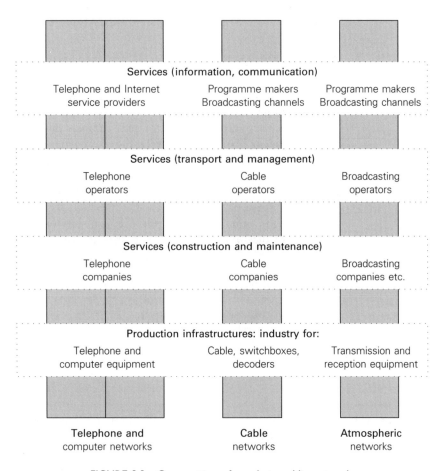

FIGURE 3.3 Composition of supply in public networks

For some decades now, a strong *horizontal concentration* – that is, concentration on the same level in the production chain (see the rows in Figure 3.3) – has been apparent in both tele- and data communications. In the 1990s the world market for telecommunications equipment has been largely controlled by 10 companies. Important names in this context are Alcatel, Siemens Nixdorf, AT&T, NEC and Fujitsu. A new round of mergers has started, and analysts expect that only five or six multinational giants will remain after these mergers.

The companies involved have to make extraordinarily capital-intensive investments and they have extremely high research and development costs. Therefore, high turnovers and profits are required. In order to survive, a company needs a vast and solid international market. Traditional links between particular producers of telephone equipment and national public telephone carriers no longer offer sufficient market share. So capital and control are being concentrated more than in any other field, though there is some outsourcing to national subsidiaries. The corporations concerned have been privatized almost completely. The French Alcatel and the German Deutsche Telekom are about the only large companies with some state control.

Regulation of the production of tele- and data communication equipment has been reduced more and more to matters of standardization. This often causes the interests of countries and companies to clash. At first, concentration in *data communications* seemed to exceed concentration in telecommunications. Within a short period, IBM had built up a monopoly in computers and company systems. 'Miniaturization' changed this situation. In the production of microcomputers, IBM was overwhelmed by competitors from Japan, Europe and the United States. There was an enormous increase in the number of independent computer manufacturers. However, after a period of heavy competition and partial saturation of the (PC) market a new concentration looms.

IBM remains the most important manufacturer for all kinds of computers taken together, but we see new 'giants' appear, such as Compaq, Hewlett-Packard, Fujitsu, Hitachi and NEC (Datamation, 1998). Two facts are striking. In the first place, the most dominant producers on the computer hardware market are Japanese manufacturers of equipment for telecommunications (Fujitsu and NEC) and electronics (Hitachi and Toshiba). However, the software market is controlled by American manufacturers (Microsoft, Oracle, Silicon Graphics and others). With its almost perfect monopoly in PC operating systems (i.e. Windows), Microsoft in practice determines what software is used by the overwhelming part of the market.

Traditionally, the production of *mass communication* equipment is closely linked to that of telecommunications. The same companies dominate. This situation has been only slightly changed by the appearance of satellite manufacturers emerging from the space and arms industry.

The convergence of manufacturing of tele-, data and mass communication equipment will be the most important future development, however. Manufacturers of micro-electronics, led by the dominating company Intel, will play a leading role. Of course, other transnational corporations active in this field of business have been expecting the convergence in the production of infrastructures. IBM started manufacturing equipment for telecommunication. AT&T got into equipment for data communication. Philips, known for its televisions and radios, diversified into computers (chips, multimedia and information systems) and telephones (mobile telephony). Telecommunications company ITT joined with the French electronics companies CGE and Thomson, thus becoming Alcatel. Ericsson switched from tele- to data communication and back again. Motorola, NEC and Fujitsu were among the first to manufacture chips and other components, allowing them to achieve a strong position in the production of equipment for all kinds of communication.

Despite rising profits, these industries with their extremely capital-intensive production do not create a rise in employment. On the contrary, in Europe and America employment in this branch of industry decreased by about one-third between 1980 and 1990 (Mosco, 1996).

Network operators and carriers

The construction and maintenance of networks are tasks largely performed by or contracted out by network operators and carriers, especially when national telecommunication companies are involved. To simplify matters, these parties are treated as one party here. In the next subsection they will be separated again.

Eroding Public Monopolies

A strong tendency to oligopolization is noticeable in infrastructure manufacturing. But in the branches of the most important customers of equipment – network operators and carriers – an opposite tendency can be discerned: one of eroding monopolies. Public networks are losing their exclusive rights to transmission because they have to tolerate private networks. In their own field they had already encountered competition before the liberalization of public telephony. This came from all kinds of specialized networks, in practice available only to a limited group of companies. Competition was spurred partly by technical problems. Over the past decades, the public telephone carriers have had great difficulties in supplying sufficient capacity for data communication. Public broadcasting corporations had problems meeting the demand for channels, frequencies and advertising facilities as well.

Significance of Natural Monopoly

In discussing the last obstacle we find political factors. Public network operators and carriers originally form a *natural monopoly* of great social significance. This means there are many reasons to concentrate management and carriage:

1 The services are of general social interest.
2 They are part of a combined system of carriage and communication.
3 They have to get as close to the customers as possible.
4 They experience peak hours and moments of unutilized capacity.
5 Demand is not flexible.
6 Competition is bound to technical constraints (standardization is desirable).
7 Using a single system usually offers advantages.
8 High continuous investments are needed.

The permanent validity of these reasons (see Chapter 5) was unable to prevent the decline of existing public monopolies in telephony and broadcasting. The decline was caused by technical factors (insufficient capacity) and economic-ideological factors (desirability of competition, deregulation and privatization). The results for the various types of network management and carriage are described in the next paragraphs.

Until recently, the most important expression of a natural monopoly in communication was the highly regulated sector of carriage in *telecommunications*. Competition was allowed first in information and communication services and in peripheral equipment. Next in line was mobile telephony.

Competitors came from cable, satellite, transportation and energy companies already possessing cables and other links which could serve as a backbone for an alternative telephone network. In fixed telephony they often still need the public telephone operators (PTOs) to connect to homes and companies. The existing regulations of interconnection compel the public telephone operators to allow competitors to use their networks, but of course they will demand the highest possible compensation. Therefore, competitors will extend their own infrastructure as soon as it is profitable, perhaps using mobile telephony.

This will create a new situation: a multiplication of infrastructure with the same facilities being constructed side by side. One of its manifestations is the construction of three or four information superhighways largely designed for the same applications (they will be described in detail below). This will lead to an overcapacity outside peak hours. This waste (from the perspective of society as a whole) could have been prevented if governments had organized investment in a joint infrastructure by public–private partnerships or by private business, in the same way that they are investing in roads and railways (here construction and maintenance have mostly been outsourced). Subsequently, all carriage and services offered on this joint infrastructure could have been liberalized. In the near future we will face countless conflicts between companies about the interconnectivity of their networks.

Public Monopolies Bypassed

However, the first infringements to the monopoly on telecommunication were caused by trends in *data communication*. Many transnational corporations and large national companies have been installing their own data networks, using not only the rental lines of PTOs but also hired and private satellites or private local networks. They no longer go first to the public data networks of the PTOs.

The explosive growth of specialized public networks is another threat to the PTOs' monopoly. Specialized value added networks* (VANs) make large profits on facilities such as special packet switching, the management of data transmission, and the supply of software for network operating systems, for the interchange of terminal equipment and for access to databases. An even more explosive growth is perceivable in company-transcending semi-public networks. Basically they are public, but – for reasons of functionality or payment – access is restricted to specific companies. Examples of these semi-public networks are money exchange networks for banks, and traffic control or reservation networks for airports and harbours. These networks only partly use basic PTO infrastructure.

In *mass communication*, public broadcasting is eroding swiftly (Tracey, 1998). While on a national and local level the public broadcasting corporations have had to accept the competition of a growing number of commercial channels, they are now being overtaken by lightly regulated international satellite broadcasting. The same kind of overtaking occurred in tele- and data communication: international satellite link-ups on the one hand and local radio traffic and local area computer networks on the other. While in the latter field the national PTOs can make a technical response, for instance by offering new services and broadband networks, public broadcasting corporations can only maintain their position by government protection or by commercializing themselves.

From Differentiation to Private Concentration

Initially, the process of overtaking causes a considerable differentiation in supply. The new services offer room for large numbers of new broadcasting channels. But initial experience already indicates that within a short period a concentration of ownership and organization will take place. (The production of programmes had already been drastically concentrated.) As long as there is tough (inter)national competition the number of channels does not have to be reduced. However, new (inter)national broadcasting corporations have been founded or swiftly taken over by large media companies such as Time Warner, Murdoch, Bertelsmann, Hersant and Berlusconi. The process of concentration of network management and services in mass communication is as fast as it has been in the manufacture of telecommunication equipment. In this field also, 5 to 10 media giants are taking control of the world market. The first in line are Time Warner with Turner Broadcasting, and Disney with Capital Cities ABC. They appeared in major mergers of the years 1995 and 1996. Next in line are Viacom in the United States, News Corporation (Murdoch) in Australia, Bertelsmann and Kirch in Germany and HAVAS in France.

From Public Monopolies to Private Oligopolies

The trend described goes from public monopolies to private oligopolies. It is important to note that both are able to manage a natural monopoly. The public monopoly does or did so on a national scale. Private oligopolies operate on an international level. There are no complete monopolies on the market – basically, there is competition – but they can split the world market among themselves, fix prices and benefit from international regulations on standardization and interconnectivity. Increasingly, large international telephone companies cooperate and merge. A handful of conglomerates are preparing to divide the world market. AT&T has started to collaborate with a Japanese and several European PTOs, linked in Unisource, to form World Partners. France Telecom, Deutsche Telekom and Sprint (United States) started to work together under the pretentious name Global One. British Telecom and MCI (United States) decided to cooperate under the name of Concert. With these conglomerates in mind there was some talk of a *triumvirate* trying to dominate the world market. Though they partly fell apart again in 1998 and 1999, this does not stop the participants from *organizing* other mergers and takeovers. The telephony giants have already shown an interest in local proprietors of cable TV systems, broadcasting corporations and all kinds of programme producers. It looks as though they want to become general media companies. The final result will be a replacement of government-controlled public monopoly without competition by a small number of private oligopolies with limited competition but no democratic supervision.

New investments in special public networks and commercial broadcasting are relatively small compared with investments in existing general public telephony and public broadcasting. The latter have to maintain their universal access obligations and comply with other strict regulations. The former are able to concentrate on the most profitable business connections (skimming the market) and on the growth market of broadcast advertising.

Employment has decreased in most public network management and carriage (Mosco, 1996; Van Tulder and Junne, 1988). Of course it has increased in special public and private network management. The former will exceed the latter for quite some time. The number of operators is steadily decreasing owing to the high level of automated switching in modern networks. Once a new digital telephone exchange and fibre-optic network is constructed, it needs relatively little service and maintenance.

Service providers

Differentiation
Supply
Service providing in the new media has just completed the experimental stage. That stage has been accompanied by decentralization and differentiation in supply. Many services are being developed. The people that start these services are often small organizations, willing to take risks and to pay for the costs of R&D themselves. When they are successful, they are quickly taken over by large telephone, software and media companies. This always happens when the services they are working on need to be offered on a large scale, such as in databanks or databases, or have high production costs, such as films. Sometimes the undertaking is so risky that government subsidy is necessary to start it.

Network Services:
Categories
Network services are divided into four categories: purely technical and organizational tele- and data communication services, transaction services, communication services and substantial information services. Services of carriage, construction and maintenance were discussed in the previous subsection.

When speaking of *tele- and data communication services* we refer to those special services needed for the development and support of infrastructures. This does not include the facilities of value-added networks since these networks themselves create and manage a specific network. But it does refer to security services and the supply of back-up facilities for large companies and institutes. Furthermore there are IT companies engaged in the development, maintenance and support of integrated business systems.

Transaction services vary from highly specialized financial activities for enterprises, banks and investment companies to simple transmissions of payments, orders, reservations and other on-line commercial services in (inter)national electronic systems. When they are business-to-business transactions they most often use systems of **electronic data interchange** (EDI).

Using open networks, *communication services* offer new exchange facilities for speech, data, text and image exchange to a wide range of businesses and consumers. These facilities include the services of so-called digital telephony (described above), radio telephony, facsimile, electronic mail and videophone.

Information services are various. First, they offer storage and processing of data (databanks, databases and data processors). Subsequently there are services for creating, editing and distributing data. 'Creating' is done by all kinds of professional consultants who have discovered 'networking': scientific, legal, accounting and architects' agencies. Involved in editing are developers of network software. Distribution is taken care of by database distributors, all kinds of electronic libraries or videothèques and publishers working with videotex or the Internet. Finally there are the broadcasting corporations, which offer their audiovisual programmes and other services in new shapes (channel bouquets and subscriptions) and channels (the Internet).

Except for public communication services, most of these services are completely commercial and deregulated.

Employment among these service providers will definitely increase. However, we might expect the disappearance of a lot of employment in this branch also, as these services replace similar off-line and analogue activities. The savings of manual and other work in postal services and (to a lesser degree) printing services, to be replaced by electronic mail and publishing, are obvious. The same goes for transaction services, owing to electronic payments and reservations. Even larger savings will result from the numerous registration systems adopted in government, trade, industry and other services, since they will take us to the users of networks (see below).

Vertical Concentration A trend towards horizontal concentration has been described, that is, among network producers and, to a lesser extent, service providers. This means mergers and collaborations between companies with similar activities, on the same level of the production chain. When we take a step further and relate the three levels discussed, we will observe important impulses towards *vertical concentration*, that is, integration of different levels in the production chain (see Figure 3.3): (a) manufacturing of infrastructure, (b) network management and (c) service provision. At the moment, the relationships between (a) and (b) and between (b) and (c) are strongest. Operators of national PTOs increasingly depend on one or two suppliers of infrastructure (Van Tulder and Junne, 1988: 191). Every PTO has its first supplier and tries to adopt two or three other suppliers to compete with the favourite one. However, this is getting more difficult owing to excessive concentration, and an increasing technological dependence on the standards and knowhow of the first supplier limits choice. Operators and carriers themselves try to become or to remain the most important service provider on their own network. This is easier to accomplish in a fragmented broadcasting system (independent broadcasters with own television programmes). In tele- and data communication networks the opposite happens because of current privatization policies. Here network operators are losing ground with their own services. They will have to compete if they want to concentrate management, carriage and service providing. In the second half of the 1990s this is what telecommunication companies and cable operators in particular have tried to do. They are working on both horizontal and vertical integration. Telephone companies have started to distribute broadcasting programmes and Internet services, while cable companies are offering telephony and Internet services as well. They are doing this on the networks they manage themselves (vertical concentration). For both kinds of concentration they buy or merge with each other's networks.

In the meantime, companies have been set up based on the vertical concentration of (a), (b) and (c). The company that has made most progress is AT&T, though this is hidden by the fact that the company was formally split into several independent companies. AT&T remains by far the most important manufacturer of equipment for tele- and mass communication in the world. The company operates most long-distance telephone lines in the United States and runs a growing number of international cable connections and satellite links. It merged with McCaw, a company in wireless telephony, joined forces with others in Unisource as well as entering into an alliance with British Telecom. In 1998 and 1999, AT&T succeeded in returning to the local communications market, buying the large American cable operator, TCI and bidding for Media One. AT&T also supplies specialist networks and increasingly secures services in tele-, data and mass communication through contracts and subsidiaries, such as America On-line. In the perspective of future information superhighways, AT&T has started to cooperate with television stations, software companies and publishers (for instance Bertelsmann).

In Europe, Siemens, Philips and Ericsson are trying to accomplish the same. Even though they are not network operators, they do have a firm grip on national operators, at least in their native countries (Van Tulder and Junne, 1988: 190). Siemens and Philips are manufacturers of infrastructure and consumer electronics and they are providers of information services in tele-, data and mass communication. International corporations originating from the data communication side, such as IBM, are trying to gain a foothold in telecommunication, for example by concentrating on specialized public networks (VANs) and business systems. This provides them with strategic positions from which they are able to advance in vertical concentration.

Effects on Communication Policy   In present-day economies, vertical concentration is a logical reaction to the technical integration or convergence in the communication field as a whole. Still, it might have political consequences which are neither logical nor desirable. The companies involved can get too tight a hold on a country's communication policy. And more specifically, they might acquire a strong influence on (inter)national standards and prices (levels and differentiation of prices for local and long-distance calls) and on technical facilities for security and the protection of privacy. In delivering integrated business systems and their operating systems or other software, they might gain disproportionately large control of the structure of organizations.

One example will be instructive enough. In 1996 Time Warner was sued by News Corporation (owned by media tycoon Murdoch). Time Warner refused to transmit News Corporation's 24-hour news channel FCC on its cable networks. The reason is evident: Time Warner owns its own news channel, called CNN.

In 1993, the breakthrough of the information superhighway perspective in the United States, Japan and Europe has accelerated these concentration processes. Many telephone, computer, electronics, software and media companies started to cooperate and to merge. Ultimately, the information superhighways will represent the peak in the horizontal concentration of telephone, data, cable and broadcasting networks. They are also an extra stimulus for vertical concentration. After the liberalization of infrastructure, manufacturers of this infrastructure decide to construct and manage their own networks, first of all in mobile telephony (for instance AT&T, McCaw, Ericsson and Motorola). Operators of telephony, data, cable and atmospheric networks increasingly start to offer services themselves.

However, this competition is not just about winners and profits. In their fever to merge, the 'warriors of the information superhighway' (Auletta, 1997) often make wrong moves. In 1997, at the end of the hype about the Internet and the information superhighway, many companies must have realized they had been too hasty in proclaiming themselves general media companies. Shares in neighbouring columns and rows in the communication branch (see Figure 3.3) have been resold and mergers have been cancelled. Some companies have gone back to their core businesses. However, the concentration and integration described here are lasting facts. The shifts are driven by continuing processes of technical convergence and economic concentration of (financial) capital.

From deregulation to reregulation

These expressions of technical and economic convergence in the media branch must face the last remnants of traditional public regulation. They mainly concern the strict regulations, varying in each country, imposed on the broadcasting system and the audiovisual industry (KPMG, 1996). The end of public monopolies was brought about by a series of liberalizations which are called *deregulation*.

Competition and Control   The reason for this fundamental change in communications policy is the supposition that all parties will benefit from competition: increased freedom of choice and lower prices, based on real costs. But the communication sector with all its natural monopolies is not a normal economic sector. The supposition of the beneficial effects of competition is not unequivocal here. Robin Mansell (1993) even claims it is based on an *idealist model* that does not correspond with the facts. These are more suited to a *strategic model*. Oligopolies control their markets according to carefully planned strategies. In some ways they work together, in others they compete. An oligopoly does not end a monopoly. On the contrary, the companies involved protect their markets, enforcing their own standards, keeping strict control of the most profitable so-called intelligent parts of networks, designing smart price policies and making deals with their rivals. According to Mansell (1993: 210), competition exists only in certain segments of the market such as the production of peripherals and the supply of international communication services. She reaches the conclusion that the increasing costs of adapting networks, provided initially for the benefit of large or specialized transnational corporations, are passed on by the oligopolies to small companies and households (1993: 213–31).

The private oligopolies and remaining public monopolies have increased the rates for local calls, claiming that the profits made in international telephony can no longer cover the losses in local telephony. This claim has been disputed, for it has never been proven. The (in)correctness of this claim will appear as soon as fixed local telephony meets competition from mobile local cellular phones, and then local prices will drop as well. In countries where local telephony was disconnected from long-distance telephony some time ago, for instance Denmark and Finland, local telephone rates are among the lowest in the world (OECD, 1993; Davies, 1994). In the past, households and small companies may have benefited from the profits in international telephony, but they have certainly made a disproportionate contribution to the huge investments needed for advanced international telephony (Mansell, 1993). Now it seems the same thing is going to happen with the increase in and broadband extension of a number of integrated networks (the different information highways to be described below) which will be constructed in parallel and will be partly interconnected. It remains to be seen whether their owners will compete with one another. They all have an interest in letting their customers pay for the huge investments.

With the need to counteract these moves towards oligopolization and to organize the rising complexity of this sector, the number of regulations quickly turned out to be increasing instead of decreasing. Institutions charged with the organization of a privatized supply on public networks have been established in all countries liberalizing telecommunications. In these countries books with regulations and standards are piling up in the regulatory offices. Clearly, *reregulation* is taking place. This is very understandable. An increasing number of networks, operators and service providers in an environment requiring a lot of organization and fine-tuning simply has to lead to more rules. For it is easier to regulate one public monopoly than a handful of private oligopolies. Furthermore, a number of social, economic and cultural values have to be safeguarded in this complex situation, such as universal service and affordable access to public networks, free competition and the protection of cultural values from outside interference. The coexistence of partially or completely integrated networks requires agreement on interconnectivity, standards, subscriber numbers, rates, rights of ownership and so forth (Noam, 1992).

Information Highways and Regulation

The necessity for reregulation will show up again in the construction of several information superhighways side by side. So far, we have the perspective of at least three types of superhighway. The first is constructed of digitalized and broadened fibre-optic *public telephone networks* extended with mobile telephony. The PTOs are currently spending fortunes to complete digitalization, to broaden infrastructure and to create new interactive services, for instance Internet services. Their competitors are doing the same, partly hiring their infrastructure.

The second type of information superhighway is developed by *cable networks*, which are extremely important in countries with high cable density such as the Netherlands and Belgium. Operators of cable TV systems are concentrating their efforts on being able to afford the high investments needed for the adaptation of their distribution networks. They have to be changed into networks with two-way traffic and they need the construction or lease of expensive digital switching nodes and exchanges. Here the need for cooperation with telephone companies is obvious – for an important goal is to offer telephony as well.

The third type of superhighway is constructed in the 'ether'. These are the digital *satellite networks* springing from (commercial) television or from telephony and data communications. Global systems of satellites close to the earth or high in space are offered as complete alternatives to terrestrial connections. Microsoft's plans for a network of geostationary satellites at relatively low altitude is a good example in this respect.

In theory, these three types of superhighway offer the same facilities: telephony, data carriage, broadcasting and audiovisual services. In practice, they will probably concentrate on one or two of these activities.

This multitude of information superhighways – and all other varieties and (inter)connections not mentioned – requires a huge amount of regulation on the issues mentioned earlier. Interconnectivity in particular will be very important. The necessity for consumers to subscribe to several or perhaps even all highways if they want to fulfil all their communication needs has to be avoided. One connection by cable or by aerial into the home should suffice. And a major issue should always be the accessibility of public information and communication facilities to everyone.

Access Systems and Regulation One of the most important facilities to (re)regulate is the access systems for computer networks and interactive broadcasting. The control of these systems will decide who will be in power on the future information superhighway. Regulation must safeguard open access for producers and consumers and prevent gatekeeping and other oligopolistic practices. The first test has already appeared in computer networks. The inclusion of Microsoft's own **browser** Internet Explorer into its operating system Windows has launched a hot legal dispute in the US and elsewhere. The fear is that Microsoft will use its predominant position in operating systems to favour its browser, search engine and other software or services. Comparable contests in digital broadcasting are to be expected. Several suppliers have developed and presented their own set-top boxes (hardware) with application programming interfaces (operating systems for interactive broadcasting), electronic programme guides (comparable to Internet browsers), television programme bouquets and **web portals**. Just as Microsoft is trying to control the supply of software and services, so a few big interactive broadcast corporations (like Time Warner, Disney, News Corporation, Microsoft NBC, Bertelsmann, Kirch and Canal+) are trying to control the gateways, instruments of selection and programme supply in the digital radio, television, audio and video of the future. These instances of vertical integration must be controlled by new (inter)national regulation for open access, interconnectivity and non-proprietary standards. Otherwise information freedom and economic competition will be in danger.

CONSUMERS: PUSHERS AND PULLED

Governments and corporations

The owners and hirers of private networks and the participators of special public networks are the most important driving forces behind the technological and economic supply of networks. Most owners can be found among the (quasi-)government bodies (defence agencies, population administrations and universities) and transnational corporations.

Defence and Space Industry

Some decades ago the largest and most advanced networks were constructed for military applications and for space travel. As early as 1970, the American global defence network AUTOVON already had cable connections of the same length as the entire American telephone network in the 1950s. It already integrated speech and data and had numerous facilities for regulating the priority of what was sent (Martin, 1978). It could withstand a nuclear attack and was equipped with several back-up facilities. Therefore it is no surprise that most breakthroughs in tele- and data communication, such as packet switching, sprung from this industry. Space travel has played an important role in the development of the satellite technology required for fast international connections.

Financial Sector

The second pioneer in the introduction of networks is the financial sector (Reagan, 1989; Castells, 1996). The present world economy, trading monetary values representing about 50 times the value of goods every day, cannot exist without the global networks connecting stock exchanges, large transnational corporations, banks and investment funds. The large international banks, insurance companies and credit card companies were among the first to invest billions in private networks connected by satellites or, if necessary, by terrestrial rental lines. The networks in this sphere of activity have stimulated technical innovation in transmission and in processing large quantities of structured data.

Transnational Corporations

The third series of pioneers consists of international industry, transportation companies and audiovisual media (Palvia et al., 1992). They are responsible for innovations in logistics, the integration of heterogeneous connections and broadband transmission.

Databanks

The large databanks and databases, sometimes connected to networks of universities or libraries, are the fourth pioneer in the development of networks. They broke new ground in the sphere of consultation and in the accessibility and interconnectivity of files with different structures.

The pioneering work of these actors in the 1960s and 1970s enabled the large-scale introduction of separate network systems by companies and public administrations in the 1980s. Their R&D efforts proved to be even more important for the first integrated networks of the 1990s. In the 1990s, the use of separate (business) networks prevailed.

Applications in Production and Distribution

The increasing power and miniaturization of computer equipment, the perfection of intelligent terminals, and the accelerating speed of packet-switched transmission enable a true revolution in data processing in industrial, financial, trade and transport companies. The need for large central computer divisions is reduced by increasing use of *distributed data processing*.

A second series of applications is *monitor systems*. These systems perform measurements, analyse, organize and report. The use of process control systems in the chemical industry, heavy industry, the graphics industry and the food industry is long established. Today there is a swift development in all kinds of safety and signalling systems.

However, the fastest developments are taking place in *transactions* of goods, services and personnel. This branch benefits most from the connections between registration systems that once used to be separate. This offers qualitatively new facilities such as fully automated booking and stock-keeping and electronic registration and control of employees.

The final series of applications in the sphere of production and distribution is *database systems*. The most important types offer marketing and credit information, legal and bibliographical reference and economic or financial news.

Applications in Administration

In the meantime, networks in offices are created by connecting formerly separated functions, equipment and workplaces (see the section earlier in this chapter about the streamlined office). The oldest applications are accounting and administration, both very suitable for computerization. But automation of the lifeblood of an office, that is word processing, is the greatest leap forward. Connecting formerly unattached word processors and documentary systems in a network is the most important step towards the streamlined office. It gives access to applications such as electronic mail, electronic meetings and digital archives. These, in their turn, are a welcome addition to management information systems. More and more often these management information systems will be connected to the systems mentioned above, thus turning them into the nerve centre of the organization (see Hawryskiewicz, 1996). All this results from the convergence of process automation, logistics and office automation, which in large companies has been going on for at least 20 years.

Households and individuals

Lagging Demand

Sharply contrasting with the demand for computer networks, hardware, software and services by big (trans)national corporations is the lagging demand by small and medium enterprises (SMEs) and households or individual consumers. Clearly, this illustrates the sequence of adoption of the new media in general: first the large enterprises; then their professional employees and people working in departments of higher education; then the SMEs; and finally, a long way behind, the mass of households and individual consumers. The adoption of the new media by the last group is essential to pay for the high investment in the large-scale infrastructure of the information superhighway of the future. This explains the desperate scramble by the IT industry in the 1980s and 1990s to bring on to the market one new medium after another. As almost all of them failed until the middle of the 1990s, these attempts may be termed *technology push*.

Market Failures   In the 1980s and the first half of the 1990s, there has been an impressive series of (consumer) market failures in the supply of new media devices and services: the videophone, the videodisk, videotex, CD-I, the first generation of personal digital assistants and the systems of (home) video on demand, to mention just the most important.

Only since the middle of the 1990s have we witnessed a partial break-through of personal computers, digital and mobile telephony and, to a lesser degree, Internet connections in households. It is partial because the broad diffusion of these new media is still confined to some Western countries, primarily in their most developed (city) regions and industrial/financial centres. Here the household penetration of PCs reaches between 30 and 50 per cent, and Internet connections between 10 and 20 per cent. However, the introduction of so-called **full service networks** – integrated networks of broadcasting, information, transaction and interpersonal communication services for households (see Baldwin et al., 1996) – has appeared to be a bridge too far in Northern America and Western Europe (see Fidler, 1997). They were cancelled or substantially cut back to a few successful single services.

Reasons for the   What are the main reasons for these evident failures of the new media on
Mismatch of   the consumer market? To answer this question one has to appreciate that
Design and   the introduction of new technologies is a matter of *design by producers*
Demand   and *domestication by consumers* (Silverstone and Hadden, 1996). Domes-tication is the appropriation of new technologies by consumers in house-holds, workplaces and other private places, making them acceptable in their own familiar everyday lives. Domestication is anticipated in design, and design is completed in domestication (1996: 46). So, it appears that design and domestication have become separated in the recent drive for adoption of the new media by households and individual consumers. Three interrelated characteristics are responsible for this mismatch.

First, a *supply-side view* dominates design, production and marketing of the new media. They are held to be so superior in features like speed, mobility, comfort and other benefits or communication capacities, like those described in Chapter 1, that their demand is taken for granted when their prices drop to a reasonable level. Therefore, unprejudiced market research before and after introduction is scarce. Rarely are user groups invited to participate in design. Of course, the new media are designed and constructed with users in mind. But putting them on the market remains a matter of trial and error instead of real and valid experiment. When a new medium appears to be reasonably successful, all bets are placed on it; when it does not catch on, it is simply dropped. In both cases there is insufficient learning about the causes of success or failure.

The second characteristic of the introduction of the new media is the dominance of *technical* design. Technicians develop most hardware and software. They are so devoted to the presumed splendid technical capabilities of their artefacts that they neglect real user perspectives and pay insufficient attention to user-friendliness. They simply cannot imagine that a particular target group will not use their technically superior products. It would not be rational to refuse them. They do not realize that the adoption of new technologies is a social and cultural affair as well. Many consumers will stick to their old habits, daily routines and emotional attachments to old technologies for personal and social reasons which go much deeper than simple utilitarian, rational objectives.

Here we encounter the third and most basic reason for the mismatch between design and domestication. In the offer of new media products a *device perspective* (hardware) or *service perspective* (software) is taken instead of a social and contextual perspective. A good example is the technical convergence of the computer and the television, as in the supply of web TV. Technically speaking it will become easy to watch TV on a multimedia computer and to use computer services like the Internet on television screens. However, this does not mean that these will become dominant social and personal practices in the real settings and daily routines of households. Computer use is mainly an individual affair, with people working and playing close to small screens with extended keyboards, usually in a study. Television viewing is both an individual and a collective activity, with people entertaining themselves watching large screens using a limited remote control, most often in the living room, kitchen or bedroom.

The simple technical availability of multifunctional computers and televisions does not mean that they will be accepted in the social settings and relationships of households. This is the heart of domestication. The same goes for information, communication, entertainment and transaction services, which are believed by their designers to be superior in use and enjoyment, but do not manage to become embedded in the daily routines of households and individual consumers. Surprisingly little attention is given to research into the social and contextual environments where the new media are supposed to work. The spatial characteristics and usage patterns in living, working and cultural places are neglected, as are the social relationships of gender, generation, status and power in households (see Morley, 1986; Silverstone and Hadden, 1996).

However, the main reason for the failure of most new media on the consumer market, at least until the middle of the 1990s, is the very rational reason that they have simply offered insufficient *surplus value* as compared with the old media. These days most observers take it for granted that the new media will not replace the old ones completely, but will be added to them. This is one of the most striking effects of media history in the twentieth century. It means that new media should have a particular surplus value of their own. At the time of writing it appears that consumers are fairly satisfied with the old media of broadcasting, the press and telephony, used separately. Moreover, they can be improved and adapted to enable more comfort, more selectivity and more interactivity. They offer so much diversity in themselves that the opportunities of choice appear to be satisfactory to most consumers. In Chapter 1 the comparatively low level of interactivity in the usage of the new media was described. The failure of the full service networks indicates that the mass of household consumers is not ready for the other main characteristic of the new media either: integration.

Expected and Actual Applications
All these rather sceptical perspectives do not imply that the new media will fail on the consumer market forever. They just mean that success will take considerably longer than the new media industry would like. Moreover, the final adoption of the new media by the mass of consumers might be different from that expected now. This is another striking feature of media history. For example, the telephone was designed to be a medium for business and emergencies, not for social talk between people, especially women (Moyal, 1992). Radio users were expected to become broadcasters at the beginning of the twentieth century, but they ended up as listeners. Computers were designed to calculate or process data and certainly not to play games with. The most important type of application of the new media in households is not yet known either. The current dominance of business and professional uses makes one part of industry think that information (services) and transaction (electronic commerce and ordering things) will be the so-called 'trigger applications' of the new media for the mass of households as well. Another part, primarily the vested interests in the media industry and telecommunications, expects that it will be primarily entertainment and communication, since they correspond to the mass applications of broadcasting, the press and telephony in the twentieth century. Both parts of industry may be right. In Chapter 6 it is estimated that the so-called 'information rich' might be most interested in new applications of information and advanced transactions or communications, while the 'information poor' might stick to new applications in entertainment and simple transaction or communication. If this turns out to be true, we would observe the growth of a usage gap in the adoption of the new media.

The growth of usage gaps is very likely, as the main reason for the more successful introduction of the new media in the future is the opportunity for differentiation, individualization or personalization of demand for the services they offer. The user is much better able to choose the time, place and kind of application according to his/her own individual needs for information and communication than with the old media. These diverging needs fit the development of modern (network) society (see Chapters 6 and 7). However, the differentiation of information and communication patterns in households makes the removal of the mismatch between design and domestication all the more necessary, as the contexts of consumption become more complicated.

POLITICS AND POWER

Network Position and Power

The central theme in this chapter is power. The division of power is one of the most important social aspects in the construction and use of networks. These media are by no means technically or politically neutral. The structure of a network enables both centralization and decentralization. The centre, nodes and terminals can be connected in several ways. In the future, the position of people in media networks will largely determine their position in society. Compared with this, the content of communication transmitted in these networks is of secondary importance. This shows how deceptive the popular phrases 'information is power' or 'knowledge is power' really are. It is not just having access to information or knowledge that is important, but also being in the right position to use it. Few would consider the outstanding creators and processors of knowledge and information in our society – scientists, information experts and journalists – to be the people in control of it. One thing is for certain: people who do not have the skill to use information belong to the powerless. Therefore, having at one's disposal knowledge or information is a necessary but not a sufficient condition for the possession of power.

Having a position in which one decides about the organizational and technical conditions for the construction and use of networks is the first and most important factor in one's position of power in network society. This applies to positions on every level. On a macro-level, the construction of networks involves the balance of power between governments and citizens, public administrations and clients, employers and employees, managers and operatives, producers and consumers. On the (meso-)level of organizations, the power shifts caused by the construction and use of networks are best displayed, as will be shown in this chapter. On a micro-level, the social and psychological effects of mediated communications are altering the balance of power between individuals, as will be discussed in Chapters 6, 7 and 8.

However, for a number of reasons this chapter will start with the most general level. People often tend to forget that control by (all positions in) a system not only increases but also decreases as a result of the introduction of networks. The system, trying to gain strength in communications, becomes dependent upon a technical medium. Media networks turn out to be extremely vulnerable technologies.

The third and fourth sections will deal with the way power is divided between the state and citizens in large political units. Networks can lead to either a more powerful state (concentration of political power) or more power for citizens and social interests (dispersion of political power). They can be used for central surveillance and registration by the state, but also for local autonomy and citizen participation in political decision-making.

The fifth section is about the transformation of power in organizations partly caused by the construction and use of networks. Both centralization and decentralization, an extreme division of tasks and an increase in teamwork, appear to be possible. Whatever happens, middle management will have to face the greatest changes.

The final section is about individual citizens, employees, clients and consumers at the network's ends, the terminals. The personal autonomy of individuals (freedom of choice) and the privacy of individuals are at stake because networks connect public and private spheres of life.

THE VULNERABILITY OF NETWORKS

Everybody knows by now that things can go wrong with computer networks. We are informed again and again of yet another hack, virus, violation of privacy and breakdown. And at the end of the 1990s worries grew about the so-called *year 2000 problem*. Many operating systems, databases, software programs and chips used for older computers and other micro-electronic equipment do not recognize the date 2000. In the year 2000, we may be painfully aware of how vulnerable our network society has become by making itself completely dependent upon computer systems. In recent decades, countless congresses and seminars about the security of information systems have been offered. And in spite of, or perhaps as a result of, the problems being reduced to concrete technical, organizational and legal proportions, fully satisfactory solutions remain to be found.

Technical Vulnerability It is remarkable how the problem of network vulnerability is reduced to aspects of technical security and the protection of confidentiality and privacy. In fact, vulnerability is a much broader problem. It is about *the stability of the entire social system* working with new information and communication technologies. The system is making itself dependent on powers over which it has no (complete) control. When technology fails, the

Social Vulnerability system cannot function any more, or only continues to function with problems, sometimes even big ones. Furthermore, it can generate internal forces opposing the use of technology, resisting the effects or even destroying them. This can happen when certain social groups or classes feel they are deprived of certain rights or pushed to the margins of society as some kind of 'misfits' in the network society. Finally, the power of the system as a whole can be threatened from outside by units that have a wider reach.

Thus, in most countries, national sovereignty is at stake because nations are conceding their grip on their own economy, culture and political policy to the networks of international broadcasting computer communications, industry and, most important of all, financial trade.

The broad idea of vulnerability developed here applies to information technology in general. But it applies to networks in particular. They possess certain *characteristics enhancing their vulnerability in daily usage*, as follows.

Characteristics Enhancing Vulnerability

Size is a network's most important characteristic. A network's reach largely determines its power and usability. At the same time, the network becomes harder for the network management to control. The chances of something going wrong increase. More than separate machines and applications, a network depends on the quality of hardware and software.

Integration of central and local sources or carriers of information, and their *multifunctionality* are also strong features of networks. However, precisely these features cause a – direct or indirect – effect across the entire network if there is a failure in one section. Clear examples are computer viruses and computer hackers; most often they can 'travel' unhindered within and between networks. A network's technical design is able to minimize the failures caused by them, but only at the expense of accessibility, flexibility and efficiency.

Accessibility for many interconnected users is one of the strong features of a network, but at the same time one of its weaknesses. The chances of ignorant and unauthorized people having access to the network increase proportionally.

Networks enhance the *complexity* of information systems in comparison with separate units. Numerous new communication problems arise. Furthermore, complexity increases as local units (intelligent terminals or PCs) become able to do more by themselves. As a network becomes more complex, the chances of failure increase in proportion. And the origin of such failures becomes harder to trace and solve.

Increasing complexity usually leads to *dependence on a few experts*: technicians and network operators. The potential drop-out or unreliability of these experts – caused by illness, a strike, incompetence or fraud – make these networks vulnerable.

A common though avoidable feature of networks is the *absence or deterioriation of back-up facilities*. When there is a failure, there is no old equipment, software or storage to fall back on. A related problem, more fundamental and harder to avoid, is the fact that old knowledge and (manual) methods and procedures will eventually disappear from workers' memories. For example, many retired designers and programmers had to be summoned back to the job to solve the year 2000 problem.

Solutions?

Most solutions to these problems in fact limit the positive features of networks. Some strategic options have far-reaching consequences: should networks be reduced in size or made less functional and integrated? This can be achieved by installing smaller networks for one purpose which can be interconnected, but do not have to be. Interconnections can be made more or less complex and secure. Furthermore, the connection itself can be kept as 'basic' as possible. This means 'intelligence' is stored at the centre and in the terminal equipment alone.

Companies often try to reduce complexity by purchasing ready-made systems instead of using a hybrid combination of old and new equipment or several stand-alone devices. Furthermore, they strive for standardization and compatibility. Access for all is the most tangible feature. It was also the first feature to be restricted. Most existing technical and organizational security is based on restrictions. Yet many experts say foolproof security of networks can never be realized. They should not support this claim solely by stating that security relies on people. The user-friendliness of a network – which everyone wants – is achieved through its size, multifunctionality and interconnectivity, and these automatically increase the chances of failure and unauthorized access. Besides, any limitation of accessibility conflicts with the distribution of knowledge and power which safeguards against dependence on a few experts.

Installing back-up facilities for hardware, software and storage capacity is a very costly process. The same goes for preserving old technology, methods of organization and operating procedures. Soon back-up is accorded a lower priority. In many cases, keeping complete and adequate facilities in reserve would make installation of a network unprofitable.

The preceding list shows how most solutions limit or even nullify the usability of networks. Some solutions increase vulnerability in new directions. Furthermore, they might have a disruptive impact on the balance of power within the social system concerned, as we shall see several times in the remainder of this book. But first, power in the social system as such, and the system's vulnerability to the social risks involved in using networks, will be discussed. The decision to install a network is first and foremost a political choice, even though it is often made under the heavy external pressures of scale extension and increasing competition.

THE SPREAD AND CONCENTRATION OF POLITICS

The Support of Democracy and Civil Rights

Without doubt, the diffusion of communication media and an increasing level of education have been the most important factors in the world-wide revival of the movements for civil rights and democracy during the 1980s and 1990s. The spread of international networks of mass communication and telecommunication had a big impact on the collapse of the Stalinist regimes in Eastern Europe and on the rise of movements fighting for democracy in developing countries. It may be said that, owing to the daily broadcasts of Western radio and television programmes and the increase in international telephone calls, the fall of the Berlin Wall and the collapse of the Soviet Union were inevitable in the long run. Even relatively 'closed' countries such as Romania, Albania and the southern Soviet republics, and developing countries weak in democracy such as China, Nepal, Kenya and Zambia, turned out to be susceptible to the influences of international media of communication.

Totalitarianism: Old and New Forms

The thesis of information and communication technologies presenting a 'lethal' threat to *traditional* totalitarian political systems, based on the centralization and control of all information and communication in a particular territory, can easily be defended. It is impossible to centrally register and control all individual activities of small-scale production and large-scale distribution across any border using these technologies. No traditional totalitarian regime can remain in power after the massive introduction of PCs, diskettes, faxes and all sorts of new audiovisual equipment. On the other hand, several new types of rule with a totalitarian flavour are conceivable using this new technology, as one of its capacities is to enable central management, surveillance and control (see Burnham, 1983; Mulgan, 1991; Gandy, 1994; Lyon, 1995, Beniger, 1996). To get a true view of these new types of rule, one should abandon the idea that they need *direct* supervision (in the Orwellian sense) or *total* control of every level of production and distribution of information. Central political and economic power only has to be wielded when citizens, workers or consumers cross one of the carefully chosen lines guarded electronically by large-scale, interconnected systems of registration and surveillance. There are methods of checking on people and their activities which are much more efficient than direct supervision, whether electronic or by eye. They allow plenty of room and freedom, but when a certain line is crossed, a 'red alarm' is triggered at some central control. See the final section of this chapter for further discussion of this dark perspective.

Technology of Freedom or Control?

In view of the contrast presented in the previous paragraph, it is no surprise that there are opposing views concerning the effects of ICT on freedom, democracy and organization. To some, ICT is a *technology of freedom* since it enhances the freedom of choice for individuals and intensifies horizontal (bottom-up) relations in networks of organizations and individuals (Pool, 1983). Others claim that, since the design and introduction of ICT are determined by leaders in governments, public administrations, businesses and other organizations, it is primarily a technology of central registration, surveillance and control. They are accused of using ICT to get a firmer grip on their organizations and subordinates (Burnham, 1983; Loudon, 1986; Gandy, 1994; Zuurmond, 1994).

Network Structure in the Political System

Let us first concentrate on the actual development in governments and public administrations before getting embroiled in this ideological discussion. This development can be mapped. The relations between all actors involved in political activities in the widest sense can be subsumed in a comprehensive model of the political system (see Figure 4.1). In the previous chapter, the manifestation of the infrastructure of the network society in the economy was described in terms of networks within and between companies. Figure 4.1 shows that the politics of the network society are also organized in a network structure. All the relations between the different actors of the political system – governments, parliaments and public

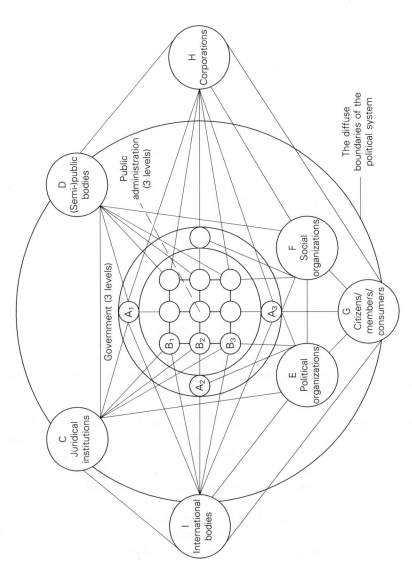

FIGURE 4.1 Network structure of the political system

administrations on a national, regional and local level, political parties and organizations in civil society, international bodies, legal authorities, (semi-) public institutions, corporations and individual citizens – can be interpreted both as political relations (of power) and as relations of information and communication. Media networks and their applications increasingly organize and shape these relations. Figure 4.1 should be seen as a model of a dynamic system, able to show how some relations and actors become of central importance while others drop out or become peripheral.

Spread of Politics In *Digital Democracy* (Hacker and van Dijk, forthcoming), the author of this book comes to the conclusion that ICT contributes to both a spread and a concentration of politics. The use of ICT enhances existing centrifugal forces in the political system, because in the heart of the system, institutional political forces have to give up some of their powers in favour of international bodies, (inter)national companies, legal institutions, privatized agencies and individual citizens and corporations sharply calculating according to their own interests. With the aid of ICT, they can start their own relations of information and communication and spheres of influence and management. Thus, they can shape a politics of their own and bypass the government's coordinating role in a given territory. Unlike a state, ICT has no frontiers.

Concentration of Politics On the other hand, networks enable attempts at total registration by governments and public administrations, strengthen the power of civil servants over parliaments, and allow the subordination of most political parties to the machinery of the state as these parties become the prime distributors of political and official functions. So, ICT also supports attempts to concentrate politics (van Dijk, forthcoming). Departments of the government and the public administration are among the first to introduce ICT on a large scale. It is obvious that they use this technology for their own primary tasks of governing, coordinating and collecting taxes rather than for the improvement of the representation of citizens and parliaments.

One-sided Visions Nevertheless, the analysis of those expecting a strong government of total registration and control to arise is as one-sided as the analysis of those who think the state will wither away or even dissolve into virtual relationships of horizontal types of organization appearing on the Internet. Frissen (1999) perceives the rise of a *virtual state* and the disappearance of traditional politics into the margins of society. Along the same lines, Guéhenno (1993) has predicted the *end of politics and democracy*. According to him they will be replaced by a system of informal relations and networks without a clear centre:

> in the age of networks, the relationship between citizens and the body of politics competes with the infinite number of connections citizens make outside this body. Politics is far from being the prime organizer of the life of people and society; instead it appears as a second-rate activity, an artificial construction no longer able to solve practical problems in a changing world. (1993: 37–8, my translation from the French)

Both visions are one-sided, since networks consist not only of (horizontal) connections but also of (vertical) centres and nodes. Furthermore, they do not float in the air. They connect actors of flesh and blood (people) and material resources (in households and organizations). In a network society, networks do not replace society, but they increasingly connect and organize its constituents. So, the state still belongs to the strongest (assembly of) actors in society. Therefore, politics and democracy, primarily operating at the level of society, are not doomed. However, they do have to be supported or corrected by political and democratic forces outside institutional politics, among other things with the aid of ICT.

ICT and Views of Democracy

Authors like Guéhenno (1993) and Mowshowitz (1992) have demonstrated why the development of ICT is not necessarily in the interests of democracy. Power might shift to less democratic or even undemocratic forces. Furthermore, the presumed positive influence of ICT on democracy completely depends on what view one has of democracy (see Abrahamson et al., 1988). There are at least six views of democracy in this respect. The first five are coined by Held (1987) as *models of democracy*. Their supporters appear to have different preferences for applying ICT in the political system (Van Dijk, 1996; forthcoming).

ICT and the Reinforcement of Institutional Politics

The first two views on democracy lead to the use of ICT for the *reinforcement of institutional politics*, that is the centre of the political system (see Figure 4.1, A and B, the actors of the government and the public administration). With the spread of politics in general and with the erosion of the national state compared with other (inter)national forces in particular, institutional politics have ended up in a perilous position, which will only be aggravated by ICT. Yet, the most dominant political forces in Western democracies are striking back, using ICT to fortify the positions of the state. The classical Western view on democracy supporting this move is *legalist democracy* – a so-called procedural view of democracy, regarding the constitution and other laws and rules as the foundations of democracy. The three basic principles are: separation of powers (legislative and executive power, the judiciary); a system of checks and balances between the government, the public administration and the judiciary; and representation. In this view, the lack of information gathered by the state is currently the most important problem to be solved with the aid of ICT. So, ICT has to bring about a strong state and an effective administration of government. Furthermore, it can help to improve public support for the government and the administration by offering more and better information in both directions.

The second conception of democracy is called *competitive democracy*. It is mainly supported in countries with a two-party or a presidential system. According to this view, parties and leaders compete for the support of the electorate. This rather elitist view of democracy emphasizes representation and efficient decision-making by leaders. ICT is first and foremost used for information campaigns and election campaigns. In the United States, a lot of experience has been gained with this use of ICT (Newman, 1994; Selnow, 1994). Public information systems and telepolling can help voters in their choice of the best leaders and policies.

ICT and the
Socialization of
Politics

The other four views of democracy have a completely different strategic orientation. Supporters of these views fight for a *socialization of politics* – a further dispersion of politics through the system as a whole (referring to the actors around the outside of the model in Figure 4.1). This implies a more prominent role for social organizations and individual citizens in particular. The assumption is that ICT will enable them to have a direct influence on politics, and even to bypass institutional politics or replace it with their own political relations. Figure 4.1 clearly shows that their relations can be created in this way (bypassing the centre). While views intending to strengthen institutional politics are mainly supported by politicians and administrators, these alternative views are defended by many social organizations and intellectuals.

The most radical view concerning existing political practice is *plebiscitary democracy*. According to this view, political decisions have to be made through referenda or plebiscites. This implies a preference for direct democracy instead of representative democracy. The opportunities offered by ICT to hold telepolls or telereferenda and to have electronic discussions have had an immediate appeal to the supporters of this view. They are said to revive direct democracy as practised in the Athenian agora. The term 'teledemocracy'* has been introduced (Arterton, 1987; Barber, 1984; Becker, 1981). Teledemocracy means that citizens and social organizations are able to directly determine at a distance, using ICT, what goes on at the political heart of the political system. See Arterton (1987), Barber (1984) and Becker (1981) on the possibilities and limitations.

Another alternative view is *pluralist democracy*. In this view, opinion formation within and between social organizations is emphasized. Democracy is not the will of the majority but that of a constantly changing coalition of minorities. Its most important value is pluralism in social and political discussion and in the media. It is a combination of direct and representative democracy, since representation is exercised not only by politicians but also by social organizations. ICT offers numerous opportunities for pluralism in public debates, among them Internet debates, and for discussions within social organizations, for example by using an intranet.

The fifth view discussed here is *participatory democracy*. Its supporters promote a socialization of politics, encouraging active citizenship. The emphasis lies on the broadest possible opinion formation about political affairs and on a particular combination of direct and representative democracy. Its most important instruments are public debates, public education and citizen participation in general. If the new media are to play a positive role in enabling these instruments, access for all is vital.

The last view on democracy has appeared as a dominant model among the pioneers of the Internet community. This does not mean that the political views behind it are entirely new. Many observers have noticed the affinity of the Internet pioneers to the radical social movements of the 1960s and 1970s in most Western countries. These views range from classical anarchism and left-wing socialism to all kinds of libertarianism.

The last are most important in the 1990s. The *libertarian view* is close to the pluralist and plebiscitarian views in several respects, as the opportunities for (virtual) community, telepolling and teleconversation are proclaimed. Specific to libertarianism is the emphasis on autonomous politics by citizens in their own associations using the horizontal communication capabilities of ICT in general and the Internet in particular. In its most extreme form, institutional politics is held to be obsolete and to be superseded by a new political reality collectively created in networks. The basic problem to be solved, according to this view, is that the centralism, bureaucracy and backwardness of institutional politics are such that it fails to live up to expectations (the primacy of politics) and is unable to solve the most important problems of modern society. A combination of Internet democracy and a free-market economy will serve as a replacement. This is well summarised by Katz (1997):

> In *The Birth of a Digital Nation* I described a new 'postpolitical' community that blends the humanism of liberalism with the economic vitality of conservatism. I wrote that members of this group consistently reject both the interventionist dogma of the left and the intolerant ideology of the right. Instead, I argued, Digital Citizens embrace rationalism, revere civil liberties and free-market economics, and gravitate toward a moderated form of libertarianism.

The preference for Internet applications such as electronic debate, virtual community building and telepolling implies that the libertarian model is both a substantial and a procedural conception of democracy and that it is much closer to direct than to representative democracy.

APPLICATIONS OF THE NEW MEDIA IN THE POLITICAL SYSTEM

Overview of Applications   The applications of the new media in the political system are so heterogeneous that clear analytical distinctions are required. The information traffic patterns discussed in Chapter 1 can offer a broad distinction as they contain a dimension of power. In Table 4.1 the major applications of the new media in the political system are displayed. They will be briefly discussed.

Allocution applications

The new media of allocution offer the best parallel to current political practice. In allocution a centre remains the source and deciding agency of the political information supplied, but some elements of consultation and

TABLE 4.1   Applications of the new media in the
political system

Allocution
Interactive press and broadcasting
Political campaigns
Government information campaigns

Consultation
Mass public information systems
Advanced public information systems (the Internet etc.)
Parliamentary information systems
Civil service information centres

Registration
Government and public administration registration systems
Computer-assisted citizen enquiries
Electronic polls
Electronic referenda
Electronic elections

Conversation
Electronic mail
Electronic debates and teleconferencing
Interactive press and broadcasting (discussion)
Group decision support systems

---

registration are added. The centre can be a body of political or public administration, a political party, a social organization or a corporation engaged in politically relevant activities. These centres offer the public more opportunities to choose and to feed back signals than in the old mass media. The latter are made interactive up to a particular level. Subsequently, the new media are used in such a way that transmission from the centre remains the predominant pattern.

Interactive Press and Broadcasting (Information)   The first applications are the interactive press and broadcasting. In 1998, this type of transmission existed only in two-way cable television or satellite television and in the publication of newspapers or magazines on the Internet. These media enable politically interested receivers and users to retrieve information on policies, parties, candidates and suchlike. Interactive broadcasting, still in its infancy, enables consumers to select particular political programmes and news from a menu. The Internet already offers the possibility of searching electronic newspapers and magazines for specific political information or of having them delivered daily/weekly to a personal e-mail account as part of an electronic cutting service. But the provider still determines what the contents will be.

Political Campaigns   Obviously these media are very suitable for political campaigns (see Rash, 1997). These campaigns become more effective since consumers ask for the information instead of having it forced upon them. Furthermore, research can be conducted as to which target group is susceptible to which type of advertising. In the United States these applications are already used frequently in permanent electoral campaigns. Computerized telephone systems, two-way cable television and the Internet are frequently used for telepolls. Reactions to speeches, advertisements and debates between candidates are registered immediately and in real time, serving as a form of applause at a distance (Selnow, 1994).

Increasingly, opinion polls are accompanied by direct marketing. A select target group of people receives a set of questions, instead of advertisements, drawn up especially for this group. So far, this has been done by telephone, letter and videotape. From now on, the Internet and electronic mail offer the possibility to get in touch simultaneously and quickly with potential voters, members and sponsors. In the near future interactive broadcasting will be a main channel. The results of electronic direct marketing are stored in huge databases. These databases enable research producing better data than telepolling on its own, since the latter's response rate is usually poor. Finally, political advertisers appear to use these media to bypass existing mass media with their 'critical' journalists and to open up their own channels to supporters (Selnow, 1994).

Government Information

The new media offer similar opportunities for government information. It looks like political advertising, but there is a difference. Public administration has to deal not only with subjects to be persuaded, but also with citizens who have a right to certain information. This is called instructive government information. In the new media, classical instruction (a one-way process) is changing into a process of mutual information (two-way). The administration is no longer the only party to take the initiative. Citizens address the administration with particular questions. Here the transition to consultation is made.

Consultation applications

Public Information Systems: Mass and Advanced

This transition is completed in public information systems. Using these systems, citizens choose not from *a fixed set* of messages for a *large* public, as was the case with traditional government information, but from *different* messages for a *relatively small* public. The latter form applies more to advanced public information systems than to mass public information systems. Mass public information systems, most often supplied by city governments, are a sort of videotex to be consulted on computer lines, on two-way cable broadcasting and on information boards in public buildings. They offer information of public interest, such as on local citizen affairs, entertainment, news, transport and vacancies.

Advanced public information systems offer far more information than mass systems. However, they do require a relatively high level of initiative, selectivity and skill from users. The Internet and so-called digital cities serve as good examples of these advanced systems. Moreover, these systems offer a lot more than just information retrieval. They are multi-functional digital platforms offering many choices such as local and national debate. Very complex and topical information can be found, at least if one has the skill and motivation. In practice this turns out to be the case for an information elite of politically interested people, professional representatives and interest groups. However, both advanced and mass public information systems have made governments and public administrations accessible to ordinary citizens.

Parliament Information Systems Governments and public administrations themselves gain the opportunity to retrieve and exchange information. They do not merely use the public information systems mentioned above. They use their own, more advanced parliament and management information systems.

Government Information Services Other promising applications of consultation are government information and service centres – locations where large amounts of data or services are integrated in one virtual desk with multifunctional civil servants and information systems. They enable better and faster services, primarily in local communities. A citizen is no longer pushed from one institution to another. All formerly separated government information and transaction services, for instance concerning real estate, are joined in one system.

Registration applications

Government Registration Systems The integration of services and information supply by the government presupposes the existence of extensive, interconnected information systems, such as extremely large *basic* registrations of persons and goods and *sector* registrations used for the execution of particular government tasks. Basic registrations are, for instance, population registers and registers of the treasury, social security and the land registry. Sector registries can be found in the police, social services, housing departments and health services among others. These registries are of great political importance. They are more important for the relationship between government and citizens than, for instance, the Internet. The latter figures more prominently in public opinion, but the government's ICT systems of registration in fact are far more important to civil rights, for example. According to a Dutch public administration scientist:

> the development of the Internet, though very interesting in its own right, takes place at the periphery of power. At the same time, at the centre of power, a process of ever larger and increasingly systematic information processing and supply takes place, linking computer files with personal data and applying all kinds of (artificial) intelligence to increase the transparency of citizens. (Zuurmond, 1996: 66, my translation from the Dutch)

Citizens, individual citizens in particular, cannot equal the power of government bodies which interconnect their own networks and link them to external corporate networks. Citizens' rights, such as the right to privacy and the rights one has as a consumer of government services, are permanently threatened.

The new media probably cause citizens to give the government more information about themselves than vice versa. This also goes for electronic citizen enquiries and referenda. The new media offer all sorts of new methods of research such as electronic panel studies, examining the quality of public services, and surveys by two-way cable television.

Electronic Referenda and Polls Electronic referenda and elections are the most controversial applications. Most often they appear in the perspective of direct democracy. This is not necessarily the case as, for instance, electronic voting machines and consultative referenda (instead of decision-making ones) are relevant to representative democracy as well. However, official electronic votes and referenda from the home will not be used for some time, because of the lack of home access and low political support. Meanwhile all kinds of electronic polls conducted independently by the media and organizations in society will continue to put pressure on political representatives and administrators.

Conversation applications

Electronic Mail New media opportunities to improve communications between citizens and administrators have had a lot of publicity. These media are said to close a presumed gap between politics and the citizenry. Electronic mail is the most obvious solution. It can be used to send letters to politicians and administrators. Furthermore, e-mail is extremely convenient for citizens to react to political views and policy documents appearing on the Internet. It will enhance the accessibility of politicians and civil servants. However, the quality and etiquette of using this medium – think about so-called junk mail or 'spam' – will have to improve considerably before people in government will take it seriously.

Electronic Discussions Electronic debates are considered to be potential substitutions for or additions to political meetings. In these debates, groups and individuals are able to contribute to political opinion formation in civil society and to policy-making in the government and the public administration. The latter is called *interactive policy-making*. In the late 1990s, hundreds of thousands of discussion lists and newsgroups popped up on the Internet. When new policies have to be made, some local authorities and national government departments in Western countries already organize Internet debates among the citizenry themselves. A serious problem is that these debates do not easily lead to consensus and conclusions (the reasons will be explained in Chapter 8). Moreover, participation is unstable and uneven: the intensity changes, and in practice access is restricted to a politically interested and well-educated elite. At the time of writing, electronic debates have had few if any effects on institutional politics.

Interactive Press and Broadcasting (Discussion) The interactive press and broadcasting are able to organize political debates as well. So-called **electronic town hall** meetings are broadcast on television, and discussion pages are opened in electronic papers enabling viewers and readers to respond to questions directly by phone, two-way cable or the Internet.

Group Decision Support Systems   The most advanced political conversation applications are systems supporting decision-making: so-called group decision support systems and electronic boardrooms. Answering questionnaires, the user can make a certain choice, a decision to vote or another conclusion after some rounds of discussion. Making choices is guided by the databases, models and questions programmed into these systems.

Conclusion   In *Digital Democracy* (Hacker and Van Dijk, forthcoming), the author of this book has drawn the conclusion that the new media will bring important changes to our political system, using the applications just described, but will not cause a revolution. These changes are expressions of the spread and concentration of politics discussed earlier. It does not seem likely that the new media will lead to an increase in citizens' participation in the political system. There are no 'simple' technical solutions to a lack of political motivation. Many have assumed that the possibility of participating in political processes at any time and place would break down barriers. It will certainly do this for disabled and ill people and for people who work irregular hours. On the other hand, a new barrier is erected against people who do not have access to the new media or who do not know how to handle them (see Chapter 6).

POWER IN THE ORGANIZATION

Networks and Organizational Structures   The previous chapter explained how networks can be used to change the *superstructure* of a (large) business organization. They turned out to support a combination of concentrating power, finance and control and decentralizing production and execution. At a lower level in the superstructure of organizations, networks may affect the formation of divisions and departments. The parallel structure of divisions in the 'Japanese' production model has already been mentioned. Such a parallel structure, or similar ones such as the division structure and the matrix organization used in project groups (see Khandwalla, 1977; Mintzberg, 1993), will supersede the classical structure of functional departments. Until recently this structure has characterized all bureaucratic organizations by putting similar functions together in one division, and in fact by urging divisions to become independent and to create their own layers of control. Networks offer the opportunity to join or unite divisions again. Tasks can be integrated in multifunctional workstations or terminals connected for computer-supported cooperative work. Whatever structure one chooses, using networks always means a need to harmonize functions and tasks within and between divisions. This functional integration must affect existing organizational structures. In the past, many managers have underestimated this effect, believing that network technology was just the next step in the technical development of their organizations.

Modernizing Bureaucracy   Not only is the superstructure, but also the *structure within* organizations, fundamentally changed by the introduction of networks. We are talking about changes in management. In the previous chapter we have seen how bureaucracy turned out to be an obstacle instead of an innovation for organizations. By modernizing bureaucracy, ICT can help to get rid of this obstacle. According to Max Weber (1922) bureaucracy has five features:

1 hierarchy of authority;
2 centralization of decision-making;
3 formalization of rules;
4 specialization of tasks;
5 standardization of actions.

The use of ICT does not make these features disappear. On the contrary, they are integrated in this technology. Frissen (1989) has demonstrated the close relationship between bureaucracy and ICT. This is obvious for three of the features just mentioned. ICT offers much better opportunities for formalizing rules, specializing tasks and standardizing actions than did the old techniques. In using computers and networks, traditional procedures are formalized by programming them in software or even in hardware. Informal solutions have to be rejected as much as possible. People are restricted to their specific tasks more strictly than before, because they know everything they do is registered. Finally, the use of computers and networks leads to an extensive standardization of actions. After all, their use supposes fixed and detailed procedures and strict fine-tuning before one is able to start cooperation in networks.

The relationship between bureaucracy and ICT is less obvious for the first two features mentioned. Many think ICT 'flattens' organizations, as the distribution of network operations requires less hierarchy and centralization of decision-making. So, these features need more detailed explanation.

From Bureaucracy to Infocracy

After having conducted an investigation in a number of Dutch social service departments, Zuurmond (1994) reached the conclusion that hierarchy, centralization, formalization and specialization in these services were decreasing. In some respects, these organizations had become 'flatter'. More teamwork took place at several levels. Civil servants less frequently recorded every step by writing it down. They acquired broader job responsibilities. Even the fifth feature of bureaucracy, standardization, was adapted. Within certain boundaries, civil servants were allowed to produce 'made-to-measure' work in the service. However, the extent of freedom for this work was strictly limited by computerization. Staff were given fewer opportunities to take important decisions themselves than before. Zuurmond claims with great emphasis that, in spite of requiring fewer traditional bureaucratic procedures, ICT causes an increase in (central) control over organization:

> Thus, an organization can create more horizontal structures, take out hierarchical levels, cancel checks and eliminate paper devouring file guiding systems because information architecture can take care of these things. In particular, (routine) coordination and (routine) communication are being

taken over by information systems. Management no longer has to control this coordination and communication: very strict procedures, designed to guide these actions, are allowed to 'disappear'. Now they are inside the system. (1994: 300–1, my translation from the Dutch)

So, the main part of traditional management's tasks is integrated in information techniques. Modern management *selects* and *guides* these techniques. Zuurmond calls his type of management *infocracy*, the successor of bureaucracy (see Zuurmond, 1996 for an elaboration of this concept in English).

Claiming that (central) control over organizations is increasing, while traditional hierarchical and bureaucratic procedures are declining, seems contradictory. What does it really mean? For further explanation we have to make clear the distinctions between the following aspects of the *infrastructure of organizations*:

1 a structure of *control*, regulation and information coordinating decision-making within and between organizational layers;
2 a structure of *authority* in a number of the organizational layers required for hierarchy and coordination;
3 a *division of labour* distributing functions and tasks within the organization.

Control

Centralized or Decentralized Control? The *control of decisions* in networks has to meet high demands. One can meet these demands by both centralization and decentralization. Mintzberg (1979) makes a distinction between a horizontal dimension (within one organizational level) and a vertical dimension (between organizational levels). Applying these concepts here, the following possibilities arise:

1 *Horizontal centralization*: the highest level of management takes complete control (see above); the most important decisions are taken away from staff members, whose only job now is to shape the information network to enable the development of manageable options.
2 *Horizontal decentralization*: increasingly complex information processes give staff functionaries more authority in the organization's management: the so-called 'line structure' (management) loses some of its influence to the 'technostructure'.
3 *Vertical centralization*: the top layers in management take decisions away from the lower levels and even from employees at the base by means of standardization, formalization and increasing routine; inevitably, lines are shorter and parts of middle management become redundant.

4   *Vertical decentralization*: standardization, formalization and increasing routine allow a transfer of decision-making power to the operational levels. They also allow a swift and flexible reaction to changes in the company's environment, an important benefit on the market and in direct relations between personnel and customers or clients.

It is important to note that all four tendencies are technically possible in the introduction of networks. Which tendency will predominate depends not only on the balance of power within the organization, but also on the type and size of the organization, its diversity and the extent of its computerization. An increase in centralization is to be expected in offices which have had a low level of automation until recently. But most organizations will have to deal with a combination of the four tendencies described. Horizontal and vertical decentralization within a centralizing framework will be the most likely combination, as it is clearly enabled by networks of ICT.

Authority

Flat Organizations?   Developments in the structure of *organizational authority* can be shown more clearly. It is common knowledge that the introduction of networks causes a decrease in the number of hierarchical levels. The network 'itself' takes over some of the supervising personnel's coordination tasks. Coordination and supervision are partly replaced by network operations. The work left for supervisors is to watch over and maintain the network instead of supervising and coordinating personnel. Lower and middle management have to give up some of their authority to higher management and staff functionaries on the one hand, and to operatives working independently with the aid of computer programs on the other. From these trends many people have drawn the conclusion that organizations are getting flatter. But this does not have to be the case at all. It would be more true to say that the line between the top and the base is being 'thinned out'. The distance that communications have to bridge is decreasing; the difference in control and authority is not.

These ideas can be clarified by the following analogy. Try to imagine an organization, formerly shaped like a spherical vase, now changed into a sandglass of the same size with a narrow waist and a bottom that is wider than the top. This metaphor is related to the well-known discussion between those stressing the appearance of an ever broader group of well-educated information workers developing new crafts, and those emphasizing tendencies towards polarization between staff and executive functions in the organization. The way in which networks are introduced in most organizations at the time of writing – cutting down middle management, increasing the strategic decision-making power and salaries of a (perhaps smaller) top management, while decreasing the power and the wages of an ever larger pool of flexible production workers – suggests the latter rather than the former tendency (see Harrison, 1994 for more arguments and data). This subject will be discussed in more detail later on.

Division of labour

Integration or Specialization?

Such a tendency towards polarization is avoidable. This opinion is supported by the observation that in the construction of networks the *division of labour within organizations* may lead to integration of tasks (task broadening and even task enrichment) as much as to further specialization (task division and even task erosion). As claimed before, integration of tasks is most likely using ICT. Opening a multitude of programs at one terminal is made easier. Furthermore, task exchanges are supported: it is easier for a person to substitute for someone or to take over for a while. Technology will help to increase the organization's internal flexibility. Looking at things from this angle, we will see tasks *broaden*. Whether this will lead to task *enrichment* for the employee involved depends on the extent of power, education and freedom of action within the programs available. With unchanged policies of task divisions within organizations, the standardization and computer programming of traditional craft or expert knowledge often leads to task *erosion*. Task broadening could serve as a compensation.

The same network technology, however, may lead to unprecedented task *division* in administrative and industrial organizations: tasks are standardized in programs that assign them to specific functions much more strictly than before. The computer system's access registration controls whether this really happens. Subsequently, the system 'itself' determines the observance of the procedures prescribed.

All this shows that network techniques are not power neutral. They are a clear matter of design, for instance in network architecture. Therefore, let us take a closer look at the *technical options* available in network construction. The most important questions in this respect are:

1 Will the main processing capacity be placed in a central or a local position?
2 Will the workstation have its own connection to a central computer or a shared one?
3 Who is able/allowed to communicate with whom over the network?
4 Which programs and files can be used by the various categories of personnel?

The answer to most of these questions is largely determined by the network's technical typology and topology, programmed in the construction and the organization of the OSI standard network layers.

Network Typology   Network *typology* has the following variations, among others:

1 centralized versus distributed processing;
2 multi-user systems of, for instance, network computers, versus PC networks;
3 'dumb' versus 'intelligent' workstations;
4 highly specialized, intelligent workstations versus less specialized multifunctional PCs.

The first option under each item best fits vertical centralization and a strict division of labour; the second option suits vertical decentralization (possibly selective) and task broadening and/or task enrichment. The revolution in micro-electronics has enabled the distributed processing of data. Thanks to miniaturization and a sharp decrease in the price of components, organizations are able to turn to local processing capacities. Now control in the organization can be divided much more easily than in the 'glory days' of the mainframe, which had a clear centralizing effect. Over the past 15 years an unmistakable shift has taken place from mainframes toward minicomputers (so-called servers), LANs and PC networks. The introduction of the network computer (NC), however, might cause new centralization.

A very common choice is the adoption of multi-user systems (in which several users depend on the capacity and programs of one larger computer) versus a PC network (with PCs having their own capacity and interchangeable programs). The aspect of power is probably shown best in the organization's choice between NCs and PCs, or an intermediary form: the net PC.

Yet the most important choice to be made is the extent of the 'intelligence' given to the workstation through its hardware and software. Such a station can be anything from a 'dumb' terminal, that is suitable only for entering data, to a highly specialized intelligent workstation used for scientific information processing.

Finally, the multifunctionality or unifunctionality of a workstation shapes the division of labour. This is mainly a matter of the software available at the station.

Network Topology   Network *topology* (see Chapter 2) is also important to matters of power and communication in organizations. It is easy to understand that a star structure, for instance as adopted in a mainframe system with terminals, centralizes power and the division of tasks and authorities. A ring structure and a bus structure, very common in local area networks, are decentralized in design and operation. A mesh structure, enabling direct links of communication between all terminals as in the telephone network or the Internet, is decentralized as well. However, the scale and complexity of mesh networks is so great that central exchanges and nodes have to regulate all traffic. It depends on the nature of the mesh network – public or private (organizational) exchange – as to whether this technical requirement is extended with a distribution of specific priorities and authorities of communication. The ring and bus structures in local area networks enable all stations to communicate with each other. But here as well, network management is able to block access to particular stations, to determine communication priorities and to impose other regimes. However, these rules can be changed overnight.

PRIVACY AND PERSONAL AUTONOMY

Now we reach the level of the individual. The use of networks can have major consequences for the power of individuals. Their privacy and their personal autonomy can be violated, but they can use the same techniques to protect themselves and to increase their freedom of choice.

We make a distinction between privacy and personal autonomy. Privacy is a freedom. It is a freedom of *individuals*, not of groups or organizations. Personal autonomy is a characteristic of an individual's *relations to others*. It determines the individual's opportunities to gain and protect freedom. Personal autonomy is a synonym for the power of the individual. Here freedom becomes freedom of choice and control – in this case in the use of ICT. Privacy is a precondition of personal autonomy. Without an individual's freedom in general, any freedom of choice is restricted. Therefore this section begins with a discussion of privacy. First, the meaning of privacy is explained. Subsequently, the threats to privacy caused by the use of ICT are discussed. Finally, there will be a treatise on existing possibilities to protect a person's privacy.

What is privacy?

Privacy Definitions   Privacy is an abstract concept bearing many meanings. It is so intangible that many people do not realize its importance. Popular descriptions are expressions like 'privacy is the individual's right to determine whether and to what extent one is willing to expose oneself to others' and 'privacy is the right to be left alone'. A scientifically justifiable definition, however, has to be based on concepts and notions accepted in legal theory, in history or in social science.

Historical and anthropological research have shown that the need for privacy may be universal, but also depends on the structure of an individual's social environment and community culture (Roberts and Gregor, 1971). At the end of extensive comparative historical research of ancient cultures, Barrington Moore (1984) reached the conclusion that the *need* for privacy, defined as the need to seclude one's intimate behaviour, to be alone occasionally and not to (have to) show certain views and behaviour to a group or community, is universal. However, *in historical practice* this need is often subordinated to a primitive social organization and technology, according to Moore. In this book we want to add that, at the end of the twentieth century, the individual is subordinated rather to *advanced* social organization and technology.

In legal theory, privacy is a particular right of freedom. It is a right of no interference, in this case of private life. Nabben and van de Luytgaarden (1996) even went so far as to call this right the *ultimate freedom,* not to be transferred on to a community and to be weighed against other interests.

The social philosopher Holmes produced one of the best definitions, in our view: 'Freedom from intrusion into areas of one's own life that one has not explicitly or implicitly opened to others' (1995: 18). In this definition of privacy, and in many others, spatial and informational dimensions are evident. Privacy is about the *spatial seclusion* of certain areas, starting with the body and its direct surroundings (private life) which are not to be interfered with. Added to this, *phases of information processing* often recur in definitions: the perception, registration and disclosure of the characteristics and behaviour of individuals.

Following Westin (1967), a distinction is often made between relational and informational privacy. Even though we shall see that these two types of privacy often mingle, particularly in the context of networks, we will maintain this division and even add a third type: physical privacy. In fact, the body and its immediate physical surroundings are the ultimate private area. This is the main reason why the act of rape is among the greatest possible violations of one's privacy.

Physical Privacy   Physical privacy is the *right to selective intimacy.* This applies to the inviolability of the body and the fulfilment of intimate human needs, allowing the presence of only a very small selection of other persons or no other people at all. This may not seem to have relevance to ICT. But in fact, biotechnology and information technology are increasingly intertwined. The most important link between them is the information code of life: DNA. Charting all genes of the human species and holding DNA tests have everything to do with a registration of personal data. In the future, DNA will probably produce the most important personal data. They will be recorded with the aid of ICT, which will also be used to link DNA data with other kinds of personal data.

Another potential threat to physical privacy is so-called biometrics. These are first of all identity checks (like eye, face, finger and voice recognition) and entrance checks (screening sensors placed on the body). In addition, analogue and digital video cameras intrude into intimate physical spheres of personal life. For instance, cases are known of employers using cameras to store and process images centrally, to control whether employees spend too much time going to the toilet.

Relational Privacy   Most of the time, camera checks will affect relational privacy: the *right to make contacts selectively.* This is about relationships and behaviour in one's (semi-)private life at home, at work, in forms of transportation (including one's own car) and other less reserved spaces. Being able to determine one's own personal relationships and conduct without other people observing and interfering with them is a fundamental right of freedom. This right might be threatened by the use of communication networks and information systems registering behaviour and relationships at a distance. Electronic house arrest and cameras in (semi-)public places serve as good examples of the registration of behaviour. Recording digital telephone conversations and tracking traffic between telephone numbers, electronic mailboxes and Internet addresses are examples of the registration of relationships.

Informational Privacy

The last type of privacy is informational privacy: *the right to selective disclosure*. In a primitive sense, this type of privacy is as old as mankind (gossip) or writing (the first registers), but the introduction of ICT has made it much more relevant. Information privacy is about the grip the individual has and keeps over his or her personal data and over the information or decisions based on these data. Unfortunately, the concept of personal data has narrowed the common notions of privacy. The protection of privacy has been replaced by the protection of personal *data*, and it is sometimes even turned into the *security* of these data. For obvious reasons, most attention in this book is directed to informational privacy, but the most important links to relational and physical privacy are taken into account as much as possible. We shall describe the integration of these three types of privacy. For instance, the words 'traceability' and 'transparency', to be used below, show the close link between relational, informational and physical privacy.

Threats to privacy

More than all previous phases in the development of ICT, the introduction of networks is a threat to all types of privacy. The threats to informational privacy are most obvious, but relational and physical privacy are endangered as well when the spatial and physical spheres of personal life are opened up.

Traceability

The danger of the *traceability* of all actions of public network users is what scares people most. It becomes a real danger, as the development of services throughout history shows. Financial services, for instance, went through a process starting with the circulation of coins, continuing through payments by cheques and printed accounts, and finally reaching electronic payment. Along this road service providers have obtained increasing amounts of information about their clients. In electronic transactions, the bank is informed of the exact place, time and nature of every transaction and the client receives bank statements of these data. In transaction services, a similar shift from cash to electronic registration is occurring. Intelligent cash registers, point-of-sale terminals, 'road pricing', electronic mail orders and reservations provide ever greater details and personal information about the consumer. This is a golden opportunity for market research, marketing and advertising. On the Internet every step in information and conversation services is recorded by so-called *tracking technologies*. If they want to, webmasters can follow every entry to and every 'click' on their sites. They have two ways to do so. Log files are kept of every step made on the Internet. These log files consist of large series of numbers containing information about the computer and the web browser used and the country they are from. Increasingly, hardware such as processors, and software such as word-processing programs, contain numbers and even the names of their owners. Often the user's electronic mail address is added to this information. This information turns log files into collections of personal data. Analysing them without advanced programs would be extremely labour-intensive. Very often, therefore, a second means is used: the user is offered an invisible *cookie**. A small file containing data on the visitor to a site is created automatically, sent back to the user's web browser and stored on the hard disk without the user knowing it. Every time the user visits this particular site the file is retrieved automatically. Thus, after some time, a user profile has been created. All this takes place without the knowledge of users. The users are often helpful in filling in all sorts of questionnaires before using a particular service. Most often, the unsuspecting user does not know that the questionnaire actually completes the user profile.

Checks on Decentralized Conversation   It is obvious that registration and consultation services cause the greatest danger to privacy because they have a powerful centre which is 'hungry' for personal data. But with the rise of digital communication networks using registration software, privacy in decentralized conversation is also at stake. For example, tapping and reading someone else's electronic mail is fairly simple. This danger does not spring only from people breaking into a centre of registration (like hackers). Increasingly the threat comes from the centre itself. For example, managers may want to (be able to) read all of the electronic mail of their employees – although more often they are satisfied with just checking the addresses they visit and the services they use. As the role of central exchanges in decentralized conversation grows, the capacity for these checks increases. In software-controlled digital electronic exchanges and switches, the duration and the costs of the connection and the number of the sender and the receiver are always registered.

Calling Line Identification   The next consideration is a much more open use of the subscriber's number in digital networks. This use is facilitated by 'digital telephony' as described in Chapter 2. Especially important in this respect is calling line identification (CLI). The display of (digital) telephones, like those used for ISDN or GSM, shows the number of the caller. From a privacy protection point of view, the most important advantage is the shift in power from the caller to the called. Ever since the introduction of automatic telephony, the caller has had disproportionate power in the process of making contact. CLI makes it harder for callers to get away with unwelcome calls, such as obscene calls and fake emergency calls. Now, emergency services only have to look at a number to find out where to go.

The most important disadvantage of CLI is that a subscriber automatically passes on his number (for blocking options see below). Marketing people, businesses in general and security organizations will use or misuse the automatic delivery of numbers to create enormous databases containing orders and purchases together with the numbers, the persons and the type and length of calls. They are able to register who has called when, how often and for what purposes. They deduce a lot of information from these data with the aid of advanced software. Furthermore, companies and private persons can enter lists of numbers to be admitted or excluded. Employers are now able to determine whom their employees can and cannot call. An obvious disadvantage is the harm to legitimate anonymous telephone calls for aid and research. Faith in the anonymity of calling will decrease.

As far as the protection of privacy is concerned, CLI has both advantages and disadvantages. The possibility of refusing or blocking this service is of vital importance. The existence of these options, however, should not allay our fears. For instance, in many cases the recipients subsequently have to justify themselves to the sender for not allowing access, or for not displaying their numbers, or, in the case of the videophone, for not showing them- selves. Technical blocking options, when available, are always linked to social and personal relationships, among them relationships of power.

Total Reachability   This brings us to the risks for relational privacy. There is pressure in all communications technology to *be within reach at any time and place*. If new facilities such as 'follow-me switches', answering machines and voice mailboxes will not see to this, mobile and cellular telephony will. The explosive demand for these kinds of facilities proves how much people have adjusted to continuous communication, but at the same time it causes the individual to be traceable to the deepest crevices of the social fabric and in all environments. Almost every place becomes a social space. It is becoming hard to avoid being accessible at any time and place. And even if one tries and succeeds using blocking options, the chances of having to *justify* oneself are increasing. This is a threat to personal autonomy (to be discussed below). Our natural space to withdraw (though this space is not divided equally in social terms) and to be left alone is shrinking. Yet this space has always been useful to the efficiency of communication. Being accessible at any time and place will lead to a sharp increase in the quantity of communication appearing to be (almost) irrelevant afterwards.

Central Control   Not only are spaces of private life in the house and the car opened up by computer networks, but also private space at work. It is fixed to particular places when people have to work at desktop computers or terminals. In this case not only the employee's achievements but also his/her spatial behaviour can be traced by management. Free movement across the department, through the building or on the road is registered and controlled. Through all kinds of passes and check cards, basically every movement is traceable. Even the use of mobile computing and telephony becomes traceable with the aid of radio telephony and satellite links. The use of teleconferences, such as video conferencing, and multimedia PCs and NCs equipped with cameras and microphones, offers a large number of benefits, but it is also a potential new threat to the privacy of employees. In video conferencing, not only formal contributions but any moves and personal exchange of notes between participants are recorded. Other parties are able to see much more than in traditional meetings, as recordings can be viewed over and over again. When computers and cameras are involved, management is able to verify whether a person is present and what that person is doing. Of course, technical facilities exist to block these options as well. However, it depends on the balance (of power) between management and employees whether this really happens. All in all, management and technology increasingly decide on the right of employees to make contacts selectively, even at work. Some managers and employers deny any right of employees to privacy at work. In any case, private space at work is changing into a more collective space.

Data Intelligence   The next threat to privacy is the establishment of relationships between data that cause no harm if they are used separately. There are many ways for information technology to help establish relations between personal data within and between files. First, relations within files are discussed. Next, relations between files, also known as links or couplings, will be described.

Within Files   Most database files are made to establish relations between individual records and fields (characteristics) in a matrix. This will produce information on individuals. As a next step, databases are created to establish overviews of all records and fields or a selection of them. Thus strategic information is obtained about groups of people, for instance the purchasing behaviour of various groups of people at various times of the day. In most cases, the information can be traced back to an individual. Enabling a company to use all these possibilities, data from several sources are brought together in one database and checked for correctness (a **Data Warehouses** clearing operation). These data collections are called *data warehouses*. Filling these warehouses with large amounts of data to be used in various contexts has become an industry on its own. Accompanying search techniques are called *knowledge discovery in databases* (KDD).

Data Mining   The next step is *data mining*: the extraction of implicitly present, formerly unknown, but potentially usable information from data. All kinds of new search techniques are developed to this purpose, based on a combination of statistics and artificial intelligence and executed by powerful computers connected in parallel to form so-called **neural networks**.

Data warehouses and data mining help to produce strategically significant information on persons. The people involved are usually not aware of this. They leave their tracks everywhere, for instance in using customer cards, savings cards and chip cards, or by filling out reply forms, thinking this will not be of any consequence to their privacy. Then, suddenly, the data deposited everywhere return to the person concerned like a boomerang. Many institutions turn out to have a surprisingly wide knowledge of an individual and appear to be able to take decisions, and not always the right ones, for the customer, employee or citizen. This knowledge can result in very interesting offers, but can also result in being turned down for a job interview, in not being granted a loan, or in having an income tax return refused.

Between Files
File Coupling More possibilities appear in the production of links between data in several different files – a process known as *file coupling*. This process can vary from simple comparisons to the actual coupling of files, enabling the use of KDD's advanced search techniques. The least drastic of these is *front-end verification*. When, for instance, someone applies for a benefit, the information entered by this person is verified *in every single case* and *in advance*. The population register is checked to see how someone is registered, and social security files are consulted to see if the person already has a job or benefit elsewhere. In this way supplemental information about a person can be obtained.

Data Matching The next technique is a systematic comparison of files: *data matching*. In this process *whole* files are compared *after* they have been created. A case that does or does not match, depending on what the file comparison is for, is called a *hit*. This technique is often used to track down errors in files or to look for tax or benefit fraud. But in fact this technique can also be used for less legitimate purposes as part of commercial, repressive or criminal activities.

Profiles Combining two or more files may lead to a complete integration of these files in one file. This integration can help to make *profiles* of a person (and a group or organization). These profiles are created using behavioural psychology and statistics to estimate the chance that someone with specific characteristics will do certain things (Rothfelder, 1992).

These profiles become more and more influential in personnel information systems and in management and marketing information systems. In all these systems the distance between combined data and the source is great. In the combination of data, in fact, new data are created (often for a different purpose from that of the original registration) and are immediately interpreted by these systems as information. The person involved is hardly ever informed of these adaptations and new purposes. It is strategic information. Yet, mistakes and inaccurate presuppositions are easily made.

The elusiveness of file combination and adaptation in networks means that the distance between the reality of individuals, the data on these individuals and the decisions based on them is increasing, and the influence of individuals on the total process is decreasing accordingly.

Defences of privacy

Without protective measures, the introduction of networks will lead to a serious threat to individual privacy. One does not need to suffer from paranoia to say this. The applications offered by networks are clearly attractive to the people in control of politics and the economy. And we are not even talking about the unwelcome rise of a more or less totalitarian administration that is offered a perfect infrastructure. For the first time in history, the network phase in computerization more or less justifies the popular spectre of a 'big brother society' characterized by far-reaching traceability and controllability of the individual. The difference is that we are not dealing with a single 'big brother' here, but with a whole series of 'little brothers'. Furthermore, most often we are not dealing with direct supervision through monitors and screens, but with indirect traceability and control. However, this is at least as efficient and effective, because (a) it can be based on summarized data and information and (b) it is totally unapparent to the victims, causing them to adjust mentally to ever present supervision, or to become indifferent to it.

Ways to Protect Privacy Fortunately, there are numerous ways to protect privacy in networks as well. They can be summarized in four categories:

1 legal protection;
2 social protection: refusal of or participation in the supply of new services and techniques by consumers and codes of conduct adopted by producers;
3 system-technical and organizational protection;
4 technical alternatives.

So far, 1 and 3 have received the most attention. However, according to the analysis below more protection is to be expected from 2 and 4 in the short term.

Legal Protection Legal protection of privacy in media networks is necessary as a framework and a backbone for the other three kinds of protection. Unfortunately, legal protection is still very inadequate. Almost all of the countries in the world have either a constitutional or a legal right to privacy (US Department of State, 1997). However, in 1995 only 110 countries had a specific provision in their constitutions about privacy and 55 some kind of privacy law (Banisar, 1995). A country can have legal privacy protection at three levels: the constitution, specific privacy law and common law (this is law based upon decisions of judges and customs instead of written law). The legal protection of privacy is inadequate, in particular with regard to networks, for several reasons.

Weaknesses First, privacy regulation and legislation are at a low level of development and effectiveness. Constitutions are very broad. They have no immediate and indisputable practical implications. In the US the part of the constitution concerned, the Fourth Amendment, is both broad and narrow, as it only protects against government infringement of a person's privacy. On the other hand, privacy laws are often very specific. For instance, the US has adopted an impressive series of privacy acts at the federal and state levels (Perritt, 1996). This has produced a complete fragmentation of privacy legislation, making it weak and capable of being mastered by juridical experts only. By contrast, the European Union has developed very comprehensive and ambitious privacy legislation, based upon the long-standing principles and guidelines of the OECD and the Council of Europe. However, the execution of the comprehensive European privacy laws takes so much effort and social support that they are difficult to put into practice. Moreover, the effectiveness of all privacy legislation is uncertain as personal data in networks are transferred across borders with different jurisdictions and because the legislation has a rather low status: it is most often civil law and common law rather than criminal law. So, prosecution and punishment for privacy offences are rare.

This brings us to a second reason. Privacy is not viewed as an absolute right of individuals. It is always weighed against other rights and interests, primarily the information and communication freedom of others and the security rights of the government. In practice privacy regulation is over-ruled by other laws and by national security or emergency regulation.

The third weakness of legal privacy protection is that it still deals almost exclusively with informational privacy. It is a matter of *data* protection. However, ICT in general and media networks in particular increasingly enter the areas of relational and physical privacy. As a result, applications such as electronic mail, calling line identification, video surveillance with storage of recordings, and all kinds of monitoring of new media use, e.g. Internet use, are poorly protected (see Chapter 5). The same goes for physical privacy, which might be threatened by biometering and DNA testing using new media (see Davies, 1994).

Finally, the most important weakness of legal privacy protection is that it always lags behind the development of technology, as do so many laws. For instance, the Dutch data protection law adopted in 1989 was designed to confront the difficulties of privacy protection in computer files with personal data. In this law, computer registration was assumed to be a static affair of producing and consulting fixed files managed by controllers who could be identified and alerted to their legal obligations. In fact, registration in computer networks is a dynamic affair of continually collecting, processing, editing, changing, consulting, using and transferring data. The European Directive mentioned above took this dynamic process as its main point of departure and forced the Dutch law to adapt accordingly. In the meantime new technological difficulties appeared once the Directive and the national privacy laws based on it were adopted: encryption, diverging international standards, monitoring on the Internet and the qualification of video registration. These problems will be discussed in the next chapter.

Self-regulation   The flaws in privacy legislation make the perspective of self-regulation by individuals and interest groups more attractive, although legislation remains necessary to guide self-regulation and to prevent the law of the jungle. After all, self-regulation favours the strongest parties involved. There are two types of self-regulation: individual and social.

Individual   Individual self-regulation consists of the attempts of ICT users to safe-guard privacy themselves using their own expertise, actions and technical means like filtering with software and using browsers to help them negotiate about their personal data with on-line service providers. The Platform for Privacy Preferences (P3) and TRUSTe are names for this kind of means. They will be considered in the next chapter.

Some users with less technical expertise simply refuse to fill out names and credit card numbers on the Internet or leave false ones instead. Privacy is a growing concern to users of the net. According to the biannual GVU survey of October 1997, among Internet users world-wide privacy ousted communication freedom from first place as their primary concern (GVU Center, 1998). The individual protection of privacy by users is stronger than one might expect. It is one of the factors preventing a take-off in electronic commerce. So, offering privacy guarantees will become one of the most important quality standards of services in networks. Many producers have prepared codes of conduct and codes of good practice on their own initiative, trying to convince consumers.

Collective   Often social self-regulation has to step in to support individual users. Increasingly, consumer organizations, user groups, trade unions and civil organizations negotiate with producers, employers and public administrations about the privacy conditions of using personal data in computer files and networks. They might be able to prevent misuse, instead of trying to cure things afterwards.

When trade unions and consumer organizations are allowed to participate in the design, construction and introduction of networks in advance, this will produce earlier and better results – broadly supported decisions in favour of or against particular solutions – than will legislation and technical or organizational measures of protection afterwards. For instance, apart from an occasional judicial decision, personnel assessment and personnel information systems, which often needlessly threaten privacy, at present can only be stopped or changed by collective agreements between employers and trade unions or works councils. Organizations of employees are able to point out how these systems may have negative effects on achievements as well, such as too much attention being directed to the quantity of production, and the stimulation of all kinds of informal resistance and escape.

System-Technical   Often the suggestion is made that privacy is sufficiently protected by
and Organizational   privacy regulations and reliable personal data protection. Yet, it should
Protection   be clear by now how vulnerable networks are. They simply *cannot* be secured 100 per cent. Besides, privacy cannot be protected by security alone which is is often regarded as a series of impartial technical measures in which social processes and clashes of interest do not play a part. In the professional literature on this issue, three terms are confused with each other: security, protection of confidentiality and protection of privacy.

Security   *Security* is a necessary but not a sufficient condition for the protection of confidential and sensitive data. Until now, most attention has been given to the system-technical and physical security of networks – things such as guarding, locking, and using access cards and the safe technical construction of networks. This kind of security almost by definition is not foolproof, for connections by cable cannot be secured as long as they are not made of fibre-optic wires. And in connections with fibre-optic wires, it is still possible to tap switches, nodes and central exchanges. Worse still, the quickest way to break security is not via connections and switches, but simply 'through the front door' by hacking access codes.

In the late 1990s, calls for procedural and organizational security have become louder. For instance, files containing personal data are left to certain functionaries who alone are allowed access to these files, whereas everyone else is denied it. These procedures are recorded in scenarios and regulations concerning access. This type of security requires training for personnel that pays a lot of attention to aspects of security and the stimulation of an organizational structure in which the protection of (personal) data, programs and equipment is a point of particular salience in daily routine.

Confidentiality   The concept of *confidentiality* is introduced here, and should not be confused with privacy. Privacy is better reserved for individuals, whereas confidentiality has to do with the data and behaviour of groups or (departments of) an organization. When people who are registered demand access to the procedures used in the information system or to the contents of their own files, they often meet with the argument that these procedures and data are confidential. In some cases those registered have virtually no rights at all, for instance when trying to gain access to the registers of the police and security agencies.

Privacy   Each of the two dilemmas described above indicates that the protection of *individual privacy* involves more than security and the protection of collective confidentiality. Even though they are based upon the power, interests and divisions of labour within organizations, the measures taken often fail to allow for conflicts of interest. When reading professional literature on technology and organizations, one might get the impression that the people responsible for keeping and securing a register themselves cannot violate the privacy of the registered, most often their own employees – as if the violators were automatically outsiders, i.e. criminals and unauthorized persons. Legislation and self-regulation are of vital importance to the protection of privacy. The interests of the individual or groups of individuals have to be weighed against the interests of other individuals or groups and organizations.

Technical Alternatives   Developing technical alternatives might be the best structural solution to the problems concerning privacy. In fact, a small number of scientists and technicians are working hard on such alternatives at the end of the 1990s. They base their work on the following four alternative network characteristics.

Local Control   *Smaller scale*   The inclination to construct single large-scale networks is decreasing. They are too vulnerable. Instead, we can see a tendency to develop a plurality of locally limited networks to be interconnected. This makes it more possible to take extra safety measures and to define regulations for each of them. Furthermore, several types of networks with different registrations can be connected without coupling their files. In this way, individual users might get more protection.

Intelligence for Users and Terminals   *An empty infrastructure*   One of the controversies in the construction of public networks concerns whether or not more 'intelligence' (exchanges, switches, set-top boxes or adapters) should be integrated in the network itself or in terminals. Of course, the manufacturers of networks champion the former solution and those producing terminal equipment are in favour of the latter. From a privacy point of view, the latter seems more attractive. It increases the possibility that the only persons having access to connection and *user* data will be network processors and carriers, not the controllers using them for their own purposes of intelligence. These data can be very sensitive for users' privacy (subscribers' personal data linked to the address, type, duration and regularity of messages). But regulations can be made requiring the destruction of these data as soon as they have been processed to produce a bill (as has been done in Germany: see Chapter 5). In this case detailed *usage* data can be recorded in the intelligent equipment of both the sender and the receiver. They remain anonymous and are not coupled to other data. (Manufacturers register the general use, consumers register their own use.)

The Centre Switched Off

More off-line equipment   The most effective solution to problems concerning privacy is to switch off the recording centre. The most extreme solution would be to use off-line equipment as much as possible. This is an overall alternative for networks *as such*. We already know the video recorder is able to tape programmes without central registration (such as a videothèque or a pay TV service). In the 1990s, the multimedia PC and CD were on the rise. They have enormous storage capacity and are a direct competitor to on-line connections. They enable individual and collective users to gain control of a lot of information.

Off-line equipment does always offer a solution to the biggest threat to privacy: the work of registration services. However, in this field a series of small off-line technical means is being developed, based on the principle of the bus, tram and telephone cards. The most primitive of these is the *magnetic strip card*. Since this type possesses hardly any 'intelligence' and can easily be copied, it can be used for limited tasks only. The *chip card* offers more. It has a semiconductor memory to be filled once. These cards can be copied too, but for small services they serve well as electronic credit cards in so-called debit systems. Next in line is the *smart card*. It is equipped not only with a memory, but also with a small microprocessor which performs operations that cannot to be influenced or controlled from outside. A card like this is able to block itself when three invalid passwords have been entered.

User Control Remains Necessary

When chip and smart cards are used in on-line connections, the card verifies the (right) identity and can thus be used for all sorts of transactions. So, evidently the on-line connection is the biggest threat to this alternative, completely destroying its potential for privacy protection. When users are somehow *forced* to plug their cards into an on-line system, where the cards are 'drained' of their most recent data which are subsequently stored in a central memory, this alternative takes privacy protection from bad to worse. Obligations to identify oneself and demands made by medical institutions could cause a situation like this to arise.

Smart cards and chip cards can also be used as a means to interconnect registrations. They can be used for several functions: as a key and as a means of identification, payment or data storage. When all these functions are combined, and when a card is introduced to serve several purposes (to pay and to identify oneself when making telephone calls, parking, travelling by public transport, visiting football matches, etc.), these cards could become a two-edged sword in privacy protection. The multifunctional chip card could become one of the biggest threats to privacy. Different functions and personal data can be separately placed on a multifunctional card, denying access to other parts, but will this really happen? That is why the *terms* by which off-line means are used will decide what happens. Users should have as much control over the applications as possible (to use or not use the card, to decide which data are handed over on-line and which are not). Then the fourth alternative becomes interesting.

Privacy-enhancing technologies   The same techniques that cause risks to privacy can also be used to protect it. In the 1990s we have seen the breakthrough of all sorts of techniques to **encrypt** information and communication in networks. Defenders of the right to privacy increasingly consider these *privacy-enhancing technologies* to be their most important weapons. But that is only after it has been determined that the registration of personal data is necessary anyway.

Basic Principles   The observation that the identity of the individual is of no importance to the greater part of the process of registration is the basic principle of these techniques. Individuals can be given a pseudo-identity which replaces their real identity in the process of registration. In registration by ICT systems, the following phases usually follow each other:

1   authorization (permission to 'enter' the system);
2   identification and authentication;
3   access control (in particular applications);
4   auditing (check and justification of the use of the system);
5   accounting.

According to a report by the Dutch and the Canadian official data registrars (Van Rossum et al., 1995a and b), the user's true identity is needed only in particular cases at the beginning (authorization) and at the end (payment). However, in all cases (when desired) and in all intermediate phases, both of them can be replaced by a pseudo-identity protecting the true identity. The following privacy techniques are used for this purpose.

Digital Signature   The digital signature is the first. It is the digital alternative to the written signature. A digital signature cannot be copied, since it consists of the unique combination of a private key, known only to the owner, and a public key, known to the other party involved, for instance a service provider. The private key is not some sort of PIN code, since this code is known by other parties, at least by the distributor (the bank, for instance). The private key is compiled by the user from a unique series of randomly chosen numbers. The private key and the public key are combined when a certain process requires identification of the individual by an institution. This combination is another key. When the combination is decoded by the institution concerned using the public key, the authenticity of the signature is confirmed. At that point in the process, it is not necessary to know to whom the signature actually belongs.

Digital Pseudonym   The second technique is the digital pseudonym. By using the same combination as used for digital signatures, users can take a pseudonym authorizing them to receive a certain amount of services from service providers. The providers are paid for the amount as a whole. A different pseudonym can be used for every service and service provider. Thus, registration and exchange of individual sales data by service providers is made impossible (consult Van Rossum et al., 1995b for technical details on digital signatures and pseudonyms).

Encryption   The techniques just mentioned do not have to be used until some sort of identification or authorization is needed, for example in a transaction or in an electronic payment system (Chaum, 1992; 1994). They can be used to protect both *transfers* and the *contents* of messages and transactions. In the latter case, they block access to a message for everyone but the addressee. These codes or *encryptions* have been designed for electronic mail, for instance. Until well into the 1990s, messages by e-mail could be opened by others fairly easily. Pretty Good Privacy (PGP), designed by the American Zimmermann, was among the first techniques of encrypting e-mail. Zimmermann was prosecuted by the American government for his illegal export of 'defence technology'. In fact, the American government had been trying to gain control of the distribution of encryption for years. First it forced hardware manufacturers to build in a so-called clipper chip, enabling the police and intelligence services to decode for criminal investigations. Later it ordered one copy of the key to be handed over to the Ministry of Justice. These measures led to a wave of criticism from business and private users of the Internet. In Europe, the proposals to hand in one key to the Ministry of Justice were softened after a few years, and it was suggested that this copy could be delivered to a trusted third party. This third party would be authorized to pass on a copy of the key to the Ministry under strict conditions, for example in the case of an official legal investigation, to decode communications by criminals, terrorists, racists and producers of child pornography.

Steganography   The latest techniques for encryption are extremely hard to track and decode. They can also be used for privacy protection. Some of them are based on *steganography*. This technique enables the user to make a message invisible by hiding it in another message. Seemingly harmless texts, videos and audio sources may contain criminal messages written 'between the lines'. In this case, the police and security organizations do not even know where to look for them. The rise of these new techniques proves that the most popular solutions of the authorities – the demands to build in chips and to deliver copies of keys – are actually rearguard actions. It will be harder and harder to intercept illegal communication in transit. Gradually, the solution will be to search at the source and at the destination – the sender and the receiver of messages – where the encrypted or hidden messages are bound to disappear from and reappear in the analogue world.

Photographs of child pornography have to be taken somewhere. Racist electronic statements are compiled, stored and printed on local computers, media and printers. Criminal deals and the theft of digital money will leave traces or lead to actions in non-virtual reality.

Integrated Protection   The most important conclusion concerning the four means used in the protection of privacy is that none of them can be omitted. They presuppose each other. Legislation will not be effective without the practice of self-regulation and the security of data. Conversely, self-regulation and social protection will be unrestrained without a legal framework of enforceable rights: they will promote a culture of the 'survival of the fittest'. We have also argued that organizational and system-technical measures are a necessary but not a sufficient condition for privacy protection. Finally, the conclusion has to be drawn that technical solutions will not cure all evils either. They have to be embedded in legislation, self-regulation (such as participation of employees and clients) and managerial practices. Most solutions are two-edged swords. They can just as easily endanger as protect privacy. Encryption can be used equally by the Ministry of Justice, by criminals and by respectable citizens. The association between the means to defend privacy shows once more that networks are not neutral technical means. In all kinds of ways they are related to power in society, in organizations and between individuals.

Personal autonomy

The conclusion just reached will be even more evident when we take the step from privacy to the personal autonomy of individuals in the choices they have to make when dealing with networks.

Networks are Systems   Networks have the character of a system. They connect several end-points or terminals. At these points human individuals are working, studying and living. These simple remarks evoke the most fundamental questions concerning power in networks. To what extent do individuals, as members of an organization, as citizens, employees, clients or consumers, have a say in whether or not they are *connected* to the network, and how much influence do they have on the *use* of the network once they have been connected?

These questions concern the control human beings have over their technical means. However, a network cannot be compared with a machine one decides to purchase. A network is *not a stand-alone instrument* just replacing or simplifying human communication and activity. A network is *a medium with a system character*. It links separate machines and their human operators and it streamlines their communications and activities. Kubicek and Rolf (1985) have claimed the necessity for an entirely different approach to get a grip on network technology. The traditional approach stems from a *machine* model: hardware and software are considered to be detached and locally or functionally confined instruments.

Their effects can be calculated and changed directly. This model no longer works in network technology. It has to be replaced by a *system* model. This model not only assesses all nodes, connections, protocols, terminals and programs separately, but also their *combinations in a system* and especially their *implementation in existing organizational and social processes*. It turns out that most often the whole organization or other social unit will change, in both their internal and external relations. Many corporations and administrations have discovered that the network phase of automation means more radical changes than the preceding phases when only separate machines were installed. The consequences are harder to foresee and calculate. They often cross borders that the organization itself has not yet crossed. This can be the case when companies are connected to a common network. This makes this technology almost intangible to works

Individual councils and other organizations of employees. For individuals, the dis-
Autonomy of: tance to places where decisions are made becomes even greater. For them, this technology usually appears to be extremely large-scale, opaque and intangible. However, from the following list it appears that networks have both positive and negative consequences for personal autonomy.

Citizens As *citizens*, individuals have become completely dependent upon their political representatives and governors concerning decisions on whether and how the government will record data on their use of networks. At best, they will get rights of access to and correction of their data. Police and intelligence agents are able to ignore privacy legislation on many issues and to shut off their networks from political control. On the other hand, citizens are able to use networks like the Internet to inform about their government, public administration and political representatives. And they can express their own opinions in electronic discussions and televotes (teledemocracy).

Employees As *employees*, individuals have to accept their workplaces being integrated in a company network, perhaps abolishing any autonomy they possessed. Trade unions and other organizations of employees are not able to stop these fundamental changes, even if they want to. Usually, they lack the power and knowledge. The network's system character and its radical consequences for work and organization force employers representatives to specialize in fields unknown to them and sometimes to retrain completely. Management and personnel information systems increase the power of executives. On the other hand, employees are able to use organizational networks for task extension and enrichment through vertical decentralization (see above) or for better and more empowering communication with their colleagues.

Clients As *clients* of a company or government institution, individuals simply have to accept that services are now offered and registered electronically. After a short period of transition, access will be granted only after entering a pass and a PIN code. This can be used to transfer personal details automatically and on a larger scale than ever before. Another consequence will be the replacement of traditional services, based on more or less informal processes of negotiation between persons, by electronic services working with fixed, pre-programmed instructions leaving less room for negotiation. On the other hand clients are able to address multifunctional or virtual desks for services of the government and private providers where all information and services are gathered. On the Internet the position of clients and consumers is strengthened by software enabling them to compare the price and quality of various sites in electronic commerce.

Consumers   Finally, as *consumers*, individuals face the constant pressure of a 'technology push' to buy electronic products. As long as the majority has not yet bought the products, the customer seems to be king. But when theatre performances and aeroplane flights are being booked mostly or wholly electronically, the potential customer of electronic services will no longer feel free to say no to them. And this freedom to say no will probably disappear completely when the vast majority has been connected. Then the crucial question will arise: will non-electronic and analogue techniques be kept in supply? For instance, as in some countries, will consumers be forced to buy digital television sets and decoders to replace their old analogue equipment?

LAW

Law at Risk   We have seen how the introduction and utilization of networks may change the balance of power at every level. The social unit as a whole becomes more vulnerable. Within this unit there can be a shift in the balance of power between state and citizens, employers and employees, manufacturers and consumers, the government and civil servants. We have also seen that the utilization of network technology tends to strengthen the positions of the first and weaken the position of the second when no protective measures are taken. The risks are growing. Liberty and equality are threatened. We would expect the law to offer some protection, for the law is a sort of legitimized power. It is supposed to regulate power, or at least to prevent excesses. But the tragedy is that the law itself, particularly existing legislation, is itself being undermined by network technology. Better protection is needed; inadequate protection is the situation at present. The legal world itself has to deal with the new phenomena of the information era. Property law, commercial law, certification and authentication law, labour law, criminal law, constitutional law, telecommunication, media and privacy law: they all need to be redefined. This chapter concentrates only on the specific legal aspects at stake when networks are involved. Nevertheless, it is confined to the main themes and structural background. Actual legislation and jurisprudence date too quickly for us to allow them to dominate the exposition.

Law, Justice and Technology   The law and justice have lagged behind new technology in almost every period in history. This is understandable, as the new technology must become established in society before legislation can be applied to it. Furthermore, the consequences of new technology are not always clear right away. That is why the legal answer usually has the character of a reaction or an adjustment of existing principles. In civil society, this character is enhanced by the principle of civil law, in which individuals initially act freely and the law subsequently makes corrections. Legislation in advance, for instance to stimulate or halt the development of a particular new technology, would be state planning. This idea does not fit well with the principle of free initiative in technological development in capitalist societies. Justice in general, and legislation in particular, increasingly lag behind micro-electronic technological development. A construction of 'second generation law in an era of fifth generation computers' is taking place (Herbert Burkert, quoted in Mellors and Pollit, 1986). In 1999, even the most basic terms such as 'information', 'data', 'program' and 'communication' have not yet been defined unambiguously and fixed in legislation. Jurisprudence is the most important weapon against misuse of these new technologies. It is created by judges who often tend to make things easy for themselves by simply declaring existing legal terminology applicable to new technical realities. Before legislation has dealt with any phase in computerization, the next phase is already happening. More than any preceding technology, networks test existing legislation. This happens for at least seven fundamental reasons.

Challenges of Network Technology

First, as preceding chapters have stressed, there is the intangible, geographically free and continuously changing character of information and communication in networks. By contrast, existing legislation depends on *clearly demonstrable, localizable and liable legal persons and ownership titles*. Information and evidence have to be, or must be able to be, set down on a data carrier that still has to be comparable to printed paper.

Second, when legislators have managed to develop and lay down new legislation for the utilization of networks, the problem of *implementing these laws* arises. Networks are connected to other networks and they are not terminated by frontiers. This causes three essential problems:

1 *perception* of the violation of the law, an offence or a crime: activities in networks are non-transparent and hard to trace;
2 *evidence* of such activities: evidence can easily be destroyed, changed or hidden in networks;
3 *prosecution*: jurisprudence differs across countries and the accuser and the accused may come from different jurisdictions, especially when international crime is involved.

Third, network technology has grown international very quickly. Laws, on the other hand, are mainly national, particularly with regard to the actual prosecution and punishment of crime. International legislation usually stops at general declarations and basic principles agreed upon by international institutions. No matter how important these declarations and principles are as an impetus to international legislation, they do not themselves have any real practical meaning. Moreover, they are usually pretexts for international political action and economic protectionism rather than genuine protection against the unacceptable consequences of a new technology.

Fourth, existing legislation is still bound to the material reality of the industrial revolution and the first communications revolution, or even preindustrial trade and craft. This explains why some juridical discussions are still about whether information is a commodity and whether communication by computers can be treated as equivalent to a 'conversation'. However, the network phase already represents the culmination of a revolution in micro-electronics which has helped to complete the rise of tertiary and quarternary services and submitted them to processes of industrialization and rationalization. Furthermore, as we have seen, the network phase is the basis for a second communications revolution. Without a thorough (re)definition of basic terms such as 'information', 'data', 'program', 'electronic communications', 'information service', 'file', 'owner', 'editor', 'controller' or 'processor' of (personal) data, and so forth, any legal grip on the consequences of network technology is bound to fail.

Fifth, existing legislation is still tied to preceding phases in economic development, the phases of free competition and monopolization, state regulation and the beginning of internationalization. However, the international concentration of capital and power, combined with decentralization of production, the creation of a 'flow economy' and the enormous growth of an elusive financial sphere, together cause a new economic reality to arise. It can hardly be controlled with existing means, and certainly not with existing legislation.

Sixth, in the late 1990s, existing legislation was still based on rapidly obsolete technological boundaries. Network technology ends the old divisions between tele-, data and mass communications and between the various media within these types of communications. Separate legislation is no longer adequate for integrated networks. For instance, the separation of press and broadcasting legislation had already started to become outdated with the appearance of cable TV information services some time ago. Obviously, a *general framework of communication and information legislation* is needed. This will have to be based no longer on concrete material technical differences, but on much more abstract distinctions of information and communication, like the information traffic patterns discussed in Chapter 1 and the horizontal layers dealt with in Chapter 3 (Figure 3.3). The information traffic patterns, based on relationships of (rightful) power and other basic rights in communication and information (which will be discussed later), can provide a useful beginning. The horizontal layers of kinds of production and services to be distinguished put together related economic activities to be regulated in a similar way.

Seventh, most new legislation is characterized by fragmentary adjustments and by (often) contradictory jurisprudence. There is no integral readjustment. Instead, detailed alterations are made to existing legislation including technical definitions that will soon be outdated. For the larger part they are economic emergency regulation in copyright, contract law, certification or authentication law (concerning orders and payments), legal responsibility and the like. The only non-economic legislation of any importance consists of freedom of information or communication and privacy acts in some countries. Fragmentary adjustments to legislation are not suitable for the regulation of large-scale networks and their far-reaching consequences to individuals and society at large. Here the failure to reach conclusions in current social and political discussion about new communication technology is felt. Such conclusions are necessary for any future framework legislation, to be worked out subsequently in more specific legislation and self-regulation.

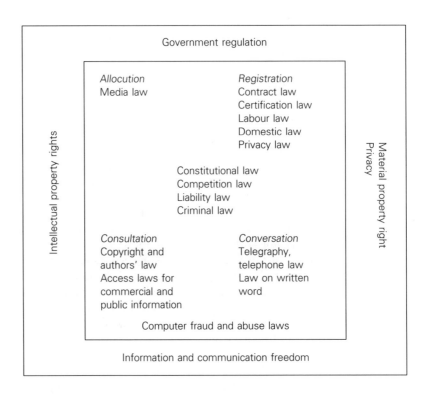

FIGURE 5.1   Divisions and aspects of the law at stake with media networks

Analytical Order of Legal Aspects

As a catalyst to the computerization of society in general, the introduction of networks has consequences for a broad range of laws. Applying analytical order is very hard. The four information traffic patterns (allocution, consultation, registration, conversation) offer the most suitable framework. Since they are based on power to be regulated, they offer insight into desirable aspects of future *framework legislation*. The five aspects around the outside of the square drawn in Figure 5.1 will play an important part in any such framework. They determine the structure of the remainder of this chapter.

GOVERNMENT REGULATION

States and Politics Losing their Grip

As has been stated, legislation cannot keep pace with technological and economic development, just at a time when we are confronted with new risks. The same can be said about 'politics'. National and international states are losing their grip on information policy owing to three tendencies taking place at the end of the twentieth century:

1 media networks increasingly crossing borders;
2 the growth of a world market of transnational corporations, operating freely and communicating through their own networks, allowing hardly any influence by international regulatory organizations;
3 current policies of privatization and deregulation of public goods and services.

Reasons for Government Regulation Every call for government regulation is suspect to those supporting the liberalization of economic commerce and information traffic associated with these tendencies. Yet there are at least two factors that demonstrate the need for government regulation of network technology which even market liberals have to acknowledge:

1 the remaining importance of particular natural monopolies;
2 the one-sidedness in the traffic patterns of allocution, registration and consultation.

Natural monopolies

Remaining Aspects of Natural Monopoly At first sight, the enormous capacity of network technology supplying channels, bandwidths, frequencies and equipment capacities in ever increasing amounts seems to oppose the arguments for a natural monopoly mentioned in Chapter 3. It looks like there is no scarcity at all. Yet, let us examine what would be the consequences of the complete privatization, liberalization and deregulation of infrastructure, management and services:

1 The commercialization of information, communication and transaction services designed for the common good would inevitably cause the exclusion of certain groups that cannot afford or are not interested in the service concerned.
2 The multitude of public and private networks still have to take part in the system as a whole, and they have a strong interest in mutual communications and exchange. In fact greater standardization is needed (to coordinate the multitude of actors) but it is harder to achieve.
3 It is harder (and relatively more expensive) to connect *every* consumer to this multitude of networks rather than to a single public provider. Increasing capacity decreases the advantages of so-called economies of scale, but they will never disappear completely. A single cable or satellite system will always be economically and technically superior to several systems needing the overheads of transmission lines, equipment and the means to access the system (different set-top boxes or decoders).
4 The price of competition is excess capacity. Several networks together have more unused capacity than one large network, for they all have to anticipate peak hours. However, it is harder to calculate the capacity that each of the separate networks requires.

5 Fixed investment costs in communications remain very high. Indeed, increasing demands for bandwith, audiovisual programming and higher levels of interactivity tend to cause a rise in costs. Completely computer-controlled exchanges will be more expensive. The same goes for multi-media program production and high-quality images. Such need for investments will promote either the support of and cooperation with states or a concentration in private oligopolies.

6 An increasing number of service providers will cause the multitude of networks to look first for common denominators on the market, for instance popular networking and programming for the largest audience in television. However, this largest segment of the market is limited too. The most likely results will be either a concentration in services or a decrease in service quality. For example, the profits made from advertisements now have to be shared among an increasing number of TV stations, but the extremely high fixed costs of programme production remain. This explains the increasing number of low-quality television channels for a large audience.

Unilateral traffic patterns

One-sided Information Traffic Patterns Three of the four information traffic patterns are one-sided from the perspective of power and communication and therefore might require regulation. Allocution is the most one-sided of these patterns. The centre is both the deciding agency and the source of information. Bordewijk and Van Kaam (1984) once claimed that allocution will and should always need regulation. The questions are *who* will regulate (government or private operators), and according to *which criteria* (being part of a cultural policy, social policy or economic policy).

In the consultation pattern, the centre is the source of the information and the local unit is the deciding agency (the questioner). Bordewijk and Van Kaam expressed the view that government regulation is not needed here. The services involved can be regulated by the market itself. However, judicial regulation according to civil law, and to a lesser extent according to criminal law, will always be necessary. There need to be guarantees of the centre's responsibility and duty to allow access (when demands have been met), and of the respect the local unit needs to have for the centre's rights of ownership and for the terms of contracts.

In this consultation pattern, the central unit is more vulnerable than the local unit. In the registration pattern, the opposite is the case. The centre is the agency that decides on the type and the conditions of the information demanded by the centre in the first place. The local unit is just the source of the information. The rights of consumers, citizens and employees have to be accorded special protection. Privacy and other vulnerable interests of a dependent party are at stake here. The registering party, on the other hand, wants to be certain about the object and content of measurement or transaction (according to contract law, certification and authentication law or obligations to provide correct information).

Finally, the 'only' thing the fourth pattern, conversation, requires from the government is good infrastructure and the protection of freedom and confidentiality of all exchange.

From this analytic framework we may conclude that those information traffic patterns having a centre as a deciding agency need the most regulation. Power is at issue here, and therefore law as a kind of legitimized power. But when we are dealing with government regulation, we should not forget that the government is a very powerful centre itself. Five reasons for regulation can be deduced from the framework:

1 protection of the local unit against the centre (for instance media and privacy legislation);
2 protection of the centre against local units (for instance rights of ownership);
3 protection of the centre of a state against other centres in the same country and abroad (for instance constitutional law and economic or cultural policy);
4 protection from a lack of centres (protection of free competition and media pluralism or diversity);
5 protection against too many centres (for instance telegraph and telephone legislation and media law).

Looking at things from this perspective, several functions remain for political, economic and legal regulation. Furthermore, the construction of public infrastructure for communications, or at least the guarantee of an adequate infrastructure for all, will be as important in the future as the construction and maintenance of roads are now. In constructing information highways a very large number of basic regulations by the government will be necessary. They have to guarantee affordable access for everyone, standardize technology, interconnect the multitude of highways to be expected (see Chapter 3), enforce so-called must-carry rules, save pluralism and diversity in media concentrations and protect the privacy of users, to mention only the most important objectives.

Remaining In the past, broadcasting was strictly regulated because of the scarcity of
Scarcities frequencies and the pressure of a particular cultural policy. Both these conditions have changed, but they have not disappeared and they will stay in one form or another (see Graham and Davies, 1997). For example, the assignment of cable channels remains necessary in an integrated two-way cable system. The available capacity will have to be divided between four traffic patterns instead of one, and between both public and private uses. Furthermore, the infrastructure will be constrained not only by its own limitations, but also by the size of the public. At present, nobody wants extreme fragmentation of channels with a small number of users. (In the future, with a massive use of interactive broadcasting and video-on-demand programmes, this might change as consumers will expect the same diversity

of selection as in a good bookshop.) This is the reason why the decline of monopolies in public broadcasting was followed so swiftly by a concentration of commercial broadcasting and oligopolization. The same goes for telephony. These processes prove that natural monopolies will be organized in one way or another.

In the 1980s and 1990s, national and (embryonic) international authorities like the EU have appeared to tolerate or even encourage private oligopolization, instead of confining it by regulations. The American, European and Japanese states all support the concentration of their 'own' transnational corporations to get a better position on the world market. This is the reason why they are always confronted with a dilemma when they have to take action against blatant cases of oligopolistic vertical and horizontal integration in their countries.

The underlying argument here is not a plea for a policy of prohibition. In general prohibitions do not solve any problems, since they are overtaken by economic and technological developments in the short term. We will argue that policies of protection will have a better chance of success using (inter)national *stimulation* of desirable developments with all the means at the disposal of governments, among them civil law and the promotion of self-regulation.

Universal and Public Service Another way is to supply the necessary *preconditions* for individual citizens, consumers and organizations to acquire open access to the goods and services of ICT. The most important precondition is an adaptation of current government regulation in universal and public service to the converging new media environment.

A definition of *universal service* is 'access to a defined minimum service of specified quality to all users independent of their geographical location and, in the light of specific national conditions, at an affordable price' (European Commission, 1996a). So, it means the supply of telephone connections on equal terms to everyone. In the course of the twentieth century, universal service has become an important obligation of telephone companies, initially the public monopolies. After the liberalization of telecommunications in many countries, the division of the existing obligations for universal service between old and new telephone companies has been in dispute. Undoubtedly, both obligations and disputes will increase with new media development. After all, the new media provoke a demand for new universal services like ISDN and electronic mail (see Anderson et al., 1995).

Public service is the fulfilment of specific needs of information and communication in the general interest of a particular society. It means a sufficient supply of accessible public connections (public pay-phones or computer terminals in public buildings) and services of health, education and public information in hospitals, schools, libraries and community centres. Public service in these institutions is broadly considered to be the best way for people to gain access to ICT in the short term. In contrast to universal service, public service is a matter of public investment, primarily of the (local) government.

INFORMATION AND COMMUNICATION FREEDOM

What Freedoms? The information and communication freedoms of citizens have been established in the constitutions of democratic states and in general international declarations such as the Declaration of Human Rights. In most constitutions these freedoms are confined to a freedom of *expression* by means of a ban on government censorship. For instance, the famous First Amendment of the American constitution ('Congress shall make no law . . . abridging the freedom of speech or the press') only protects against interference of the government or a public institution performing state action, not against private interference (Perritt, 1996: 263ff.). A logical corollary would be that the freedom to *receive* expressions should be protected as well. Constitutions and declarations are less clear about this legal principle. In practice there is no guarantee, as regulatory bodies, cable operators and other service providers decide what channels, programmes and services can be received. One can even go a step further and say that the freedom of opinion *formation* should be protected. However, that would mean strong support for public service and an active role for government in public information and media supply. This policy has some (declining) support in Europe, but it is rejected in North America.

So, it is important to observe that current legal rights of information and communication freedom offer a passive protection (against interference) and not an active protection (supply of conditions). Further, they mainly protect against government interference, not against intrusions by private conduct. This means that the infringement of these freedoms in new media practice, for example by increasing information inequalities or gatekeeping media monopolies, is not covered by them. These problems have to be confronted by other laws (of privacy and free competition, for instance) and by public information services.

Conflicting Rights A second point is that information and communication freedoms are not absolute rights. The right to information and communication freedom is not absolute where individual and state autonomy are concerned. At the individual level, one person's freedom of speech and right to reception ends where another person's right to privacy, security, identity, dignity ('reputation') and personal material interest begins. At the state level, the right to entirely free (inter)national information traffic conflicts with a state's right to sovereignty, national security, public order, cultural identity and economic interests.

These conflicts are inevitable and can never be resolved completely. This is even expressed in the essence of the descriptions of information and communication freedom, all of which reveal at least some internal tension. Thus in the discussion on international traffic of data, jurists use expressions like a 'free *and balanced* flow of information' (Freese, 1979) and 'everyone is free to . . . as long as this does not . . .'. This means values have to be weighed against each other in legislation. Such considerations can be made in national legislation. Internationally, legislation can have little effect while international declarations of human rights are too general and their sanctions are too weak to provide a solution. The biggest problem is that the right to state autonomy is being undermined by the free flow of information in cross-border networks. In addition to the legal aspects, this right also has economic, political, military and cultural aspects, as follows.

Law and State Autonomy Undermined

First, in the *legal* sphere, international networks can be instruments to evade national legislation. They enable not only extremely fast file transfers from one country to another, but also a division of the parts of information processing between the most advantageous countries – which means the cheapest and least regulated countries. Data are gathered in one country, edited and stored in another, and distributed and used as information in yet another country, thus avoiding taxes, rights of ownership and privacy legislation. Some countries are already known as *data paradises* or *data-free havens*. One just picks a country where there is little or no sanction against a particular wrongful act, or even a crime, and makes sure one has access to an international network.

Second, in the *economic* sphere, states increasingly miss out on income because taxes are imposed only on data carriers and not on the contents and the production of these data, which are usually worth a lot more than the carriers. It is impossible to install 'gateways' to serve as a kind of customs in every network at the point where it crosses a border. In the past, Brazil tried to do this, but very soon had to give up its attempts.

Material goods (CDs, books etc.) ordered over the Internet are not the biggest problem. They have to 'surface' (out of the virtual economy into the material one) once they are imported or delivered. Then, import duty and VAT might be collected. Intangible services, on the other hand (digital information, transaction services), offer simpler ways to evade taxes. By the late 1990s this had become a big problem for governments. Experts put forward the wildest solutions, such as the introduction of a *bit tax*. To realize this, a bit meter would have to be installed in all computers to count the number of bits used. Subsequently, some sort of VAT would be imposed. However, in the Declaration of Bonn (July 1997) the governments of the EU member states, the United States and Japan agreed that the development of the Internet should not be restricted in this way. Only a limited number of elementary international rules should be drawn up to secure data, to regulate electronic trade and to define legal responsibility for the use of the Internet. The United States in particular supports free trade on the Internet, in other words, no import duties or other taxes. That country, well known for its attempts to control public communications, criminal activities and threats to state security on the Internet and other networks – for instance the Communications Decency Act and the resistance to encryption – takes a very (market-) liberal stand on economic affairs on networks. This stand is obviously inspired by economic self-interest, for the US has the bulk of the global market in information and communication services and a huge surplus in the trade balance of these services.

Third, in the *political* sphere, the (exclusive) use of information can be of great interest to a country. Most countries want to have crucial information stored on their own territory to make sure they are not completely dependent on others in cases of emergency. Many developing countries in debt discover the importance of the exclusive use a country has over its own data at the moment the IMF presents an austerity plan based on far more advanced processing of a country's own data than it is capable of doing itself.

Fourth, the *military* importance of a country's information sovereignty closely relates to the political. Passing on confidential data can cause a threat to national safety. What is more, international information networks are gaining importance as military instruments. At this point, the United States has taken the lead. The networks controlled by the Pentagon, the CIA and the NSA are vastly superior to anything else that exists in this field. Defence experts expect that future wars will increasingly be *infowars*. Networks have become so important for a country, and at the same time so vulnerable, that putting them down will prove to be a decisive military action.

Fifth, the *cultural* identity of poor, less developed and in general non-Western countries or of closed communities is seriously threatened by broadcasting satellites, international computer networks like the Internet, and the powerful databanks and databases of the rich Western countries (see Hamelink, 1994).

A country's autonomy should not be absolute either. This would oppose the information freedom and material interests of other countries and, in particular, the country's own inhabitants. In order to disguise this opposition, countries often use false arguments. For instance, countries regularly use arguments about the protection of national sovereignty and culture as a reason to restrict the information and communication freedom of their own citizens. Pure economic protectionism often hides behind claims of legal, political or technological sovereignty.

Other Problems Implementing the Law

The rash and uncontrolled development of the new media, the Internet in particular, appears to offer a refuge for anyone who wants to escape prosecution for offences against information and communication law. That is why it is viewed suspiciously by governments, security organizations, regulatory bodies and all kinds of interest groups. The conduct of criminals, terrorists, slanderers, racists and (child) pornographers is more or less controlled in the old media. How should one try to regulate the same conduct in the new media? The groups mentioned are among the heavy users of the Internet. Evidently, they threaten the freedom and safety of others and of society at large. There is a growing consensus that the law should apply to both old and new media, including the Internet as a public mass medium. What are the problems, then, with this application? Some of them are fundamental. The most important follow.

Blurred Character of New Media

First, what is the character of the new media? They are in a process of convergence, blurring many of the distinctions between the old media. Should the new media be modelled on the press model, the common carrier (telephone) model or the broadcasting model? The press has acquired most freedoms of information and communication in the last two centuries. In contrast, common carriers and broadcasters have been subject to rather severe infrastructure regulation (telecommunications) or both infrastructure and content regulation (broadcasting). By the end of the 1990s most governments in the Western world and Eastern Asia had tended to accept the press model for economic freedom (on the market) and the common carrier or broadcasting model for social, cultural and political freedoms in the new media environment. These governments try very hard to stimulate global electronic commerce while at the same time trying to implement new restrictions, or to apply existing ones to the social and cultural uses of the Internet.

A related problem in applying current legislation is that many words for the old media are used in laws and even in constitutions. For instance, the First Amendment mentions (only) 'speech' and 'the press'. Some legal experts say words for new media should be added or more general expressions invented. Others claim the old expressions remain valid and only require a broader interpretation.

Blurred Public– The second problem is that the new media blur the distinctions not only
Private Distinction between media themselves but between social spheres of living as well, especially the public–private distinction. This blurring of spheres of living is analysed in Chapters 6 and 7. It has immediate consequences for new media legislation. The Internet is both a mass medium and an interpersonal medium. In offering web sites it is a mass medium, and in the facility of electronic mail it is an interpersonal medium. But what about the increasing list of Internet applications having both public and private functions: more or less closed news lists, electronic billboards, chat rooms and multi-user dungeons (MUDs)? They operate somewhere between mass and interpersonal communications.

Traditionally, the regulation of information and communication freedom in mass and interpersonal communication has been rather different. What is left free in private and personal communication, for instance obscenity, may not be allowed in mass communication. The question is how the different applications of the Internet should be rated. There is no difficulty in treating web sites and news or discussion lists, billboards and MUDs with open access as mass communication. The e-mail between persons will probably be treated as private communications, although there is (as yet) no legal right to confidentiality of e-mail in most countries. But what about completely closed discussion lists or chat rooms and private mailing lists? A large number of norms and observable facts have to be invented to specify things like membership, accounts, passwords and encryption as indicators of the private or public character of these applications.

The last problem to be mentioned here is that of the extremely volatile, dynamic and perhaps encrypted nature of network communication crossing many borders and jurisdictions. This makes criminal behaviour of all kinds, obscene, indecent and defamatory expressions, violations of human rights like privacy and other offences extremely difficult to trace, investigate, prosecute and prove. These activities are very time-consuming

TABLE 5.1   Types of solutions for legal ICT problems

Legal solutions
Adaptation of laws and regulations
Product standardization

Self-regulation
Codes of conduct and good practice
Hot lines (reporting offences)
Market regulation: licensees, public domain software, relationship marketing, advertising
Information agents (self-service)
Rating and filtering systems (self-service)

Technical solutions
Rating and filtering systems (software)
Built-in hardware: V-chips etc.
Embedded software, scrambling and coding techniques
Encryption: encoding messages, digital signatures, pseudonyms and watermarks
Data metering
Monitoring and tracking (log files, cookies)

for the police and security agencies. So even when an offence is detected, the chances are small that someone will be charged and convicted.

Three Kinds of Solutions   There are three kinds of solutions to these problems, which have already been mentioned in Chapter 4 and reappear several times in the next sections: legal solutions, self-regulation and technological protection. It is one of the most important claims of this chapter that they are only effective when used in combination. Table 5.1 shows a list of instruments to choose in realizing these solutions.

Adaptation of Legislation   The adaptation of legislation and other regulations in the field of ICT remains necessary, however great the difficulties mentioned. It produces a legal framework and protection for all the more or less voluntary solutions to be described below. This will take considerable time, as the technology in question and its uses in daily practice are still maturing. However, some governments have been seized by panic, observing the apparently anarchic nature of Internet use. They have hastily adopted emergency legislation. A clear case is the Communications Decency Act signed by President Clinton in 1996. The aim of adopting this act was to limit access to and prosecute offences in expressions of violence and obscenity on cable broadcasting, the Internet and on-line computer services. It subjected these media to more severe prohibitions than those existing in traditional media like free-to-air broadcasting and the press. Only one year later the act was overruled as being unconstitutional by a judgement of the American Supreme Court. It is interesting to observe that the Court stressed the right of freedom of inter-personal communication on the Internet as protected by the First Amendment, while the Decency Act primarily classified the Internet as a medium of mass communication. Restrictions on the freedom of communication on the Internet have been made by Eastern Asian governments as well. The European Union has adopted a *Directive on the Protection of Minors* and a *Resolution on Illegal and Harmful Content of the Internet*, urging the member states to adapt their laws for Internet regulation accordingly.

Self-regulation   In view of the fundamental problems with the adaptation of legislation mentioned above, it is no surprise that for the time being the two other classes of solutions have received more attention: self-regulation and technological alternatives. Urging some kind of self-regulation, but in fact trying to use them as an extension of the law, the authorities have approached service providers on the Internet and cable networks concerning their presumed liability in controlling and surveying all traffic on their networks. Many of them react by saying that they are not the police. Most access providers assert that they have no control over the messages they carry, just as the telephone companies do. They claim not to be editors or suppliers of cable programmes. However, for the service providers that offer content, the claims must be different: consensus is growing that they are liable for the content of their services.

The access and service providers themselves propose self-regulation as the best solution, offering codes of conduct and self-censorship in refusing subscribers, sites, programs and files which might run them into trouble. Moreover, they introduce special addresses serving as *hot lines* for their own clients to report child pornography, racism and other potential violations of the law.

Rating and   By the end of the 1990s so-called *rating and filtering systems* had emerged
Filtering Systems   as (perhaps) the most important protectors against illegal and harmful content on computer networks in the coming decades. In fact, these systems are a combination of self-regulation and technology. Rating systems mean either a self-rating of content by providers themselves or an assessment by professional rating services specializing in particular sectors of content. The quantity and quality of items like sex or violence are rated on a scale which is attached to a service or site to be rated and is presented in browsers. Then the software of the filtering systems installed by the users themselves is able to offer whatever nature and level of protection are required by parents, educators and in fact any other kind of authority. Future users will be able to include them in their personal information selections.

The best-known organizer of rating systems in 1998 was the Platform of Internet Content Selection (PICS) offered by the World Wide Web Consortium. Well-known filtering systems had the meaningful names of Net Nanny, Cybersitter, Net Shepherd, Surf Watch and Cyber Patrol. The government of the United States and the European Commission increasingly put their faith in these solutions after the disaster of the Decency Act and the problems they had with adapting and executing legislation. From a libertarian point of view they are strongly supported by Internet experts like Esther Dyson (1997). She opposes government regulation of the net and offers self-regulation by means of rating and filtering systems as the most important alternative. She expects these systems will become the most important quality standards of service providers. Unfortunately, in giving this support she neglects any relationship of power in society and on the Internet. Governments and other authorities may well enforce the use of these systems of a specified nature and quality. At the time of writing the government of Singapore already screens sites on the Internet using filter systems. American parents demand in court that schools install them on their networks to censor the information available to their children. Moreover, the supply and design of rating and filtering systems will most likely be controlled by all kinds of vested interests. Minority interests might become marginal or blocked entirely. So, the adaptation of legislation remains necessary to protect the information and communication freedoms of all. Another disadvantage of these systems is that they are easy to escape by the target group, especially children. They just go to friends, neighbours or public places offering a lower level of protection in filtering. Or they will use one of the many small mobile devices offering easy access to the Internet in the near future.

Technical Solutions   For this reason, and others, still more effective solutions are being looked for in technology. Rating and filtering systems will be included in any operating system and search engine and they might even be programmed in hardware. The introduction of the so-called 'violence chip' in televisions is a precursor to this option. Scrambling messages in programs or blocking them by some kind of encryption will be increasingly 'popular' techniques. So, just like self-regulation these technological solutions are a two-edged sword. They both protect and threaten information and communication freedoms. They are indispensable as solutions, but to strike a balance in using them in a right, justified and equal way the adaptation of legislation remains vital.

RIGHTS OF OWNERSHIP

Information Freedom versus Ownership Rights   Information and communication freedom can clash not only with limitations of public communication and autonomy, but also with rights of ownership. The latter conflict is even harder to resolve than the former. On the one hand, many people consider information to be a social product that should not be exclusively appropriated by private interests. On the other hand, information has become one of the most important economic products in the modern economy and it should therefore be submitted to the principles of the market economy like any other good. This contrast **Special Characteristics of Knowledge** can be derived from four special characteristics of a more or less fixed kind of information: _knowledge as a product_. (See Chapter 7 for the difference between knowledge and information.)

1   The production of knowledge demands far greater investment than its distribution and use. Knowledge is produced once, but it can be used endlessly.
2   Every time knowledge is produced or used, risks are taken: one can never be 100 per cent certain about producing useful results. This is why scientific research is subsidized by the government and why the reliability of a knowledge supplier is crucial to the consumer.

3 Knowledge is an intangible product. Unlike a material good, it cannot be transferred from one owner to another, giving the new owner the exclusive permission to use it. On the contrary, knowledge is shared. After transfer, knowledge is owned by both senders and receivers. A person is able to 'acquire knowledge' without the producer losing any of his own.

4 Knowledge is a result of both individual and social labour. It is hard to place a dividing line between them. For this reason the protection of individual achievements is a problem and solutions are always temporary.

Problem: The Socialization of Knowledge

These four characteristics offer arguments for both the production of knowledge as a property (the first two) and the free disposal of knowledge (the second two). The existence of networks weakens the arguments of the first two and strengthens those of the second two. Networks simplify and expand the possibilities for exchanging and duplicating knowledge. Knowledge in networks (data, programs, information) is at the disposal of numerous users without losing any quality or intellectual value. Increasingly it is passed on to multiple users in licence agreements (passing on the right to use the information), and decreasingly it is transferred in strict sale agreements or hire agreements (passing on ownership). *Without doubt, networks add to the socialization of knowledge*. This makes it even harder to protect the ownership of knowledge passed on in networks. Most legal instruments to do so are faulty and outdated (see below).

The socialization of knowledge, and the problem of its private appropriation in digital environments in general and networks in particular, explain the enormous efforts made by governments to protect the billion-dollar interests of the copyright industry and to adapt the legislation of intellectual property rights accordingly. They tend to make it even more rigid than it used to be in the analogue environment.

Legal Solutions

Legal adaptation is the first kind of solution to the problem of protecting intellectual and material property rights in the use of the new media. The others are, once again, self-regulation or self-organization on the market and technological solutions.

Intellectual Property Rights

Let's deal with the problems of intellectual property rights first; later we discuss material property rights. Intellectual property rights consist of three basic parts: the right of *publication* of a work of unique creative effort (authors' right), the right of *reproduction* (copyright) and the right of *distribution* (for instance in broadcasting and on stage). We must recognize that continental European legislation is more concerned to protect (cultural) authors' rights, while American and English legislation tends to put (economic) copyright first. That is why the American law is called the Copyright Act, while the Dutch law is called the Auteurswet (Authors' Law).

Copyright and Authors' Right in a Digital Environment

Now, the most important fact concerning new media intellectual property rights is that communication in computer networks links the acts of publication, reproduction and distribution. It is the process that becomes central. For example, making a web site with hyperlinks and files to be copied blurs their distinction. Therefore, the question arises of which of the three rights mentioned will be emphasized in new legislation. For fundamental reasons concerning the development of authors' rights in a digital environment (see above and below) and for historical reasons, that is the rise of corporate power and privatization, it is very likely that reproduction and distribution rights will be defended most. The rights of authors as the protectors of creative effort will be threatened. There are fundamental difficulties in protecting them in the digital network environment.

First, authors' right and copyright only protect the *form* of an idea, concept, procedure, method of operation or discovery, not the *content*, that is the facts and ideas embodied (see Perritt, 1996: 421ff.). In content one encounters the cultural heritage of society: one never knows exactly where this heritage ends and the original expression of creators begins. This was already a basic problem for works created in analogue media. Using digital media the problem appears to be insoluble for the following reasons. In digital environments the content changes continuously and it soon acquires a general public character. The recognizable artistic content of the age of simple commodity production, clearly visible in paintings, sculptures and books, is lost in digital signs which are very easy to manipulate, reproduce and exchange. Moreover, the form can be changed just as easily. Computer programs are adapted continuously, both by producers and by users. Databanks contain more or less automatic summaries and abstracts of forms and pieces of information. For these reasons infringements of authors' right and copyright are extremely difficult to prove.

Second, all existing laws of intellectual property right only protect works that are *fixed*, enabling their originals to be copied and multiplied. In the dynamic digital environment of computer networks this point of departure is untenable. As has been argued above, the process of creation, re-creation and reproduction will replace fixed forms.

Judicial Solutions   These fundamental problems lead to the conclusion that any authors' right solely based upon the protection of the unique creativity of products of the mind will become untenable in digital environments. A clear case is the problem of computers creating computer programs themselves. The rights to these programs are granted to the owners of the technologies concerned. Other cases are judicial decisions mentioning the added or surplus value of new computer programs, the new composition or reworking of data in databanks or the production of new information out of existing data. More and more, judges and lawyers speak about the protection of *labour* effort instead of creative effort. In this way, authors' rights move from a cultural into an economic sphere. This is an essential change, unnoticed by many people.

In the practice of using software and information services this evolution of intellectual property towards economic property goes yet further. Here one can observe the shift from property right to *usage right*. All kinds of licences and contracts between producers and business or household consumers become ever more important. In these cases one buys not a copy of the original but a licence to use it.

In the American and European proposals for the adaptation of intellectual property rights in the years 1995–8, the fundamental shifts mentioned above were reflected. European proposals moved in the direction of the basic American assumptions of an economic conception of intellectual property rights. Both American and European proposals tried to meet the terms of digital technology. However, we will argue that they did this so zealously and so much influenced by economic interests that essential freedoms of information and communication have been at risk.

In 1995 the Clinton administration adopted the White Paper 'Intellectual Property and the National Information Infrastructure' which was prepared by the National Information Infrastructure Task Force (1995a). The goal was the adaptation of existing legislation, first of all the Copyright Act. It was proposed to give copyright owners control over every publication, reproduction and distribution of works in a digital form. The dynamic qualities of computer networks were taken to heart in the most radical way, by calling every digital copy of a publication, even a temporary one technically required in a network such as in cache memory, and every transmission of it, a right of the copyright owner. Fair use rights traditionally attached to intellectual property rights, like personal use and use by libraries and schools, were strictly curbed to allow licensed use only. Another traditional right of the user, the so-called first-sale right, of a book for instance, meaning the right to use and forward the copy purchased as long as this does not harm the commercial interests of the producer, was also cancelled in this proposal. To prevent digital copying and to track every use of protected works, so-called *electronic rights management systems* and protection by means of encryption were proposed. Every attempt to circumvent these technological solutions would become illegal. On-line service providers would be held responsible for the report of these offences and for the protection of pay-per-use rules.

In the meantime the European Commission prepared a *Directive on Certain Aspects of Copyright and Related Rights in the Information Society* very similar to the American White Paper. It was a bit less severe in fair use rights to be allowed and it still mentioned 'related rights' – referring to authors' rights that were in fact swallowed by copyright in this Directive – but its basic assumptions were the same.

In December 1996 a diplomatic conference in Geneva accepted the WIPO Copyright Treaty on Performances and Programs (WIPO: World Intellectual Property Right Organization) mitigating the radicalism of the American and European proposals (Samuelson, 1997). Temporary copies made for transmission and browsing on networks were not protected – but downloading them was – and the curb of fair use rights was slightly moderated. Access providers were not held responsible for monitoring whether electronic messages are authorized, though content providers like web site publishers still are. At the time of writing, the WIPO Treaty still has to be approved by national parliaments and incorporated in national legislation. This will take several years. For instance, the final proposal of the EU Directive mentioned above (European Commission, 1997a) does not have to be expressed in national laws before 2003.

There is considerable opposition in American Congress and the European Parliament to the proposals. Critics have called attention to the fundamental shift they introduce into intellectual property rights (Samuelson, 1996; Miller, 1996; Catinat, 1997). The balance in existing legislation between creators' and copyright owners' interests on the one side, and the public interest of the diffusion of ideas in fair use and limited copying on the other, has clearly shifted to the benefit of the former, the copyright owners in the first place. Perritt argues that 'the justification for copyright is to reward new contributions, not merely to increase the revenue for old contributions' (1996: 423). The latter will happen when (fair) individual users, libraries, schools and research institutions will have to pay for uses which are free now on a non-commercial basis. With the proposed legislation impending, the groundwork is laid for extensive and unprecedented tolling on the Internet and the future information superhighway. This is especially so because the technological solutions to unlimited copying of digital works – all kinds of encryption and rights management software – are strongly backed by this legislation.

Self-regulatory Solutions In the meantime the second type of solution is increasing in the daily practice of new media use. With the transformation of property rights into usage rights described above, all kinds of self-regulation or self-organization appear on the market of intellectual value. An increasing number of suppliers of software and information services allow its use more or less free. Considering software, we now have *public domain software* (free to distribute and to change), *freeware* (free, but exploitation and change are not allowed) and *shareware* (free until the software is actually used, then a licence is to be obtained). Licences have become the prime type of transaction in the new media market of intellectual value.

Another method is advertising. Increasingly software and other information services are paid for by advertisements. According to Esther Dyson (1995), intellectual ownership on the net is being gradually replaced by advertisements for intellectual services and products which really are profitable: all kinds of support; advanced services in searching, collecting and processing scattered information; and, last but not least, selling the latest version of a program. The provider's main occupation is (customer) *relationship management*, which will be the service provider's main source of profit for the future. In this way, the information sector increasingly organizes its own business without appealing to copyright.

Another example of self-regulatory protection of intellectual property rights is the free adoption of codes of conduct or codes of good practice by service providers themselves. Sometimes they promise to assist property owners in searching and charging violators of their rights. To an increasing degree they are able to use search engines and software screening for content and for broken conditions of access to and usage of protected works. These information agents will serve as the private and public 'copyright police' of the future.

Technical Solutions

However, probably the most effective solutions to the problem of illegal appropriation of digital works are technological ones. The copyright industry and the producers of encryption software are working hard to develop and introduce all kinds of technical means to control any access and usage of these works. To begin with, they can be encrypted like any electronic message. In this case one only gets a key after payment. A special kind of encryption is a *digital watermark*: a product is equipped with invisible codes which scramble the image in the event of unauthorized use. Again, hardware players (multimedia computers, CD players) have been developed which can no longer make illegal copies: they automatically register what rights a particular user has to use a certain product, and allow access only by payment. For instance, listening to a CD on the Internet might cost the user 25 cents, whereas to buy a copy would cost $5. This solution comes pretty close to so-called *data metering*: a built-in chip or a small device connected to a television or a computer registers the use of a certain product in the same way as an electricity meter. (Supporters of a bit tax – see above – suggest the use of this technique.) Chip cards are a means of payment. However, data metering might become another great threat to privacy, since all use can (also) be registered in central processors and files.

When these technological solutions are backed up by legal enforcement, such as that envisaged in the American and European proposals for legislation, the present situation on the Internet and in other new media of uncontrolled illegal copying on a massive scale will be completely reversed (Miller, 1996; Catinat, 1997). No longer will the rights of copyright owners be in danger, but instead the rights of (fair) users, authors (except for the financial protection by their publishers) and the public at large will be at risk. The balance between owners' rights and legitimate public usage will be lost and the scale will tip towards the former. So, while in principle computer networks support an unprecedented distribution and socialization of information, and though technological means are able to protect both owners and users, the practice of our free-market economy will lead information into an (attempted) level of private appropriation as never before.

Material Property Rights

The material property right at stake through the use of information technology has been safeguarded much earlier than the intellectual property right. It is so crucial to our economic system in the digital age that it is defended by every means. This has been done right from the beginning. All kinds of statutes about computer fraud and abuses have been adopted in criminal law. It is no surprise that the range of electronic services, electronic trade and electronic payments is marked by increasingly strong legal and contractual protection. However, problems remain as network transactions increase in size and quality. The problems are greatest in information services. Here we find problems of the liability of databanks, for instance (see Perritt, 1996). Other remaining problems of economic trade in general and EDI in particular are: fixing on-line agreements; providing evidence in electronic messages and claiming responsibility for mistakes made in them; enforcing the use of particular standards; and exacting the rules and obligations in message storage. In other words, the main issues of contract law, certification and authentication law, liability legislation, laws of open competition and storage obligations are at stake. These problems are all caused by the replacement of paper by other carriers of data. An increasing amount of data is never recorded on paper. However, the faith of the law and judges in paper is not completely unfounded. It is easier to demonstrate manipulation of data on paper than manipulation of data stored in computers or on networks. And what is more, data on paper can never be moved from one paper to another. Data in computers or on networks can easily be moved to another computer or network.

THE RIGHT TO PRIVACY

Legal Framework The legal framework for the protection of privacy consists of the following three parts:

1 national legislation;
2 international legislation and treaties;
3 codes of conduct and professional codes.

On a national level, the right to privacy is covered in most constitutions. On an international level it is described in the Treaties of Rome and Strasbourg (European Council) and the Treaty on Civil Rights and Political Rights (UN). To them we can add more general declarations such as the Universal Declaration of Human Rights, and more specific and locally valid ones such as OECD and European Commission guidelines.

Codes of conduct as a result of organizational self-regulation are available in electronic banking or information services and in collective agreements between employers and trade unions or between producers and consumer organizations. Professional codes are made for researchers and information workers or for medical staff and social workers. Both kinds of codes are a valuable addition to legislation. In times of fast technological change, they serve as a buffer or as emergency legislation for some time.

Legal Protection First we will discuss the legislative protection of informational privacy. Legislation and self-regulation in this field are often guided by the eight principles formulated by the OECD and the European Council as early as 1980. The following four are the most important of these:

General Principles 1 The *use limitation principle*: the smallest possible amount of personal data should be gathered and used for the purpose given.
2 The *principle of purpose specification*: only personal data for strictly specified purposes should be collected and processed.

3 *Quality*: the personal data must be correct, complete and up to date. Furthermore, they have have to be well protected by means of security.
4 The *principle of transparency or openness*: the people involved have the right to know what personal data are collected, to what purpose, who has access to these data, what will happen to these data when they are passed on to others, and to whom they are passed on.

National Legislation The EU Directive called *The Protection of Individuals with Regard to the Processing of Personal Data and the Free Movement of Such Data* (European Commission, 1995) is based on these principles. At the end of 1998 all EU member states should have had privacy laws founded on them. The United States has no general and comprehensive privacy law and no other legislation following these principles. They have only been adopted in an advice of the Privacy Working Group of the National Information Infrastructure Task Force (1995b).

United States The US has an impressive number of privacy-related acts dealing with specific issues (see Perritt, 1996: Chapter 3). The Electronic Communications Privacy Act (ECPA) is the broadest of the federal statutes. Then there are Computer Fraud and Abuse Acts, dealing only with intrusions that cause certain harm after it has happened. These forbid certain actions of intruders and eavesdroppers in computers and their networks, but impose no duties on controllers and processors of personal data (1996: 88). The federal and state privacy acts impose these duties only on government agencies.

The fragmented nature of American privacy legislation leads to a number of weaknesses and loopholes (see Miller, 1996: Chapter 10). For example, medical records are not protected. Most often one has to appeal to the constitution in general or to common law. The results are unpredictable. According to Michel Catinat:

> most of the attempts to improve the legal environment fall short because of the lobbying of businesses including the marketing industry, federal intelligence and law enforcement agencies, and others. All these actors have diverse interests in maintaining easy access to individual data. (1997: 53)

The European Union finds American privacy legislation so defective that, according to the Directive mentioned above, no export of personal data to that country is allowed. This may force the US to adopt legislation protecting their international business interests.

Europe The EU Directive on personal data protection is the most stringent in the world. This does not mean that it is an unconditional defence of the civil and human rights concerned. Not for nothing does its long name carry the expression 'and the free movement of such data'. The Directive tries to balance the economic interests of global, primarily European, commerce and human or civil rights. According to some critics it even legitimizes current economic practices of handling personal data with a large potential for privacy intrusion. The economic interest of free movement of data, including personal data, is suspected to be the prime motivation. The Directive offers some safeguards only afterwards.

No matter how one judges the motivation for producing this Directive, it is a step forward in the legal protection of personal data. Four essential characteristics are worth mentioning here.

Assets of the European Directive

First, it is technologically appropriate as it takes the processing of data in networks as the main point of departure. The Directive covers the 'collection, recording, organization, storage, adaptation or alteration, retrieval, consultation, use, disclosure by transmission, dissemination or otherwise making available, alignment or combination, blocking, erasure or destruction of all personal data' (European Commission, 1995: Article 2). Personal data 'mean any information relating to an identified or identifiable natural person . . . directly or indirectly' (Article 2). This dynamic approach is considerably better for computer networks than the static approach of taking the existence of single computer files and their exchange as the main assumption for data protection legislation. This static approach marked the first generation of privacy laws, like the Dutch one which applied from 1989 until 2000. Moreover, the broad definition of personal data just mentioned makes the new legislation valid for all multimedia registration as video and audio recording are protected as well. The same goes for biometrics.

A second advantage of the Directive is the full application of the OECD principles of use limitation, purpose specification, openness and quality of personal data referred to earlier. These data may only be 'collected for specified, explicit and legitimate purposes and not further processed in a way incompatible with these purposes'. The data should be 'adequate, relevant and not excessive in relation to the purposes' and they should be kept up to date (Article 6). A controller is held to be responsible: a controller is any agency or body determining the purposes and means of processing personal data. Controllers have to take care of all the actions of processors processing data by technical means on their behalf.

The openness of personal data registration is supported by the demand for prior consent by the so-called 'data subjects' concerned. They have to be informed about the purpose of and all events subsequent to the registration, such as passing the data on to third parties. Prior consent is not required when there is a legal obligation or when the registration is part of a contract to which the 'data subject' is a party. However, in any case there is the right of access to one's own data (Article 12).

A third advantage of the Directive is that the strong obligations it imposes on controllers and processors are enforced not by governments but by independent supervisory authorities like national data protection registrars (Article 28). Controllers have to notify these authorities about the purpose and other features of their processing activities. They are bodies of consultation, investigation and legal intervention or redress. Although the Directive is supposed to be a sound legal solution by itself, it strongly encourages self-regulation by codes of conduct and good practice and by the appointment of independent protection officials inside organizations.

A fourth plus-point is the list of special categories of personal data which one is not allowed to process at all. They are 'data revealing racial or ethnic origin, political opinions, religions or philosophical beliefs, trade-union membership, and the processing of data concerning health or sex life' (Article 8: see this article for exemptions). Though it is not the category of personal data *per se* which makes it more sensitive than others, but the combination of categories and the context of appropriation, this list is very instructive as these kinds of personal data are those most misused.

Shortcomings of the European Directive

However, there are a number of shortcomings to this Directive and the national laws based on it. First, its most decisive assumption, the principle of purpose specification for processing personal data, makes it vulnerable. Marking out separate registrations with their own purposes is the Achilles' heel of the Directive. Controllers will either have great difficulty putting this into practice, or they will prove to be very creative in defining divisions and combinations of purposes which circumvent the meaning of the Directive and its principle of specification. They may control several registrations or appoint other controllers instead of themselves.

A second weakness is the protection of personal data in international networks crossing borders of jurisdiction. Of course, the Directive is only valid in member states of the EU. Many networks, the Internet in particular, move through numerous countries. The prohibition of a transfer of personal data to countries outside the EU which have no adequate level of protection (Article 25) – the US is considered to be such a country – is difficult to enforce. The Directive is applicable to data protection issues across the Internet because domain names or e-mail addresses are identifiable personal data and because Internet access providers are both controllers and processors, while content providers are controllers and network providers are processors (see Walden, 1997). However, the Directive does not apply where a user of European personal data is not established in a European Union member state or does not use a server in such a state – perhaps only passing nodes on their territories in technical transmission, which is allowed (1997: 53).

The greatest disadvantage of the Directive is that it is very difficult and expensive to put into practice and easily leads to bureaucracy. There is much complaint about this among European controllers and processors. This piece of legislation will therefore only work with the help of organizations supplementing it with self-regulation and 'data subjects' being conscious about their assets and defending their own personal data. So here self-regulation is a necessary counterpart of the legal framework.

Individual Self-regulation

At the level of individual solutions we have the development of privacy rating systems by special software like P3 and TRUSTe (see Chapter 4). These show great promise. Nevertheless, they also have disadvantages. If they are promoted, the accountability for and burden of data protection may be shifted from the controllers actually responsible for the registration to the subjects themselves (Working Party on the Protection of Individuals . . ., 1997). Further, individual responsibility assumes a level of knowledge about the extremely complicated affairs of data protection in networks which cannot be expected from most people. Organizations offering personal help and information in this regard are not well established.

Collective Self-regulation

At the level of collective solutions one can observe a large number of codes of conduct in the business of electronic banking, direct marketing, personnel information systems and specific information and communication systems. Let us take the last of these as an example. The best solution for (self-)regulation in information and communication systems is to make sure that a clear division exists between the tasks and responsibilities of the carrier; the system operator; the service provider; and the bank or other financial account provider. The more these tasks and responsibilities coincide, the bigger the potential threat to privacy. For instance, a provider of information who manages the network with the databank *and* charges users is able to apply both user details and data on the use of the network to create full profiles.

A complete organizational division of roles was realized by the French videotex system Teletel. In this system, the French PTO is not a service provider but only a carrier and system operator.

Legal measures might be better than a code of conduct. Germany provides a good example: the 1983 Bildschirmtext Staatsvertrag. In this videotex system, the German PTO is both carrier and system operator. However, according to this Treaty it has to maintain separate systems for the transmission data it receives as a carrier and the account data it receives as an operator. The transmission data have to be destroyed when the connection has been realized. The account data should never give specifications on time, duration and contents unless the user asks for these data explicitly. The contact between providers and users is also regulated in detail.

Regulation of Relational Privacy

The laws and self-regulation mentioned have been directed almost exclusively at informational privacy. Even though *relational privacy* is covered by most constitutions in a very general sense, in the context of networks it is not (adequately) supported by specific legislation concerning, for instance, trespassing, and secrecy of telephone conversations and posted mail. The legislation concerned is based upon the technical possibilities of the past. 'Entering' someone's home through interactive media, telemetrics or electronic house arrest is not considered to be trespassing, as the law presupposes only a physical entering of the home. And what is more, the law assumes the resident has given permission to enter after accepting the installation of equipment. (Of course, this does not apply to electronic house arrest.)

The confidentiality of electronic conversation is not sufficiently protected, as usually the exchange of digital messages is not treated as an equivalent to telephone speech conversation, and making contact with a computer system is not considered to be equal to addressing another person. In most countries it is not clear yet whether the confidentiality of traditional mail and telephone conversations covers electronic mail, or when this will be the case.

Relational privacy in digital telephony and in company networks electronically tracking employees is only protected by most constitutions in a very general sense. There is hardly any jurisprudence. This type of privacy is still scarcely discussed. It is just another example of a technology slowly and secretly changing relations between people. The sociological and psychological aspects concerned are barely known. Apparently they are so abstract that their importance is not recognized – all the more reason to explain them in the following chapters.

Technical Solutions Finally, we have the technical solutions for privacy protection described in the previous chapter. Cryptographic techniques show great promise for privacy protection. In the field of digital cash, privacy-enhancing systems are offered, although they are not yet adopted by banking on a massive scale. Another encryption technique, designed for all messages, is Pretty Good Privacy (PGP). Other ways of message protection are so-called anonymous remailers (services forwarding your mail anonymously) and anonymous access by means of public Internet terminals, anonymous e-mail addresses and prepaid access cards.

These means put the question of the right to anonymity in electronic environments on the agenda. Anonymity is (ab)used by all kinds of criminals and networkers displaying improper behaviour. So, these technological solutions are a two-edged sword, as has been explained before. According to the Working Party on the Protection of Individuals (1997), a body advising on data protection registrars to the European Commission, the right to anonymity should preserve the same level of protection in on-line as in off-line environments. So, anonymously sending messages, browsing websites, purchasing goods or services and telephoning should be as possible on the Internet as it is in the off-line world of sending letters, looking at shop windows, buying with cash and calling anonymously.

Further advice of the Working Party is to adopt the same careful balance between the fundamental rights of privacy and freedom of expression on the one hand, and the prevention of crime on the other, as we aspire to in off-line environments. After all, at the end of the 1990s we observe all kinds of overreactions of governments adopting measures of control affecting the right of anonymity and freedom of expression on public computer networks. Examples are keys of encryption which have to be delivered at government security agencies or trusted third parties where they are put into (vulnerable) databases to be opened for judicial enquiries on request. The Working Party argues that this should only be allowed in certain specified cases, with all the juridical safeguards required in traditional media (opening letters, eavesdropping, search warrants etc.).

The author of this book would like to add that current government attempts to confront or to break into encryption systems to combat crime will prove to be rearguard actions, as encryption techniques like steganography (see Chapter 4) are progressing much faster than the countermeasures of the authorities. It is better to reorient the search methods of the police and security agencies to traffic analysis (tracking the use of electronic networks in log files among others) and to investigations at the source and destination where criminal actions go into the digital under-world and have to return to the analogue surface again (a suggestion to be found even in official documents of the European Commission, e.g. 1997b: 14). Most police officers investigating child pornography know that the images concerned – which are less of a problem than the acts of produc-tion, where irreversible harm is done to children – are difficult to trace on the Internet when they are encrypted. Most often this is not even the case. Therefore these officers first analyse the sources of images, the persons on them, and their destinations and distribution lines (pictures and videos).

Reductions in Privacy Protection

All the solutions described scarcely address any type of privacy other than informational privacy. It has been argued that privacy protection is reduced to the protection of personal data, if not the technical security of these data. Relational privacy and physical privacy are neglected, while their importance in communication networks and biometrics increases by the day.

SOCIAL STRUCTURE

Social and Technological Infrastructure

The technological infrastructure of networks is influencing the social structure of society. This is an important part of the argument of this book. No less important is the opposite argument: a particular social structure influences the design and use of the technological infrastructure of networks. This chapter deals with both arguments. In doing this, social structure is viewed in three dimensions. We will start by discussing the vertical dimension of social stratification. After all, the issue of *social inequality* closely relates to the division of power discussed in the previous chapter. Then we will analyse the horizontal dimension of communication infrastructure. We will consider the relation between *media networks* and *social networks*. We will try to find out whether media networks add to the erosion of old communities and to the development of new ones. Closely related is the third dimension, which intersects the other two: the dimension of *social cohesion*. Are media networks causing a decrease in society's social cohesion, stimulating social inequality and individualization and the segmentation and fragmentation of social structure? Or are they adding to a society's cohesion, improving channels of communication, socializing individual space and creating direct links between formerly divided public and private spheres? In other words: are the new media primarily bringing us together, or are they tearing us apart? These are questions about the (infra)structure of society.

The Bias of Power

In the previous chapter it was stressed again and again that the use of a network is able both to disperse and to concentrate power. However, in practice there is a particular bias: we observe a tendency towards concentration of power when no adequate measures exist for the social and legal protection of less powerful actors. After all, the centre takes the role of deciding agency in almost every new media initiative, planning, introduction and installation. In theory, networks can add to a better diffusion of information or knowledge and to a decrease of distance between social classes. In practice, however, existing 'information gaps' between several social categories are increasing. This will be demonstrated later, using evidence of differences between nations or regions, between social classes, between the sexes and between ethnic minorities and majorities.

Uneven and Combined Global Development

Contemporary globalization of production, distribution and consumption is a process of uneven and combined development. From the command centres of transnational corporations and developed states, the division of labour is being made more selective and more encompassing than ever before (see Barnett et al., 1998). Media networks are the most important infrastructure for this process (see Chapter 3). Nowadays information processing is spread globally. Philippine programmers produce on-line software ordered by American companies: they may be paid only a third of what programmers in the US demand as a salary. Irish data typists process the claims of a New York insurance company at wages about 20 per cent below those in the US. At first sight, these examples appear to add to the diffusion of employment and therefore to social equality world-wide. In fact, the positive effects of this transfer of employment to less developed countries are disappointing, since this kind of employment is highly selective and limited. The tasks are designed from the perspective of the needs and interests of the centre and not from the perspective of a better organic development of the region concerned. Therefore, we might observe increasing differences in the number of telephone connections between rich and poor countries, while at the same time the latter are being connected to ultramodern international networks. The negative effects of this transfer of employment for the developed countries, on the other hand, may be greater than expected because simple administrative and programming work is disappearing rapidly. Moreover, it could add to a further segmentation of the labour market in Western countries. This process is sometimes referred to as First World countries partly resembling the Third World or a Fourth World (Castells, 1998): in developed countries there are enclaves of economic activity with conditions close to those of developing countries. The employment structure created is characterized by high-quality jobs at the centre, usually Western capitals, carefully selected according to criteria of logistics and management. Simultaneously, it is marked by relatively low-skilled jobs at the periphery of the system, selected just as carefully and located all over the world. The economic effects on the immediate environment of both the centre and the periphery are much less important than the emanation of the traditional infrastructure of production (factories, offices) and transportation (stations, harbours, airports). The networked economy stands alone as a system within traditional economic environments. Streams of products, goods, services and information initially flow *inside* (inter)national networks. This observation is of crucial importance to any regional or national economic policy and to every local geographic plan (see Harrison, 1994). The importance of spatial frontiers and proximate areas decreases in a global network economy.

The result of this global network structure is a diffusion and division of jobs all over the world (combined development). For instance, these days there are computer programmers almost everywhere, and even the poorest country is connected to the Internet. At the same time the quantity and quality of jobs in the global economy across countries and regions is becoming more unequal (unequal development). Without measures of prevention these inequalities will increase. Moreover, the spatial distance between the poor and rich parts of the global networked economy is decreasing. For example, top executives, high-tech specialists and financial

TABLE 6.1 Expected trends of employment in the network sector of the economy (0 equal level; + growth; − decline)

Producers of infrastructure/equipment	0 or −
Network management:	
carriers	0 or −
operators	+
Network producers (service providers)	+
Network consumers:	
business/government (process innovation)	−
households (self-service)	+

experts, while coming home from work, run into beggars on the street and people working in sweatshops. This might have great consequences for social cohesion in a particular area.

Networks and Employment
The evidence becomes stronger when we make an inventory of the expected results of network technology for the quantity and quality of employment in each social category concerned. We shall do so for social classes, for the sexes and for the relation between natives and ethnic minorities. However, we will start with a bird's-eye view of the entire employment structure to be expected in the 'network sector' of the economy.

The total extent of present and future employment in the 'network sector' of Western economies varies considerably across the divisions of this 'sector' (see Table 6.1). The production of *infrastructure* offers decreasing employment in both a relative and an absolute sense. It requires extremely high amounts of capital and high productivity. Producing an entire telephone line with an electromagnetic switching system took approximately 10 hours of optimizing work; many years ago, the use of a digital switching system had already brought this down to 20 minutes (Ungerer, 1988: 122). The construction of ISDN, fibre-optic networks and other hardware extensions to build information superhighways will compensate for this decline in employment in the short term. Furthermore, Europe, North America and Japan will create jobs from the delivery of telephone systems to less developed countries. However, the balance of employment will remain stable at best. In the production of hardware, a shift towards the production of peripheral equipment is taking place.

In *network management*, a distinction has to be made between the function of carrier and the function of operator. Employment for carriers decreases once a network has been constructed (Gershuny and Miles, 1983: 194ff.). For instance, few basic telephone operators are needed in a fully automated system, and less maintenance is required. The function of (advanced) operating, on the other hand, will offer more employment. It involves all kinds of telephone services, value-added network services and the exploitation of the Internet and cable or satellite broadcasting channels with interactive services.

A substantial increase in employment is to be expected among *service providers*, first of all in services of so-called 'content'. Currently, this primarily concerns intermediary *producer* services, that is services for producers. Leading in this field are business services (financial services for companies provided by banks, brokerage, research and advice agencies, legal services etc.) and computer services. They partly replace existing employment in non-electronic services and in the higher ranks of sub-contracting companies. Compensating for this loss of employment, companies contract more technical (tele- and data) communications personnel themselves to manage their own networks. And in the future, service providers will produce a lot of jobs in multimedia services of 'content' for consumers. This will happen with the final breakthrough of the Internet and interactive television in households.

However, we don't know for sure whether this new service employment will be maintained in the face of the self-service it will provoke among the customers concerned. Tele-activities like distance education, health services, financial services and interactive media services, at home and in schools or workplaces, will require a lot of research, development and programming at the start. Subsequently, efforts shift to self-service guided by professional services: independent distance education, self-diagnosis of health and distance monitoring, self-service in reservations, electronic transactions and self-selection of programmes in the electronic programme guides of interactive audio, video and television.

Employment Conclusions

It seems safe to predict that the 'network sector' itself will not cause a meaningful increase in employment. When we look at the old parts of the communication sector the future looks even less bright: these sectors, such as printed mail and newspapers, will not disappear, but they will provide less employment. The question remains as to what effect the 'network sector' will have in the rest of the economy. In Chapter 3 network technology was said to be contributing to *process* innovation. Many jobs were lost in the course of the 1990s as a result of flexible automation in production, improvement of logistics, reduction of distribution and delivery times, cuts in administrative operations, and even the complete elimination of human beings from certain processes, such as electronic payments. Only after a completely new infrastructure has been established, reaching most companies and households, will *product* innovations of some importance produce new employment (see Chapter 3). The size of this employment will crucially depend upon the amount of real new services (for many of them are merely a partial or complete replacement of existing services) and upon the flexibility of demand for products decreasing in price after process innovation.

With the estimations just described, we have to take into account that network technology will be the core of information and communication technology as a whole. If one tries to stimulate this technology in order to create employment in the long term, one has to support network technology from a strategic point of view. This is why America, the EU, Japan and other developed or developing countries strongly back the development of telecommunications and information technology. It will be the backbone of every future high-tech economy.

Nevertheless, for the time being the conclusion made above still holds: network technology in itself does more to increase than to decrease the problems of employment in the short and medium terms as process innovation largely exceeds product innovation.

Networks and class structure

Influence on Class Structure   Regarding the subject of social inequality, the *type* of employment being created or disappearing is even more important than the extent. In the broadest sense, we will have to deal with the question of the influence of networks on *class structure*. This question first appeared in this book in Chapter 3 when the future of middle management in organizations was discussed. Following Erik Olin Wright (1985) we want to define social classes with the dimensions of (a) ownership of means of production, (b) control of organization and (c) ownership of skills and qualifications.

Ownership   *Ownership of the means of production*   The decentralization of production will lead to an increase in the number of formally independent companies or agencies. In the ICT sector, these corporations relatively often consist of one or a few persons. Many independent companies are created in service provision. This mainly concerns professionals running all sorts of agencies. There is no great barrier preventing people from entering the market, since a single network connection already gives access to large-scale means of production (such as the Internet) and only a small amount of starting capital is needed. Providing services on the Internet is fairly simple. The increase in the number of independent businesses resulting from this situation is only moderated by the fact that successful projects are partially or completely taken over by larger companies within a short period.

Organizational Control   *Control of organization*   In Chapter 4 we have seen how the use of networks is able to change the ways organizations are controlled. Traditional middle management and supervision are replaced by top executives and technical staff controlling the organization with information systems on the one hand, and executive personnel working with the same systems on the other hand. A polarization between top management and technical staff with increased power to control, and executive staff working with a selective, electronically controlled set of tasks and under flexible conditions, is the most likely development. Other possibilities were described in the same chapter, but this one is the most likely. However, in all cases supervisors and middle managers are replaced by technicians and information staff managing and maintaining networks. If this observation is correct, the use of networks will increase the almost unbridgeable gap between groups of employees with different skills and qualifications that is starting to appear in larger organizations. Promotion within the organization, from the bottom of the shop floor to top management via supervisory work and middle management, will become nearly impossible.

Skills and Qualifications

Skills and qualifications So, having skills and qualifications will be even more important than it used to be. At first sight, information and communication technologies seem to create a lot of high-skilled jobs and make redundant low-skilled ones, particularly in transportation and administration. On the whole, levels and standards are increasing. On closer analysis, however, we find that in most categories, real daily work matches these standards less and less. Insufficient use is made of the resources and skills gained in education. A typical example of this situation is the work of a checkout girl in a supermarket: she is required to have completed secondary school, but all she has to do is pass articles over the sensors of an electronic cash register connected to central supply and payment systems. Only for a small part of the working day will she be confronted with more complex tasks requiring higher levels of education. As many jobs in our technological society do demand such skills from time to time, low-skilled workers are increasingly excluded from the labour market. However, this should not blind us to the fact that new skills are underused and old skills, such as the traditional expert knowledge of craft workers in industry, transport, retail and administration, are made redundant by the introduction of networks in companies and organizations, especially the core networks of production, supply, retail and administration. Most often, actual daily work is deskilled until it can be automated completely. Contrary to this, at the other end of the spectrum of jobs and tasks, higher skills and qualifications are needed than ever before.

Polarization?

So, the *actual* possession and execution of skills and qualifications is polarized. When making an inventory of research in organizational automation in the Netherlands, Huijgen and Pot reached the following conclusion: 'The application of new technology often goes hand in hand with a polarization of labour organization. A division takes place: a segment comprising difficult work on the one hand, and a segment consisting of standardized, relatively simple work on the other' (1988: 306, my translation from the Dutch). The authors add the conclusion that segmentation and polarization increase as automation advances. In one segment, so-called 'new skilled work' is created. Work in the other segment runs the continual risk of becoming completely redundant in a subsequent phase.

The division as it is presented here may be too rough, but it is clearly perceptible in networks that have been in operation for some time and have the chance to streamline production processes. In these networks, 'new skilled work' is found in network management and network services. Standardized work is found mainly among the operators and users of networks in factories, in trade, transportation and retail companies and in offices.

Position of Women

It is well known that the number of women is lower in the first segment than in the second. An important part of 'female' employment, in administrative and partly in low-skilled commercial work, may even disappear from the second segment. But apart from this, female employment is not particularly threatened by the introduction of networks. Other sectors employing mainly women, such as care and education, cannot easily be fully automated and transferred to self-service. We would probably expect an increase in employment for women in these sectors. Much more important for the future of 'female' employment, and from an emancipatory point of view, is the estimation that network society will increasingly require a lot of communicative, didactic and commercial skills. These capabilities, for which women have a particular affinity according to the current divisions of labour, gender roles and gender identity, will gain importance in all segments of the job market in network society. So, the position of women on the labour market of the future might be much better than it was in the twentieth century.

Position of Ethnic Minorities The future is considerably less bright for foreigners and ethnic minorities in a network society dominated by natives and ethnic majorities. Usually they lack skills and, what is worse, they do not speak or command the native or dominant language sufficiently. So, they run the risk of missing out on the technical and communicative skills required in a network society. The major handicap is having insufficient command of the dominant language. The only exception is to be able to speak and write in English. Without the command of either the dominant or the English language in a particular country one is not even able to do simple terminal work at the level of data entry. If this situation is not improved, ethnic minorities will undoubtedly be among the 'misfits' of network society in every respect (both in work and in social communications).

Barriers to the new media

(In)equalities among Consumers The social categories described above appear to demonstrate great and even increasing differences among people in production and education. But what about the *consumption* of new media hardware, software and services? Several barriers appear to exist that prevent people from using the new media. These barriers will be described as four hurdles that have to be **Four Hurdles of Access** crossed successively to enter the network or the information society. These four hurdles are specifications of the multifaceted concept of *access* to the new media.

Lack of Skills and Computer Fear The first hurdle concerns those who want to use electronic devices in general and computers in particular, but shrink back because they think it is too difficult or because their first experience with such devices has been unpleasant. In 1996, the Dutch Centre for Innovation in Education (CINOP) conducted research among the Dutch population to gather data on their so-called *digital skills* (Doets and Huisman, 1997). It showed that a considerable proportion of the Dutch population aged 18 to 70 had problems performing the following electronic actions: playing a CD (33 per cent), consulting teletext on TV (23 per cent), playing a VCR (52 per cent), programming a VCR (62 per cent), withdrawing money from a cash dispenser (15 per cent), paying with a PIN card (22 per cent) and buying a train ticket from a vending machine (61 per cent). A small majority of the Dutch population (52 per cent) claimed to be able to use a PC in 1996, but the following applications were not used, or were very poorly used: word processing (54 per cent), using spreadsheets (85 per cent), transferring money (93 per cent), playing computer games (81 per cent), sending e-mail messages (89 per cent) and looking for information on the Internet (92 per cent) (1997: 14–16). Striking differences appeared between old and young people and between people with low and with high levels of education. Not being able to perform electronic actions (well) was considered a personal shortcoming: it was considered important, but the people concerned were unable to perform these actions (properly). Some 26 per cent of Dutch people below the age of 50 experienced not being able to operate a PC properly as a great personal shortcoming in 1996. Over 40 per cent of people over 50 felt this way (1997: 22). These data illustrate the expression 'information *want-nots*' as opposed to the expression of 'information have-nots' used by people who belittle the problem of information inequality.

Apart from the objective degree of complexity of operating such devices and the lack of experience in doing so, to be discussed later, there are subjective and emotional factors which are largely responsible for the lack of basic skills in this field. The experience of personal shortcomings (leading to insecurity), the fear of being excluded, and the negative attitude towards these techniques by people who do not master them, give rise to 'computer fear' or 'button fear'. The operations mentioned are said to be difficult and people are afraid to start mastering them.

One might suppose it is just a matter of time before people cross this first hurdle. It mainly concerns elderly and unskilled people. The growth of the 'digital generation(s)', the dying out of the older generations, the increasing penetration of computers in society, and the increase in education about computers, should 'automatically' provide a solution. This supposition is only partly true and, furthermore, it is ethically unacceptable. After all, the research referred to earlier indicated that the majority of the generation below the age of 50 experienced personal deficiencies in the use of a PC. Besides, many elderly people want to learn how to operate a computer: in 1996, 39 per cent of Dutch people between 50 and 56 and 20 per cent of people between 64 and 70 said they wanted to learn to operate a computer (1997: 42). This shows it would be unethical to 'write off' the older generations from the information society in which they still have to live for many years.

No Access to Computers and Networks Those people who cross the first hurdle, and who are willing to use the equipment involved, inevitably confront the second hurdle: not having a computer or a network connection themselves or not having access to one at work or at school. This fact dominates public opinion on the question of access to the new media. All research on the social characteristics of computer and network users has shown large differences in social groupings.

The majority of users are male, relatively young and well educated, having a relatively high income and living in a rich Western country, often the most affluent part of it. (See CommerceNet and Nielsen Media Research, 1996; Cyberatlas, 1996; GVU Center, 1994–8; Nielsen Media Research, 1996; and the CINOP research referred to earlier, amongst many others.) A representative survey of the American population based on official statistics has shown that most of these differences increased between 1989 and 1993. This occurred among all the social categories mentioned above. Simultaneously, young and well educated people with a high income living in rich Western countries and regions have *increased their lead* on elderly people, less educated people, and people with a lower income and from poorer countries and regions (Anderson et al., 1995). There is only one exception to this increase in *relative* differences in access to computers and networks: the gap between males and females is decreasing, though this is happening much faster in Northern America than in Europe (Anderson et al., 1995; GVU Center, 1994–8).

At this point, many economists and media experts will note that this is a normal pattern in the adoption of new media, like those for the introduction of the telephone, the radio, the television and the VCR. Some people are much faster in adopting new technologies than others and, in fact, pay for further development. In that case, the adoption of computers and networks will have just left the phase of the 'pioneers' and the 'early adopters' and will be now taking its first bend upwards in the well-known S-curve. Indeed, such a curve may occur in this case as well. But when it does, it remains to be seen whether this curve will rise as fast and as high as has been observed in the diffusion of the radio, the television and the VCR. The adoption pattern of the telephone, a comparable medium linked in networks, seems much more likely. The telephone needed over 70 years to become more or less generally diffused as a medium in the developed countries. And even now, about half of the world population does not have access to a telephone, and in the rich Western countries about one-quarter or one-fifth of the low-income households in particular cities or regions still has no telephone. It would be fair to assume that the new media are more likely to follow the adoption pattern of the telephone than that of television. If this is true, it cannot be expected that computer networks will reach a level of diffusion of 80 or 90 per cent within the next decades, even in the most developed countries. Several arguments can be put forward for this view:

1 In general, the new media are more expensive than the old media, because they become outdated much more quickly and new peripheral hardware and new software have to be purchased all the time.
2 The old media do not disappear: new media are acquired to be used side by side with the old media, having a cumulative effect on expenses. However, there is little elasticity in total domestic budgets for media and communication, at least in the budgets of lower-income households.

3   The development of multimedia causes a rise in the need for interactive audiovisual services requiring much more capacity and payments for intellectual property rights.

4   Optimum use of the new media means having to be motivated and trained in searching for information; possibly, this capacity is the one most unequally distributed among the population (Rogers and Picot, 1985: 119; see also Chapters 7 and 8).

5   The new media are especially suited for searching and finding specialized information; and those mostly interested in this type of information are those who are already 'well informed'.

6   According to many observers, too little attention is paid to the needs of users in the development and design of new media (see Leeuwis, 1996); this applies in particular to the communication needs of the lower classes, of women and of ethnic minorities.

7   The general diffusion of the old media, such as the TV and the telephone, took place in a period of strong economic growth and the consolidation and levelling of incomes. The new media are being introduced in a period of relative economic stagnation, of increasing social and cultural differences and increasing income inequality in most countries of the world. The diffusion of the old media was backed by a policy of universal and public service from governments and public administrations. By contrast, the diffusion of the new media and the construction of information highways are almost entirely left to business enterprise, causing commercial interests to gain prominence and universal and public service to come under pressure.

Lack of User-friendliness and Unattractive Usage Style

Nevertheless, it is quite possible that, within about 20 years, a large majority of the population in the developed countries will own a PC and will be connected to a computer network at home or will have access to these facilities at work or at school. One has to be careful in mentioning percentages such as these. Computers and networks are brought on to the market in ever simpler and cheaper forms. Apart from simple game computers and home computers, we are now confronted with palmtop computers and network computers. In the late 1990s, primitive versions of the Internet are distributed by cable (web TV) and mobile telephony. However, even if the primary conditions for simply gaining access to the new media are met within two decades, questions remain concerning their *accessibility* for users in practice. What possibilities will the new media offer to users? And will users actually use them? Here we meet the third hurdle.

PCs and computer networks were known for their user-unfriendliness until well into the 1990s. Major improvements were made with the introduction of new graphical and audiovisual interfaces. However, the situation is still far from satisfactory, as was proven by the limited computer skills of the larger part of the Dutch population, mainly caused by the user-unfriendliness of hardware, software and operating manuals. Of this population, 14 per cent wanted to purchase a PC in 1996 but did not do so because they thought it was too complicated, and 23 per cent of PC owners did not use their machine for this reason (Doets and Huisman, 1997: 38, 39).

A broader interpretation of the term 'user-friendliness' is what the new media offer as their *usage style*. Some say this style does not appeal to most women, less educated people and ethnic minorities (Van Zoonen, 1994; see also earlier). The style offered is said to insufficiently meet the needs, preferences and searching behaviour of these groups. Little has been demonstrated empirically on issues of usage style, but in fact it would not be a surprise, according to the theory of technology as human effort, that the design of new media techniques carries the imprint of the social-cultural characteristics of its producers: predominantly male, well educated, English speaking, and members of the ethnic majority in a particular country.

Lack of Significant Usage Opportunities

However, user-unfriendliness and the unattractiveness of the usage style offered do not seem to be the most important reasons for the lack of primary skills described earlier. Both can be improved and extended, and the ICT industry will probably take care of this to some extent in the near future. The lack of experience with PC applications, in turn caused by the limited and unequally divided opportunities to use them, seems to be much more important. This brings us to the fourth and ultimately most important hurdle.

In practice, word processing turns out to be by far the most important application of PCs. It is followed at a great distance by the other applications mentioned earlier, which in 1998 were only used by an average of 10 to 20 per cent of the Western populations (the Internet, electronic mail and the like). An exception is the use of computer games as this is very common among young people. To the average user, however, the PC is nothing but an enhanced typewriter. It is well known that this multi-functional device is utilized far below its capacity. Applications other than word processing, computer games and, recently, reference and education using CD-ROMs, are with minor exceptions used only by professionals for work and education. Household applications are still lagging behind. Many home computers, purchased through subsidies for PC ownership by students and employees or bought for the benefit of the children, are left unused in the study or the attic.

In the meantime the usage opportunities for professional applications at work or at school are increasing rapidly. This is so to such an extent that many users feel they are not able to catch up any more. A new version or update is already available before the old one is mastered. However, this is a reality for about 20 or 30 per cent of some Western populations. Those who have nothing to do with computers in education or at work are probably not going to use them on their own initiative. The only exception is that of parents of children attending school, who are among the most important purchasers of home computers: they have the opportunity of learning to master a computer, often with the help of their children.

A Usage Gap   Further analysis of the domestic use of computers shows well-educated people making far more use of applications in work, private business and education. The favourite applications of people with little education and the young are entertainment and/or computer games, followed by education (Nielsen Media Research, 1996). Here a *usage gap* appears (a better expression than the familiar ones of 'knowledge gap' or 'information gap'). The important thing is that it is likely to grow, instead of decline, with the larger distribution of computers among the population. If this turns out to be true, the difference between advanced and simple uses will increase.

It cannot be ruled out, and in fact it is likely, that in the long term the first three hurdles of access to the network society will be crossed by the majority of people in the developed countries. However, in saying this, one has to acknowledge that a considerable minority will continue to be excluded. At the time of writing an average of 10 per cent of the adult, non-handicapped population in the developed countries is still a real illiterate or a functional illiterate (United Nations, 1998). The number of 'digital illiterates' will probably remain much higher for some time. Primary skills will gradually increase and 'computer fear' will diminish. In time, ownership of and access to computers and networks may reach the majority of the population. Great improvements can still be made in respect of the user-friendliness of hardware, software and manuals, and the user style offered can be made more appealing. However, all this does not rule out an increase of differences in usage. How can this be explained? Why should a technology, so much suited to the *spread* of information in society and into the world, in practice lead to more *private appropriation* and greater inequality in the use of it?

This contradiction can be seen in a large number of problems of network society that appear to be difficult to solve. Take the protection of the right of intellectual and material property in the context of ICT (authors' rights, copyright, safety of payments) and the right of privacy. The difficulty in maintaining these protections in digital environments is both an expression of the socialization of information and the desire to keep it in our own hands. The trend towards socialization is technologically supported by the ease of registration and copying by digital media. However, in current (Western) societies there are a number of strong counter-tendencies supporting the opposite trend, that is private appropriation.

Background to Increasing Information Inequality   The first tendency is a social-cultural one. It is a combination of processes of social-cultural *differentiation and individualization* in (post)-modern society. ICT supports these processes because its most important medium, the computer, is pre-eminently a device to be used by individuals, although it is also able to connect individuals within groups and communities through networks. Social-cultural differentiation is also supported by computers and networks because their uniform digital substructure helps to produce and spread all kinds of cultural artefacts of whatever kind and quantity desired. So, increasing information inequality might just be an aspect of general social-cultural differentiation in society.

However, there is more, as we see when we look at a second tendency which is a part of current social-economic development. It is the rising *material inequality and income differentials* seen in all Western countries to some degree since the beginning of the 1980s. This tendency causes increasingly unequal division of material resources and in extreme cases even an exclusion or marginalization of segments of the lower social classes living on welfare or minimum wages. The means of information and communication are a part of these resources. In this case increasing information inequality might be a consequence of the rising costs of information and communication in general and the goods and services of ICT in particular, while the household budget is shrinking or remains the same.

The third tendency is a political one. It serves to tolerate rising material inequalities. It is the *policy of privatization and stimulation of the free-market economy* in most countries. It leads to the commercialization of formerly public information supply and communication facilities and the surge of private education. Inevitably it increases the opportunities for information inequality.

Finally, we must mention the continually *diverging areas of application* of ICT. This technological tendency originates from the multifunctional capacities of computers. The most important property of these devices is their (re)programmability for extremely diverging activities. One can use computers for very advanced and difficult applications, but also for familiar and simple matters. Computers are used for complex economic and political decisions and for high-level education. They are also applied – sometimes even the same computers – for relatively simple actions like paying and receiving money, ordering products, typing letters and playing games. The multifunctionality of ICT is much more extended than it is in old media like the press, broadcasting and the telephone. The press and broadcasting only have information contents of a different kind and level. The telephone allows all kinds of interpersonal communication. The extended multi-functionality of ICT is a neutral property in its own right, but in particular circumstances it offers many more opportunities than less functional media and techniques to expand existing information inequalities.

Structural Information Inequality Such a combination of circumstances is the key to understanding present information inequality. *When the four tendencies described above come together and interweave they produce a force easily inducing greater information inequality – a force difficult to counter by those who might wish to do so.*

Of course, information inequality is not a new phenomenon. This type of inequality has existed ever since the development of writing – and it will probably remain. Perhaps we will even have to accept the fact that information inequality will increase in the network society. It might be an inescapable side-effect of social and cultural differentiation. However, we have to be very careful not to let *structural or basic* inequalities arise within a society and between societies. This would certainly undermine political, social and cultural democracy and strip formal civil rights from their actual substance. Structural inequality would appear when on the one hand an 'information elite' strengthens its position, while on the other hand those groups already living on the margins of society become excluded from communications in society because these are practised in media they do not possess or control. The differences become structural when the positions people occupy in networks and other media determine whether they have any influence on decisions made in several fields of society. Here we can refer to Chapter 4 which explains the importance of positions in networks for the exercise of power.

No Simple Two-tiered Society
So, the picture is not the usual simple one of a two-tiered society, or of a gap between information 'haves' and 'have-nots' as two clearly separate groups of the population. On the contrary, the pattern described is ever more complex social, economic and cultural differentiation. A better representation would be a continuum or spectrum of differentiated positions across the population, with the 'information elite' at the top and a group of 'excluded people' at the bottom.

THE SOCIAL INFRASTRUCTURE OF NETWORK SOCIETY

This section will show how the use of media networks is linked to several fundamental social changes taking place in modern Western society at the end of the twentieth century. We are talking about processes such as individualization, privatization and socialization which together shape Western society's new infrastructure. The importance of networks for this infrastructure can be shown on several levels of abstraction and generality. Unfortunately, the following account has to be fairly abstract.

Time–Space Distantiation
One of the most abstract and general historical processes is *time–space distantiation*, which was described in Chapter 1. It was explained how Anthony Giddens uses this term to show that space and time are important dimensions of any society. With the introduction of global networks reaching into every (Western) home, *the process of time–space distantiation seems to be approaching its limit, at least in Western societies.* Many take it for granted that we have a 'global village'. Distance and time seem to lose any relevance. These popular ideas are partly wrong, however. All in all, the process of time–space distantiation is marked not only by the extension of space and time, but also by the contraction of space and the compression of time. As a result, time and space in some respects gain importance, instead of losing relevance. The technological capabilities of bridging space and time enable people to be more *selective* in choosing coordinates of space and time than ever before in history.

Increasing Selectivity of Space and Time
Many examples can be given to support this statement (see also Ferguson, 1990). The enormous growth in telephony and the explosive increase of demand for data communication already show that more value is being placed on bridging distances of space and time. Nobody will deny the extreme relevance of (clock) time in the most advanced nerve centres of

ICT, the stock markets. Hesitating for a second or failing to make a fast connection to another financial market can mean the difference between profit and loss. In companies, the coordination of labour by means of information and communication technology leads to an increase of the relevance of logistics and time registration. In mass communication, the importance of time schedules for broadcasters of programmes and commercials is still increasing, for they want to reach very specific target audiences. The Cable News Network (CNN) gloriously won the first media battle in the Gulf War, by always being in the right places and broadcasting their scoops 24 hours a day. The dimension of time is becoming more important for viewers as well, as new concepts of global time (produced by satellite TV and Internet communication) overlie the old ones (marked by local, daily rhythms and routines) (Ferguson, 1990: 155).

In the dimension of space the same applies to all the fields we have just mentioned. In Chapter 3 it was stressed how selective transnational corporations have become. They are extremely careful in strategically choosing the right places for their departments and computer network nodes in the world, assigning them particular functions. Increasing control over space enables them to choose between the quality of particular places (Harvey, 1989: 294ff.).

Expansion and Compression of Space and Time

So, expansion and compression of space and time are two sides of the same coin. They represent the most general expression of the idea of the unity of scale extension and reduction that is one of the threads running through this book. Increased control over space and time in a local context by a small social unit can only exist thanks to increased control over space and time over long distances by a larger social unit. In Chapter 1 we pointed out that the privatization of local units to become smaller units has always been enabled by means of large-scale infrastructures of the supply and transportation of energy, matter and people. The need for communication and information flows by media networks is now added to this list. In households, the need for these infrastructures has grown with the development of four dimensions of privatization:

1   decreasing density of housing (settlement);
2   increasing size of a single house with more individual rooms;
3   decreasing household size;
4   a cultural process of spending more time at home and in family life.

In companies, the combination of decentralizing production and centralizing control described in Chapter 2 causes an increase in the need for all kinds of communication channels. Both at home and in companies, the expansion of communication and of information processing over long distances goes hand in hand with an increasing intensity of information activities in local contexts (using an 'intelligent home', an 'intelligent' workstation or a local network).

The historical process of both socialization and individualization of space and time in society runs side by side with the scale extensions and scale reductions mentioned above. In the following pages we will consider the spatial dimension, and forget the time dimension for the present. The spatial dimension is aptly described by Burgers (1988) as 'the detachment of society from geography'. The natural environment as a relevant context is replaced by or interwoven with social environments constructed by people. Simultaneously, natural time is outstripped by the increasing importance of clock time constructed by society (Bolter, 1984; Rifkin, 1987). Communication and information networks more or less complete these processes (Meyrowitz, 1985). In a manner of speaking, they spatially enlarge society – in the late 1990s mainly Western society – and they reduce the size of the world. Transmission takes place in 'real time' and messages have to be sent and received at any desired moment. With the shifting limits of natural time, the meaning of socially constructed time becomes more important. The socialization of time even seems to become total as people think time is no longer relevant in the new media environment. So it seems – but in reality the natural (for instance biological) substratum will continue to exist, of course.

Socialization of Space
The social and mental consequences of these processes have a large cultural impact. This will be demonstrated in the next chapter. In this section we want to point out four immediate social and mental consequences of the socialization of *space* and the role played by networks (see Burgers, 1988: 16–22). These are discussed in detail in the following chapters as well.

In the first place, an *upgrading* of the social environment is going on. Although individual environments remain decisive for individuals, of course, people acknowledge the shrinking relevance of these environments in social contexts.

> The moment the world is brought into the home via the mass media, the interest in individual experiences seems to shrink to insignificant proportions. Viewed from the perspective of modern society, the ups and downs of individual life are less and less important and the individual is well aware of this. In relation to the physical environment this means that really important events seem to be taking place elsewhere. (Burgers, 1988: 17, my translation from the Dutch)

Second, the social environment is made more *objective*. The social environments made by humans increasingly adopt the character of a natural environment. Individuals therefore feel that they face an anonymous, opaque, inaccessible and uncontrollable reality. Symptoms of alienation and uprooting are widespread. Social and economic crises begin to resemble natural disasters. Media networks, which enable more direct communications between the micro-level and the institutions of the macro-level, do not reduce these experiences. On the contrary, we have argued that, in the late 1990s, computer networks both subjectively and objectively tend to enhance opaque and uncontrollable processes.

In the third place, a *fragmentation* of social environments can be observed. They comprise fewer concrete, continuous and collectively used areas, and more abstract, dispersed areas used for special purposes. And what is more, homogeneous communities are being gradually replaced by all kinds of diffuse social networks. This will be discussed in greater detail later, for the communication capacities of media networks seem to fit perfectly with these trends.

Finally, we perceive a *generalization and a standardization* of social environments. 'Human activities seem to become more uniform after the scale extension of social communications; the same activities are happening in ever more places' (1988: 21). The exchange of experiences through networks on a global level has led to a general diffusion of Western urban culture. It is made dominant by Western economic and technological strength and it has produced a loss of the particularity and identity of other, less materially strong cultures. On the other hand, elements of the latter cultures are adopted by Western culture (see the next chapter).

Socialization and Individualization of Space and Time

In the twentieth century, this general socialization of space was pursued within a particular dialectical process, that is a unity of opposing tendencies: a particular socialization of individual space on the one hand, and a particular individualization of social space on the other. One social scientist will emphasize the first development whereas another will emphasize the second, but in fact both processes are active simultaneously and both are supported by media networks. Again we are dealing with an expression of the unity of scale extension and scale reduction. The second tendency suggests individualization and privatization – social processes visible to everyone in modern Western society. A nice description in this respect was given by Burgers: 'It seems as if a process of detachment of society from geography "in the second degree" is taking place: we try to detach ourselves from our direct social environment in the same way as we have liberated ourselves from our "natural" environment' (1988: 21). Instead, solitary individuals are withdrawing into their own (ever smaller) households and are participating in all kinds of 'communities without propinquity'. This term is from Webber (1963) and refers to the multifarious, more or less diffused and large-scale social networks of modern society. The result of this process is a strong *erosion of public space* as we know it. Instead, we find a completely different type of public space, to a large extent realized by media networks. This will be discussed in the next section. Well-known analyses of individualizing public space have been made by Richard Sennett in *The Fall of Public Man* (1974) and Christopher Lasch in *Heaven in a Heartless World* (1977).

The often neglected opposite tendency is a particular socialization of individual space. Some critical, emancipatory or liberal social scientists speak about 'colonization of the world of daily life by the system' (Habermas, 1981) or about the increasing intrusion into private life by the authorities and by fellow citizens (Shils, 1975). Usually, they describe these tendencies as linear historical processes produced by public authorities and private corporations, previously operating from a distance and now increasingly penetrating the private life of (for instance) households. When these tendencies are solely described as a linear process, it is hard to

understand how a socialization of individual space can go han
with an individualization of social space. There is no reason to can
conditions of the nineteenth century a 'golden age of privacy'. In the close-
knit, socially controlled communities of those days, the privacy of citizens
among themselves and in relation to local authorities was not considered to
be relevant. Only in the twentieth century has the penetration of authorities and market organizations into the private life of households and
other more or less private spaces increasingly run contrary to the process of
privatization and the attempts to protect these households and other
spaces. This conflict has made privacy an increasingly important value to
modern Western people.

It is extremely important to understand that media networks offer an
infrastructure for both the tendencies described above. They are a potential
social threat to privacy in private life, and at the same time they are a
condition for the fulfilment of the need for social communication and
information in the same spheres of privatized life. This contrast is a fertile
breeding ground for future social conflicts.

**'Lost'
Communities and
the Perspective of
Virtual
Communities**

The history of the twentieth century reveals a disintegration of traditional
communities such as families, neighbourhoods and groups of workers, into
associations which on the one hand are declining in size (caused by
privatization and individualization) and on the other hand are extending as
they become more diffused and spread over greater distances. In the eyes of
many social scientists, planners and citizens, we are dealing with a 'lost
community'. After World War II, town planners tried to create a counter-
balance to this presumed social uprooting by saving communities and (re-)
creating them ('saved communities' in the terms of Wellman and Leighton,
1979). In the late 1990s these attempts can be dropped far more easily.
Most people accept the strong trend towards privatization and individualization and the rise of diffuse communities. The introduction of the
new media, in particular the Internet with all its sites and discussion groups,
has raised hopes for a recovery of community in electronic environments.
So-called *virtual communities* are considered to be a renaissance of lost
community by the early adopters and advocates of the Internet (see
Rheingold, 1993a, 1993b in particular). The reality of such virtual community building can be judged by comparing these communities systematically with *organic communities* (see van Dijk, 1997a).

**Virtual and
Organic
Communities
Compared**

Virtual communities are associations of people not tied to time, place
and other physical or material circumstances, other than those of the
people and media enabling them. They are created in electronic environments with the aid of mediated communications. Organic communities are
bound to time, place and natural environments. They are mainly based on
face-to-face communication. Every community has its own particular
structure and activities, a social organization, a language and modes of
interaction, and finally its own culture and identity.

Composition

An organic community (in a neighbourhood, quarter, extended family or
workplace) is a relatively stable unit with many short and overlapping
communication lines and joint activities (see Figure 1.6). Virtual

communities, on the other hand, are loose affiliations of people that can fall apart at any moment. For instance, leaving a group on the Internet is simple and may hardly be noticed. Virtual communities consist of people with a particular interest or range of activities. Therefore, they are called *communities of interest*.

Social Organization
A virtual community's social organization is not bound to a particular time, place and material environment. Many think these fundamental co-ordinates of life are redundant in virtual communities. This is a misunderstanding. The contents of communication in networks, and therefore in virtual communities, are largely determined by the reality of the organic communities with which one is familiar, as will be explained in Chapter 8. This is the origin of the many expressions containing 'virtual this' and 'digital that'. People take the reality they know with them, as a kind of baggage, when they surf the Internet and take part in virtual communities. The constitution of people is shaped entirely by their physical and mental condition and environment. Furthermore, we have just seen that the importance of place and time in using networks is increasing instead of decreasing. Attempts to ignore time, place and other physical conditions result in the extremely fragile organization of most virtual communities. Some think leadership and coordination are unnecessary in such communities, because technology enables all members to participate at the same time. This supposition is also false, as social-psychological research has made perfectly clear (see Chapter 8). Electronic discussion and interaction require more organization and coordination than face-to-face discussion, not less.

Language and Interaction
One of the reasons for this requirement is that for the time being almost all signals in the communication of virtual communities are restricted to verbal utterances of a particular type (texts on a screen). The rich potential of verbal and non-verbal communication in organic communities is sorely missed. This is compensated for by consciously using artificial paralanguage such as smileys (tokens of emotion added to the keyboard, such as ☺) and asynchronous types of interaction (the language of the answering machine). See Chapter 8 for further information.

Culture and Identity
Members of a virtual community usually have only one thing in common: the interest that brought them together. They are heterogeneous in everything else. In an organic community, on the other hand, people have several interests in common, which makes such a community relatively homogeneous. This provides an organic community with better chances of building and maintaining its own culture and identity than a virtual community.

Supplement Instead of Replacement
From this short comparison (see van Dijk, 1997a for an extended one) we can draw the conclusion that virtual communities cannot make up for the loss of traditional community. They cannot *replace* organic communities, because they are too limited and unstable to exist without them. However, increasingly they will become *added* to traditional communities. A mutual improvement and reinforcement will be the real challenge for the future. The interrelatedness of virtual and organic communities was illustrated in Figure 1.7, a sketch of the infrastructure of network society.

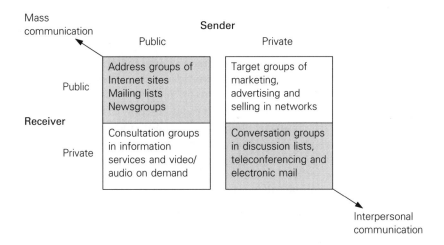

FIGURE 6.1   Electronic groups between interpersonal and mass communication

New Communication Groups   The rise of diffuse social networks and the support given by networks create new communication groups, and even new types of communities, with at least one thing in common: *they fill the field between interpersonal communication and mass communication*. These groups and types can be analysed by placing them along the dimensions of public versus private and sender versus receiver (Figure 6.1; compare McQuail, 1987: 301–3). For they exist between one extreme, a combination of public sender and public receiver, and the other, a combination of private transmitter and private receiver.

Receiver Groups   In the mass communication relationship between public sender and public receiver, a clear *segmentation of public receiver groups* can be perceived. This means these groups acquire a more private character. This trend will be discussed in the following chapter where the question will be posed as to whether this means the end of mass communication.

Consultation Groups   Segmentation of the public is completed in new media *connecting public senders to private receivers*. The dominant pattern is consultation. We are referring to video and audio on demand and to information services. But one can also identify phenomena springing from the segmentation just mentioned. James Beniger (1987) has referred to the strong tendency in current mass communications to create or suggest a 'personal' relation to receivers. He has shown the correspondence with the boom in 'personal' direct mail and in marketing backed by research into special consumer groups. In this way 'pseudo-communities' are created, according to Beniger.

Target Groups   In the Fordist age of mass production, communication between *private senders and public receivers* has expanded enormously (see Beniger, 1986). We are referring to target groups in public relations, advertising and all kinds of propaganda. In the current age of specialized production, this type of communication is enhanced and directed towards *semi-public* reception aimed at specific target groups. The new media offer all the necessary

facilities. And in fact they do not provide these facilities merely for commercial and party political purposes. The number of networks for experts,
hobbyists and activists is increasing rapidy. For instance, networks of
medical experts, computer hackers and environmentalists are multiplying.

Conversation
Groups
The latter phenomenon also creates new and improved opportunities
for communication between *private senders and public receivers*. In the
narrowband networks of today (used by discussion groups and other groups
using electronic mail) people cannot talk simultaneously, but it is possible to
converse alternately. In broadband networks, groups can talk simultaneously in video and computer conferencing. This type of conversation is no
longer restricted to sounds, but also contains images, texts and data. In the
meantime, all kinds of facilities are being added to the traditional communication medium, the telephone, thus increasing the facilities for group
calling and for selective contacting (persons, times).

All the initiatives mentioned above indicate the birth of more or less new
types of communication and community operating *between* interpersonal
and mass communication. They are constructed deliberately and selectively. Therefore, many observers expect the growth of all kinds of on-line
subcultures which will communicate only among themselves and will break
up the social cohesion of our societies. Is their concern warranted?

UNITY AND FRAGMENTATION: SOCIAL COHESION RECONSTRUCTED

Social Unity and
Fragmentation
In the previous section it was argued that scale extensions and scale
reductions, including socialization and individualization, are two sides of
the coin of modernity. This *duality of social structure* has been noted by
many theorists of high modernity or postmodernity, notably Giddens
(1991a), van Dijk (1993a), Lash and Urry (1994), Featherstone et al.
(1995); Barber (1996) and Castells (1996; 1997). Modern society simultaneously reveals aspects of growing homogeneity and heterogeneity,
integration and differentiation, unity and fragmentation. This is not some
kind of compromise position of social scientists who refuse to take a stand.
It really is characteristic of all spheres of modern society, as is shown by the
authors just mentioned, and as it is claimed in this book in the context of the
role of the new media in society. Usually social scientists have to argue in
favour of the existence of homogeneity, integration and unity and against
simplistic notions of a fragmenting society. It seems as if sociologists'
classical nightmare of a society falling apart returns with every modern and
technological development.

Against people expecting a break-up of American society into subcul-
tural clusters of race, religion, ethnicity and gender – a process supposedly
reinforced by a fragmented media system of countless cable channels, pay-
per-view programmes and Internet sites – Meyrowitz and Maguire contend
that 'the current trend is towards integration of all groups into a relatively

common experiential sphere – with a new recognition of the special needs and idiosyncrasies of individuals' (1993: 43). According to them, television and other electronic media have made the divisions between social groups more visible and permeable. 'Current media, then, continue a trend towards greater homogenization in one way and greater fragmentation in another. Traditional groups are bypassed in both directions: individuals experience more diversity and choice, but traditional group cultures are overlapping, losing identity and blurring into each other' (1993: 45). This goes for broadcasting as well as for (new media) narrowcasting. Television has bridged the lives of people living in different physical and informational spheres. The Internet goes even further in offering the opportunity to connect by direct interaction both people of the same origin and different people or environments.

Media Unity and Fragmentation
So, we may observe a *duality of media structure* closely corresponding to the duality of social structure in society. According to 'medium theory' (Meyrowitz, 1985; 1997) media have their own characteristics, producing social contexts that foster certain forms of interaction and social identity. They are both defining and enabling, just like the communication capacities described in Chapter 1. Meyrowitz claims that oral media in traditional societies fostered a homogenization of relatively small communities ('us against them'). Opposed to this, the diversity of print media in early modern societies produced a compartmentalization and specialization of social groups and simultaneously supported the unification of nations by a single official language. This duality returns in the history of broadcasting. At first, radio and television unified national and local societies with a single or a few network(s). After the multiplication of channels and the advent of pay TV, audiences became fragmented again, while keeping many similarities and overlaps. For example, audiences actually choose a handful of broadcasting channels among a much larger number, and broadcasters or advertisers still prefer the mass market (the common denominator).

Duality Increases
In the new media the duality of media structure increases once again. They are both mass and interpersonal media and they offer new types of media in between: the so-called virtual communities or new associations of communication analysed in the previous section. They are media of allocution, consultation, registration and conversation in a system of integration or convergence. The new media are individualizing media, mainly because they are based upon individual human–computer interaction, and they are media to be used collectively as these computers are connected in networks. This huge plurality of potential applications enables both divisions and commonalities among users and audiences. So, the actual result of the duality of media structure is defined by the unifying and fragmenting trends in society, that is the duality of social structure.

The Divisions of Marketing
Both dualities are eagerly adopted by electronic traders on the Internet who have discovered the concept of virtual community and are translating it into new opportunities for commercial relationships. Hagel and Armstrong (1997), for example, make a number of proposals to exploit people's desire

to congregate on the net for basic needs of (common) interest, relationship, fantasy and transaction in their book *Net Gain*. This definition of virtual communities as new types of association fits to that supplied above. The authors claim that the more a community can be split or segmented, resulting in smaller electronic groups, the better it is for the depth, coherence and commercial exploitability of this community. So, they start with a complete fragmentation of potential communities along so-called 'vectors' (differences in geography, demography, topics of interest and business functions or categories) from the point of view of the marketeer. However, these are the abstract conceptual inventions of marketing, not of the concrete organic groups trying to organize themselves on-line and off-line.

A widely held view is that the narrowcasting of the new media based upon these techniques of categorizing and direct marketing, trying to reach extremely specific groups in advertising and sales, will (further) divide society. That is why Joseph Turow (1997) has called his book *Breaking up America*. Turow claims that direct marketing with new media exploits growing social divisions and exacerbates them. According to Meyrowitz and Maguire (1993: 43–4), this is wrong. The target groups that narrowcasters and direct marketeers are trying to reach are 'thin age/sex bands (such as pre-teen girls, nine to twelve) or "lifestyle clusters" based on interests, tastes, values, attitudes and consumption patterns'. They are conceptual categories constructed by marketing people, not organic groups of social class, race, ethnicity and gender acting and organizing themselves and (still) having a number of overlapping commonalities.

Future of the Public Sphere
Will the new media primarily bring us together, or will they tear us further apart? This is a question about the future of the public sphere. The most popular answer to this question emphasizes fragmentation as well. The reasons are evident. At first sight, three conditions of the modern public sphere, as we have come to know it in the twentieth century, disappear in the new media environment:

1 the alliance of the public sphere with a particular place or territory;
2 the presumed unitary character of the public sphere that is transforming into a patchwork of different and partial public spheres;
3 a public–private distinction that is becoming blurred.

A short explanation will be sufficient here. As to the first condition, members of a particular organic community or a nation are no longer tied to a given territory to meet each other and build collectivities. They might use old media like the press, the telephone or satellite broadcasting, and new media like the Internet in particular, to (re)construct their own public sphere and form imagined communities (Anderson, 1983) or virtual communities. The pattern of the Jewish and the Armenian public spheres, for instance, which was not confined to Israel and Armenia long before the advent of the Internet, will be multiplied.

Second, what binds people in a contemporary public sphere is not a fixed number of common situations, views, habits and other social, cultural and political characteristics. It is an extremely diversified and shifting complex of overlapping similarities and differences, particularly in the growing number of multicultural societies. The 'common ground' of the unitary nation or mass society is an idea from the age of national broadcasting through a few channels. It is still rooted in the minds of the intellectual political and media elite of the nations concerned, though it was never firmly based in reality (Meyrowitz and Maguire, 1993; Keane, 1995).

Finally, the imagined borders of every public sphere in modern society become blurred, as has been demonstrated in many earlier sections. Public affairs become private in home television viewing, radio listening and surfing the Internet. The private becomes public in the numerous invasions of privacy by computer registration, in the pouring out of intimate affairs in talk shows and reality TV, and in the personalization of politics. The new media, the Internet in particular, add a new dimension to the blurring public–private distinction as new kinds of association and communication appear between interpersonal and mass communication.

Reconstruction of the Public Sphere   Does this mean that the three conditions of the modern public sphere will disappear completely and that all common ground for societies at large will dissolve? No, it just means that the conventional idea of a single, unified public sphere, and the accompanying ideas of a distinctive public opinion, a common public good and a particular public–private distinction, are obsolete (see Keane, 1995). Instead we get a 'complex mosaic of differently sized overlapping and interconnected public spheres' (1995: 8). The Internet itself, with its hyperlink structure of connections and its numerous overlapping discussion fora, is a perfect model of this mosaic. It is complemented by the increasing number of cross-references and cross-fertilizations between new and old media, like newspapers and television programmes referring to websites and vice versa.

So, the three conditions mentioned will reappear in different forms, and public spheres will be reconstructed in ways we cannot exactly anticipate yet. What we do know, however, is that the imagined unity of modern public spheres will transform into much more complex and differentiated unities. The public–private distinction may blur, but it will not vanish. New distinctions will be negotiated in struggles for privacy and personal autonomy, for more public or more private, market-based information supply, and for the soul of the family and spheres of living and working. Finally, public communication will be less tied to the parameters of time, place and territory then ever before in history. But this does not mean that the physical, social and mental make-up of the people engaged and the material environment of the resources used in this type of communication will no longer matter. In Chapter 8 (on psychology) it will be explained that this popular idea is wrong.

CULTURE

Several significant cultural aspects can be perceived in the trends of fragmentation, segmentation and individualization of social reality currently appearing at all levels of Western society. The contention is that 'mass society' or 'mass culture' is eroding and a huge increase of cultural diversity is taking place. In previous chapters this contention has been qualified. However, the question as to whether these trends of fragmentation will mean the end of mass communication remains a valid one. Unfortunately, most often this question and the concept of mass com-

Opposing Trends munication are neither carefully defined nor given a balanced treatment. Yet this most important question deserves a balanced answer. This immediately becomes clear when we note opposing trends, such as the globalization, generalization and standardization of cultural expressions. Moreover, plenty of opportunities for the types of mass communication created by developed countries in the twentieth century still exist in developing countries. In comparing these opposing trends, we will once again observe a combination of scale extension and reduction.

A number of developments that might indicate the end of mass communication have been observed in the preceding chapters. Most important were the shift from allocution to consultation, registration and conversation; the expansion of communication in the gap between public and private communications; and the birth of new types of communities and communication between mass communication and interpersonal communication. All definitions of mass communication include the following three characteristics: it is *public*; it mainly goes *one way*, from sender to receiver; and it is aimed at a *large audience*. All three characteristics are subject to change.

Aspects of Mass Communication at Stake The public nature of mass communication is affected by two developments. In the first place, publicness is fragmented by drastic segmentations of the public. In theory communication remains public, but *in fact* it is limited. Segmentation is far more extensive for the new media than it was for the old media of the press and broadcasting. Second, accessibility of ever more types of mass communication is restricted. Currently, the new media are only accessible to a minority. In the future, access to the new media will be commercially determined and segmented in groups able or willing to pay (subscriptions and pay-per-view).

TABLE 7.1 Opposing tendencies in the field of mass
communication

Category	Scale-extending tendencies	Scale-reducing tendencies
Geographic scale	Globalization	Localization
Producers/senders	Integration	Differentiation
Consumers/receivers	Massification	Segmentation
Products/services	Generalization	Specialization

Furthermore, one-way traffic in traditional mass communication is replaced by two-way traffic and multilateral communication. New media are interactive to a certain extent. As has been said before, they reveal a shift from allocution towards consultation, registration and conversation. This does not imply that the receiver in traditional mass communication views and listens in a passive manner only. In any case, in using new media the so-called active receiver in more recent theories of mass communication (Fiske, 1987; Ang, 1991; Silverstone, 1994) acquires many more means to return signals. The active receiver now has the opportunity to become an active sender. However, it remains to be seen to what extent this will actually happen. In the late 1990s, the way the Internet is used (still) looks a lot like traditional mass communication. Zapping along television channels has just been replaced by 'surfing' websites. Users read and view a lot more than they make contributions themselves. And newsgroups and discussion groups on the Internet also have many more readers or passive participators than active news producers or contributors to discussions. Each group usually has a small hard core of members. Nevertheless, the possibility remains that, after some time, these classic patterns of participation in public media will become more balanced ones.

Finally, the size of the public of mass communication is at issue. As has been mentioned earlier, audiences are fragmenting. However, this does not mean the quantity of fragments is small. They are spread all over the globe. An extremely specialized website, for instance, can still be visited by thousands of people. What really matters here is the fact that the field in between interpersonal communication and mass communication is enlarged. The size of the public in this field is usually smaller than the size of the public in traditional mass communication.

So, the expectation of the imminent demise of mass communication seems to be right. However, we think it is inspired by a one-sided view of the contradictory trends current in mass communication. It is entirely based on the trends given in the right-hand column of Table 7.1.

Scale Extension and Reduction The scale reduction going on in the limited public nature of specific audience groups and local communications, using electronic mail, local broadcasting or company television, for example, is only able to exist under the umbrella of the scale extension of current mass media. Concerning infrastructure (connections and other equipment), market organization and programming, local communications depend upon the larger media of broadcasting and telephony expanding and concentrating on the (inter)-national market.

Globalization and Localization

Localization of media is opposed by a striking (inter)nationalization taking place at about the same speed. The shift of local and regional media to national media occurred in the nineteenth century. The return to local broadcasting and computer networking going on at present is accompanied by an opposite shift to satellite television and international press and programme production. The growing importance of global media events, such as the Olympic Games and the soccer World Cup, both watched by billions of viewers world-wide, do not provide strong support for the end of mass communication!

Integration and Differentiation

The producers of mass communication multiply and diversify activities on a local scale. Simultaneously, their economic organization is concentrating in huge media enterprises. In Chapter 3 it was claimed that soon five to ten of these enterprises will dominate the world market. Undoubtedly this will lead to an increase in the number of programmes made for a global audience and covered with a local dressing.

Massification and Fragmentation

The consumers and receivers of mass communication are not just an audience disintegrating under the influence of technology, increasing supply and social processes of individualization and fragmentation. This would be an unhistorical and one-sided impression of affairs. In culturally divided countries like the Netherlands, there was a much more extreme fragmentation of society and mass media in the past than there is today. In the 1980s and 1990s, these structures crumbled under the influence of a generalization, massification and commercialization of culture. Today, fragmentation does not have to lead to fixed segments of the public: it may just as likely result in constantly shifting publics overlapping in many ways. Within this diffuse set of publics both the common denominator, addressed by many senders (broadcasters and press) in prime time with average subjects, and a whole range of much smaller audiences (of a special music channel or a quality newspaper, for instance), can be observed. So there is no question of decreasing massification in media consumption: masses simply appear in other forms. Audiovisual media reception approaches consumption on other markets where the combination of manufactured and custom-made goods has been known for much longer. Receivers might no longer view and listen to the same channels and programmes, but they certainly consume similar contents.

Generalization and Specialization

So, media products not only become more diverse and more specialist, but also more general. This corresponds with the trend towards generalization and standardization of social environments discussed in the previous chapter. To give just a few examples: Western popular music and film celebrities are known throughout the world; the same applies to their products and symbols, such as music and clothing. On the other hand, exotic expressions of culture (such as African music, Oriental religions, Chinese cuisine and all sorts of souvenirs) are entering the Western world (see Barber, 1996). Though these expressions are merged with specific local interpretations to preserve identities, the most important trends remain the dispersal, blending and equalization of cultural products (see Featherstone, 1990; Meyrowitz and Maguire, 1993).

Changing Connotations of 'Mass'

So, the question about the presumed end of mass communication will receive neither a positive nor a negative answer here. It is an unhistorical question. It would be more appropriate to say that the term 'mass' acquires new meanings. They can be expressed in five connotations of the term 'mass' in mass communication:

1   We are dealing less than ever with an *undivided* mass. The segmentation described indicates that masses are dividing into diffuse 'component masses'. The components are not necessarily smaller than the original mass. On the contrary, we might be dealing with mass on a global scale.
2   The mass is less *anonymous*. People are screened by all kinds of market research. Besides, more and more pseudo-personal relations are established between sender and receiver in current mass communications (as discussed in Chapter 6).
3   The opportunities for selection, feedback and interaction offered in the new media enable the mass to become less *passive*.
4   We are dealing less than before with mass in the sense of a *crowd*, in the Western world at least: new types of communities appear largely or partly based on mediated communications.
5   Finally, we are dealing less and less with a *detached* mass (of individuals or groups totally separated from each other and hardly communicating): the traditional boundaries between interpersonal communication, communication within and between organizations, and mass communication are disappearing.

Tendencies and Norms

The question concerning the end of mass communication is not only unhistorical, it is also loaded with *normative views*. The *centrifugal* trends in the right-hand column of Table 7.1, indicating the decline of mass communication and enabling increasing cultural diversity and opportunities for individual choice, are rated *positively* (particularly by liberals) because they are considered to be aspects of modernization and increasing individual freedom in present-day society. The same trends, however, are rated *negatively* (in particular by social democrats and Christian democrats) because they are presumed to be enhancing the social isolation of the individual and to be curbing traditional publicness. People supporting the latter view are afraid that individuals will start to show symptoms of alienation and uprooting and they fear the presumed manipulative power of segmented media over their own audiences.

The *centripetal* trends in the centre column of Table 7.1, indicating an extension of mass communication and a standardization of cultural expressions, are viewed *positively* (in particular by social democrats and Christian democrats) because they would satisfy the individual need for collective identity and the public need for social cohesion. These same trends are valued *negatively* (particularly by liberals) because they increase the chances of paternalism, of registration and of control by the centre.

Finally, they are supported by all kinds of elitist cultural pessimists who fear the decay of culture and the loss of identity.

THE BLURRING SPHERES OF LIVING

One of network society's most important characteristics is the fading away of boundaries between the macro-, meso- and micro-levels of social life, between the public and the private sphere and between the spheres of living, working, studying, recreation and travelling. Therefore, telework and telestudy are among the most discussed applications of the new media. So far, these tele-activities have not yet proved themselves. The over-estimation of their adoption is caused not so much by a lower than expected introduction of the infrastructure required, but by an inaccurate view of existing relations between spheres of living and by a strong underestimation of the social and organizational difficulties involved in tele-activity. Most people assume that the spheres of living, the domestic sphere in particular, will become *multifunctional*. At the same time it is assumed that people want to perform their activities *in a single place* (except for travelling, of course), preferably at home. Both assumptions are only partly correct. The fading away of boundaries between the spheres of living, described earlier, is caused not so much by the multifunctional use of spaces enabled by communication technology, but by the *linking of spaces that remain and are used primarily for special purposes*. A network's most fundamental technical characteristic is the connections it makes, and one of its most important social characteristics is the combination of scale extension and scale reduction. In this way, multifunctionality and specialization can be linked.

Multifunctional or Connected Spheres of Living

The opportunity for an increasing multifunctional use of *spaces* in spheres of living cannot be denied. The same applies to the multifunctional use of *time* for that matter. The new media enable working, studying and entertaining oneself at home at every hour of the day. In the meantime, workplaces are also provided with opportunities for study, entertainment and mediated conversation with friends, acquaintances and relatives at a distance (although there is a limited chance that this will be allowed). Direct links to companies will enable students to gain work experience while sitting at the school desk. And people will be enabled to work and have conversations while travelling and being entertained (by way of portable PC, mobile phone or car telephone and by way of audiovisual equipment). Finally, the workaholics among us will be able to work while having a holiday (for instance by taking a laptop to the beach).

Telework

However, there are several limitations to a predominantly multifunctional use of space and time. But before these limitations are discussed, we will briefly survey the first experiences with telework and telestudy, which already show these limitations. At the end of the 1990s, the number of real teleworkers must be rather disappointing to the advocates of this type of work. According to the IDC (1996), real teleworkers are employees having a formal agreement with their employers which allows them to spend some part of the working week at some location other than the bureau/office (for instance at home or at a telework office) using ICT. So, teleworkers are not simply people who have always worked at home, who were mobile workers before, or who have a business of their own. On the one hand, teleworkers are professionals usually working independently (such as programmers, consultants and system designers); and on the other hand, they are functional workers undertaking activities such as data entry, data processing and selling goods and services. Finally, there is a group of professionals often working at home, and most often working overtime.

Advantages and Disadvantages   The advantages of telework are obvious. Employees need to travel less and they are able to plan their own days. Moreover, telework can be combined with other activities such as household work and looking after children. However, the disadvantages appear to be numerous in the first experimental phase of teleworking. They can be summarized thus:

1 The *conditions of labour* for (in particular) teleworkers having functional tasks are poor. Like all people working at home in flexible labour relationships, they have little protection. They have almost no chance of making a career within the organization. Trained professionals often work overtime without receiving any extra payment.

2 *Impoverished communication* with management and co-workers affects the quality of the tasks to be performed. The work is routine and it lacks informality and crucial non-verbal aspects.

3 A consequence, disadvantageous to both management and functional personnel, is that *little support can be given* by management. Not only is supervision unsatisfactory, but there is little opportunity for suggestions (for improvements) and coordination between colleagues.

4 *Social isolation* of employees working at home is considered to be the most important problem. It can reduce productivity to such an extent that it is noticed by management as well. This is why, in some cases, companies decide to start local telework centres.

5 Doing telework at home makes it *hard to separate work* from other domestic activities. A teleworker is required to have strong self-discipline. When several members of one household spend more time at home than before, tensions may arise.

Telestudy: Advantages and Disadvantages   The advantages of *telestudy* can be compared with those of telework: less time spent travelling, being able to plan one's own day, and the possibility of combining activities. Furthermore, teachers can correct and grade assignments sooner and sometimes even faster. In the late 1990s, however, the practice of distance education was confined to an elite of people in higher education having some experience with computers and used to working independently. The disadvantages of telestudy also resemble those of telework:

1 Telestudents *completely depend* upon communication with the educational department offering this facility. It is much more difficult for them to consult other students if they have study problems requiring collective action. Telestudents work more individually than traditional students, though they may send each other messages by e-mail.

2 In fact, *interaction* between teachers and students reaches such a *low level* that the quality of education completely depends on the programme, which has to be repeatedly tested and improved.

3 Many students cannot handle the *independence* and *self-discipline* required. Direct supervision and help, beyond instruction at a distance, are sorely missed. Drop-out rates in distance education will be at least as high as in present-day correspondence and lifelong learning courses.

4 Telestudy is a *socially isolated activity* as well. Students can no longer lean on their fellow students. A traditional educational institution serves as a meeting place, a place of socialization and a means of creating a daily study routine. It is therefore highly unlikely that distance education will become the predominant way to educate children and adolescents.

5 As is the case with telework, separating study from *other domestic activities* is extremely difficult. This division has to be enforced by, for instance, putting the PC in the attic, which can have negative effects on living together. Both too many and too few contacts may lead to tensions in a modern household.

General Problems of Tele-activity

These disadvantages of both telework and telestudy involve a number of structural limitations to tele-activity and the multifunctional use of spaces in general:

1 In practice, tele-activities are still bound to certain places, even though they can be performed in numerous places in theory and by technical means.

2 They remain dependent upon an external centre.

3 They encounter difficulties concerning the separation of activities.

4 They have to deal with a limited quality of communication.

In part, these disadvantages are the same as the limitations of traditional work and study at home. However, mediated tele-activities considerably intensify these limitations because the demands are much more ambitious and because the number and complexity of distance activities increase. People think activities formerly performed in centralized and face-to-face situations can now be performed locally and in mediated contexts. Furthermore, adequate and frequent or even permanent communication between the centre and the local units is assumed to exist. And finally, the local units are expected to make unhindered use of their own multifunctional spaces and terminals. These assumptions are realized only in a limited number of cases, as is shown by the following series of problems.

First, all tele-activity except mobile networking is actually tied to one place and leads to symptoms of social isolation. This applies not only to telework and telestudy, but also to working at a terminal in general. So far, most labour has been carried out in face-to-face or telephone conversations with colleagues and by moving around the company and meeting colleagues everywhere. In computer work it seems that the terminal has become the closest colleague and the nearest partner in conversations.

Second, most tele-activities are tied to a particular place, which conflicts not only with the need for social contact, but also with the *need for mobility*. Daily travel to work, school and shops and regular trips to meetings are not merely undertaken to get there. They also fulfil the need for a change of scene, for chance encounters or impressions – and for adventure. An accumulation of several types of tele-activity can stop these needs from being fulfilled sufficiently.

Third, dependence on a centrally controlled and integrated medium of communication that does not respond to all individual needs directly *clashes with the pursuit of individualization* in present-day Western culture. People not only want more control over their work, their study and their spare time, instead of less, but also want more space of their own, with a telephone, a TV etc. Those who do want a room to be used multifunctionally, want this room to be an individual place. In the light of most current situations at work and school or in the home, it will be impossible to fulfil this need. Besides, it acts against the need to prevent social isolation. The dependence described also counters the wish of modern individuals to manage extremely heterogeneous activities and contacts in their own times and places. So, a desire for separate rooms with specialized equipment/monitors could arise instead of the need for a single multifunctional room with all the equipment.

Fourth, a multifunctional use of all times and places does not provide people with the daily routines and rhythms needed to *distinguish and coordinate activities*. It is not without reason that most people want to do one activity in one place and another elsewhere, or one activity at one time and another at another time.

Fifth, in Chapter 1 the *limited social presence and the information richness* of new media communication were claimed to be major obstacles. So, the reluctance of managers to stimulate telework and of teachers to experiment with distance education is no surprise. Their resistance is not merely based on conservatism or a wish to save their own jobs and to keep workers and students under supervision and control. They really do have legitimate problems, as the quality of communication at a distance is still lacking.

Tele-activity: Replacement or Addition? One can reach the conclusion that there are so many limitations and contradictions attached to tele-activities that they are not likely to dominate work, study, travel and recreation in the near future. At least for some time they will merely serve as an *addition* to similar traditional activities. Professionals will partly *combine* work or study at home and at the office. This conclusion emphasizes that the distinctions between spheres of living will become blurred rather than disappear altogether.

LIVING IN A DIGITAL CULTURE

The Meaning of Being Digital Views differ as to which technical part of the new media has the greatest cultural impact. Many think it is the fact that they are *digital*. At least, this word is very popular in all kinds of prefixes: digital revolution, digital city and even digital being (Negroponte, 1995). Used in this way, the word suggests more than it says. In Chapter 2 it was explained that digitalization is only one of the technical characteristics of the new media. What effects could it have on culture? To answer this question we will have to dig deeper than is usual in popular accounts of digitalization.

Digitalization means that every item can be translated into separate bytes consisting of strings of ones and zeros (called bits). This applies to images, sounds, texts and data. They can be produced and consumed in separate pieces and combined in every manner imaginable. From now on, every item can be presented on screens and accompanied by sound. All items can be stored on digital data carriers and retrieved from them in virtually unlimited amounts and at virtually unlimited speed. In the preceding sentences, digital technology and cultural impact have already been linked. Thus, at this point in the discussion, the reader can gather that digitalization increases the *chances* of:

1 a standardization and differentiation of culture;
2 a fragmentation of culture;
3 a collage of culture;
4 an acceleration of culture;
5 a visualization of culture;
6 a larger quantity of culture.

Pre-programming and creativity

Unlimited Choice? In popular literature on the new media, the suggestion is made that these media will create unlimited choice from our sizeable cultural heritages and a new creative potential among the population, as people are enabled to create their own works of art and other products with multimedia. In *The Road Ahead* (1995), Bill Gates claimed ICT will offer new ways for people to express themselves. Apparently, ICT offers 'unprecedented artistic and scientific opportunities to a new generation of geniuses' (1995: 154). Indeed, these opportunities do exist for people with the means and the skills to use them. However, the chances that we are dealing with a 'new and original type of work', in the terms of Dutch copyright law, are decreasing. More and more often we will be processing, reworking or adapting things other people have created. This is just the next phase in the evolution of art. In the course of (modern) history, the work of art has been taken away from the artist step by step and put into the hands of consumers. After the era of large-scale technical reproducibility of art (Benjamin, 1968), we are now entering an era enabling people to create their 'own' works of art consisting of all the bits and pieces of the cultural heritage. Multimedia encourage users to make all sorts of video collages and images, to sample and compose pieces of music from a CD, to decide about the ending of a film by picking one from several scripts, and to create their own abstract Mondrian-style painting from red, yellow and blue squares. Of course, professional and popular art have always been a matter of reworking and adapting the cultural heritage. But now we are taking

Preprogrammed Creativity one essential step further. Qualitatively more means are inserted between source and result. There is more than pencil, pen and ink on paper and paint on canvas. The means of production offered by digital media are (pre-)programmed themselves and they partly work automatically. They only have to be adapted by the user to gain some craft. The material worked upon is not empty, but it is filled with existing cultural content. In this way creativity is put in an entirely different perspective.

The same can be said of the presumed infinite options in digital media. In fact, the whole thing is about options from a menu, in other words entirely pre-programmed. Usually, the user is able to make general choices only. Allowing users to choose among details would require too much pre-programming work.

Anyway, these options do lead to both a differentiation and a standardization of culture. The number of contents from which one can choose is increasing. At the same time, however, these contents increasingly resemble one another. Everything is arranged in similar (menu) structures. Sources of information that used to be separate are combined in multimedia. Under certain circumstances, this may lead to diluting sources of information and eroding contents (see below).

Fragmentation and collage

Effects of Fragmentation on Cultural Contents Digitalization causes a technical division of analogue sources into bits and bytes. This enables an unrestricted division of the contents of these sources. Digitalization and processing of analogue sources by multimedia equipment have already had a fragmenting effect on our culture. Michael Heim (1987) pointed out this trend some years ago by analysing changes in texts caused by word processing. Texts are provided with a pointed structure. The argument is structured in advance and divided into separate subjects, items and paragraphs. Items can easily be added or deleted later on –

which may result in some loss of the course of the argument. Another example is the structure of the Internet. The contents of websites are spread over several pages and images which can all be accessed in one click. In this way, the traditional linear processing of contents is replaced by the making of links, jumps and associations.

Finally, we come to the contents of pieces of music and films processed by using interactive programs. Interactive music CDs are composed of separate, accumulated layers and fragments which may be easily isolated, manipulated, sampled and (re)combined. This *modularization* quickly causes the unity of a creative work to be lost. For the idea is to give listeners the opportunity to create their own collages. Many traditional artists, designers and producers find this anathema. They think the unique construction and coherence they have made is the essence of their creation. They dissociate themselves from the results obtained by the consumer, or accept them only because it pays to do so.

Acceleration

Digitalization allows a considerable increase in the production, dispersion and consumption of information and the signals of communication. In hardware, 'fast' has become the key word: fast computers, fast modems, fast lines, fast programs. The hunger for speed is never appeased. This is all the more reason to believe that the popular assumption of the irrelevance of time in the new media is wrong. On the contrary, the importance of time is radicalizing (see Chapter 6). Saving time is immediately followed by new needs to be filled and created.

A Culture of Speed The need for speed is determined by motives in the economy (maximization of profits on the surplus value of working time in capitalism), the organization (efficiency) and consumption (immediate fulfilment of needs). Driven by a swift increase in technical capacities, these motives call into existence a *culture of speed* (Virilio, 1988; Miller and Schwarz, 1998). This means our culture changes substantially as well. The following examples may be useful. First, expressions of culture date quickly. Trends follow each other at high speed. In the modern world various trends exist side by side, competing for popularity. Second, information is sent in increasing amounts, ever more frequently and at ever higher speed just to attract attention. This phenomenon is called information and communication overload (see below). The result is shallowness in the perception of cultural expressions, a fact producers are anticipating and reinforcing. Furthermore, communication and language have increased to such a speed that we cannot sit down to think about a message, such as writing a letter or starting a conversation. Instead, we immediately pick up the phone and give *ad hoc* answers by telephone, or by e-mail. Language also changes under the influence of the new media. This will be discussed in the next chapter. It acquires an abrupt style (like staccato) and contains increasing amounts of jargon with innumerable abbreviations. The final example is the rising importance of images in our culture, a type of data that is presented and consumed much more quickly than the others (speech, text and numbers).

Visualization

The Centrality of Screens

The fact that monitors are increasingly being used for the *presentation* of cultural contents has the most visible and direct effect on human perception and understanding. The monitor is everywhere in network society. It is not merely a medium for reproduction which increasingly dominates mass communication, thanks to the rise of audiovisual media; it already characterizes data communication as well, and in the near future it will also symbolize telecommunications (by means of the videophone and video conferencing). Monitors in data and telecommunications will have the quality of current and future (HDTV) television screens. They will be able to contain several images at once and they will serve as touch screens. This means a single monitor can be used for tele- as well as data and mass communications. They will be not only the *window* to our world, but also our *second front door* – a most important, perhaps even the most important entrance to and exit from our homes. This will give the monitor a position in society important enough to have profound effects on our culture. There is no way to predict what the consequences will be, because monitors and terminals may change considerably in the next few decades.

Likely Consequences

Yet, it seems worthwhile to make an inventory of a number of probable and lasting consequences of the dominance of the screen.

From Active Reading to Passive Viewing?

Replacing older means of communication The rise of the screen as a means of communication will lead to a partial replacement of texts on paper, of separate audio and of direct physical transmission of signs in face-to-face communication. The last replacement is a much more basic development than the other two. That is why it is one of the central themes of this book. The current replacement of reading printed texts by watching television or looking at images in other media, together with the transformation of listening to the radio and to audio as a main activity into using them as a background, have been judged by intellectuals and culture pessimists far too easily as signs of blunted culture and losses of creativity and imagination. The Flemish expert in audiovisual semiotics Jean-Marie Peters (1989; 1996), has convincingly challenged these opinions. Peters (1989) opposes the popular assumption that watching and understanding images takes only a small mental effort, claiming that all sorts of imaginative thinking are required. Even the simplest image is very complex: it contains a large amount of symbols to be perceived and interpreted simultaneously. Comparing reading and listening on the one hand and watching on the other, one has to realize that all three can be performed with full or partial attention. Peters opposes the idea that an image cannot have any depth, given that readers and listeners are themselves urged to employ abstraction and creativity by calling images to mind. He argues that images have not only the capacity of reproduction and representation, but also symbolic and creative values. Viewers are able to discover and shape these symbolic and creative values themselves (Peters, 1989). From this line of argument he also challenges the assumption of a culture of images smothering creativity and imagination. Perhaps people who have been raised in a culture of reading have forgotten how to look properly?

Simplification or Complication?

Extending Peters's argument, we may say that the most important problem concerning the replacement of texts on paper with audiovisual display is *complication, not simplification!* Future screens will contain large amounts of information. They will be able to present images, texts, numbers, graphics and visual augmentations of sounds, close to each other and in extremely complex shapes. In audiovisual entertainment we have already become acquainted with the rise of a 'staccato culture' containing a bombardment of stimuli growing stronger and stronger: brief, flashing, swift and full of action.

Intellectuals or culture pessimists should worry less about the decline of reading and listening (even in a culture of images, these activities will quantitatively increase rather than decrease) than about *writing and speaking* and about the extent of *activity and initiative* required. With the rise of the new media, the pattern of allocation shifts to consultation, registration and conversation. This seems to indicate an increase in the extent of local activities and initiatives, but this does not have to happen. Even though receivers of messages of allocution are able to reshape them in their minds, they are and always will be transferred messages. Consultation also means choosing from an offer, and registration includes answering questions. Conversation is the only pattern requiring active multilateral communication. Yet, this pattern has advanced the least in the new media until fairly recently. Videophony has not yet been introduced on a large scale. Electronic mail is becoming the most important new media application. Still, it remains a rather limited mode of expression (see the next chapter). The exchange of more advanced types of expression, like self-made audio, video, software and all kinds of graphical designs, is still an activity for a small elite.

Excessive Use of Screens

The cumulative and one-sided pressure of screens   The increasing presence of screens in all spheres of living leads to an accumulation of similar activities. And this will apply even more when the accompanying, omnipresent use of push buttons is taken into account. It is conceivable that, in the near future, many people will spend eight to ten hours a day in front of screens of all kinds. For example, people in the US watch television or video for about five hours a day. The acceptable amount of working time spent in front of a computer screen is five hours a day, but this is often exceeded in practice. The use of mobile equipment with displays will perhaps add an hour to the daily total. An excessive use of screens can have negative consequences in terms of the physical and mental pressure it causes.

The influence of universal screens will increase even further when opportunities to relax in other environments and in face-to-face communications are reduced. In their leisure time, screen workers are confronted with similar activities. Verbal and non-verbal behaviour in face-to-face communication, with the physical exercise accompanying it, still have important functions of relaxation for human beings – functions left largely unfulfilled in mediated communication. Thus, an excessive amount of time spent in front of screens will restrict physical and mental development.

Adaptation of Communication Contents

The selective limitation and articulation of communication contents Mediated communication is always marked by some kind of adaptation to the technical characteristics of the medium concerned. Obviously this has consequences for the contents of communication. The screen as a medium of reproduction has both possibilities and limitations. They differ according to the target and the type of communication desired in tele-, data and mass communication. However, there are also substantial similarities.

The power of screens is the attraction of human attention. The biggest problem in mass communication nowadays is that attention is slackening fast. The stimuli offered become ever shorter and more powerful in an attempt to prevent the slackening of attention. Short and impressive newsflashes, fast shots full of action in films or video clips and sparkling shows tend to fragment contents. Background information and reflection disappear or are pushed to the sidelines. According to many media critics this will result in shallower mass media contents, though we have seen that the form of images is becoming more complicated.

In data communication, one may expect the partner in communication to have enough self-discipline to continue following the contents of the screen. Here communication has been disciplined by the general characteristics of computer language: formalized, standardized and programmed in algorithms. It is a well-known fact that this will lead to the accentuation of one type of contents and the limitation of another type. Signs of qualitative information are replaced by quantitative ones. In data communication, compressed data, tables, graphs and the like are the most favoured signs presented on the screen, for understandable reasons. This is done in a pre-programmed order. Take for example someone who consults data in videotex or in a databank. The information is compressed in short chunks fitting (part of) a screen. Long texts, for instance background information, are not feasible. Main points or abstracts are preferred. Chunks of information are ordered in entirely pre-programmed search structures. Consulting such information is a completely different cognitive activity from reading a newspaper. In the latter the reader has much more freedom to decide on the speed and intensity of reading, on stopping, skipping and starting to read again. Furthermore, no knowledge of search structures and operations is required.

Early experiences with telecommunications consisting of conversation that was not only sounds but also texts and/or images seem to reveal a selective limitation and articulation of particular contents. In the next chapter the abrupt and *ad hoc* manner of communication in e-mail is discussed, for example. Many sentences are either shortened or left unfinished. Many stopgaps and abbreviations are used.

Disappearing Contexts

The dilution of information sources As communication media integrate further, more types of senders and messages are presented on the same screen. In theory, allocution, consultation, registration and conversation can all use the same screen as a medium of presentation. As a result, receivers may have problems distinguishing between these patterns and the various senders and messages they are getting. Well-known specific contexts disappear. This can be explained with a few examples.

First, people tend to look at the source of a message to determine its plausibility and reliability. Many investigations in mass communications have shown that reception of messages on television is considered to be more trustworthy than messages from newspapers and magazines. Audiovisual media are trusted more than printed ones.

Second, in the separate mass media of the late 1990s, receivers were still able to make a clear distinction between allocution, consultation, registration and conversation. This is evidently more difficult when working with integrated media. The situation has already changed with the advent of teletext. This medium is considered by some to be allocution (as it is linked to television), whereas others say it is consultation (it looks like an electronic paper). The fact that new media can be 'interactive' in several ways may also lead to misunderstandings. The choice from extensive menus in allocution may be viewed as free consultation, whereas consultation in a medium in turn may be considered a kind of conversation with this medium. Consultation and registration (for instance addressing an electronic mail order catalogue) can be veiled types of advertising (that is allocution).

The final example is of people thinking they are taking part in allocution, consultation or conversation, whereas actually they are also being registered without knowing and wanting that.

Increasing presentations of information and communication on screens may also lead to blurring the distinctions between types of information and communication *within patterns*. We already know this phenomenon from allocution by TV. News, current affairs, entertainment, information programmes and advertising increasingly resemble one another. They are combined in overall programmes or presented in a similar manner. Advertisements are inserted in and between programmes as commercials or as hidden and clandestine advertising. In the future forms of allocution and consultation, sources of information, propaganda and advertising will be hard to tell apart. In newspapers or magazines, one glimpse usually suffices to know whether you are dealing with an advertisement. On a screen this can be veiled much more easily. Take, for example, the ingenious ways of advertising on Internet pages and on the screens of commercial television.

Images as a substitute for personal experience

> The fact that *all* of these cultural expressions have to be communicated through the screen transforms the culture into spectacle. Our civilization tends to substitute images for experience: journeys become window viewing and slides become souvenirs; gymnastics a TV program; music a video-tape. The old media of culture based on a process of symbolic *exchange* do not work any more in the new media. (Sabbah, 1985: 221)

The most fundamental result of the universal presence of screens is undoubtedly the gradual replacement of a person's direct personal experience and direct interaction by observation through glass and camera lenses, usually someone else's, and by mediated interaction. This is one of the first psychological aspects to be dealt with in the next chapter. There is a danger

Artificial Reality   that people will start living in an artificial reality offering less room for personal experience and experiences shared directly with others. People become dependent on the nature and quality of images produced by the various media with their more or less limited communication capacities. Debord (1996) speaks about a *society of the spectacle*. However, attending a football match is a completely different experience from watching that same match on television. Going out shopping cannot be compared with teleshopping. Meeting a friend will always be different from communicating over the best videophone imaginable.

Individual   Replacing direct personal experiences with produced images will have
Perception   more social impact as the process of individualization continues. The *individual* is increasingly confronted with a world made up of images. Conversations about the images offered are decreasing, both at work and in one's leisure time. People travel home, perhaps listening to a personal stereo, from their more or less isolated work behind a monitor, to watch their own favourite programme on TV. Watching TV all night as an entire family is becoming history. The number of individual options has increased so much that it has become almost impossible to talk to others about one's own observations. This is the main reason why some social scientists fear a culture of images, as they fear social cohesion will be undermined through a combination of this culture with social segmentation and individualization.

The fascinating screen   Watching a screen is not only fascinating, but also compelling. As said before, screens are exceptionally powerful in attracting attention. Even during interpersonal conversations, we are easily distracted by nearby screens. People can also be 'glued' to a screen. When immobile equipment is used, people are bound to their workplaces too. However, the latter trend will be reversed when mobile equipment makes a breakthrough.

Manipulative   The fascinating and binding effects of screens can be a threat to human
Impact?   freedom in several ways. In the past, the manipulative impact of the television and other visual media has been overestimated. Today, a more modest role is ascribed to these media, namely that of setter of the agenda

and the topics of conversation. To a large extent they help to determine what people talk about and what (they say) they think is important. The universal presence of screens and the selective articulation of their contents are able to reinforce the agenda-setting capacities of visual media.

Qualifications The aspects of the culture of images described will mainly be considered negative. This impression has to be corrected, for several reasons. In the next chapter, on psychology, we will stress that visual perception and visualization are the most important perceptual and cognitive mental capacities of humans. Perhaps these capacities have been underused in the history of linguistic media. In that case a further visualization of culture might mean progress.

This description has to be refined in two other ways. In the first place, the results discussed only apply to the extent to which screens will *dominate* all media of presentation and the extent to which they will *push aside* other types of mediated communication as the most visible type. In the second place, we have not taken into account the educational and cultural policies trying to confront the negative effects. Their first priority might be an adjustment of teaching courses in language(s), information and computer science, social studies and the humanities. These subjects should be used to teach students an active and conscious engagement with our visual culture and to give them (some) insight into the shape, the contents and the selection processes of visual communication. Cultural pessimists might better use their energy in these ways than in futile attempts to restore the reading of printed texts as the presumed most important type of intellectual activity.

Larger quantity

Seemingly, the new media enrich our culture with a huge increase of information and communication. We might get the impression this is true in both a quantitative and a qualitative sense. But is this impression correct? On second thoughts, many critical comments can be made here. First, we will have to explain the distinction between information and **Definitions of** communication. Information* consists of data or signals that have been **Information and** interpreted by people. Here, the process of interpretation by the receiver is **Communication** emphasized. Communication*, however, is a transfer of information from a sender to a receiver, the former being aware of the existence of the latter. Here, the emphasis is on transfer: the social processes of transmitting (allocution) and exchanging (consultation, registration and conversation) information. Communication presupposes information, as the transfer of signals should not be represented as some kind of delivery of post parcels or the exchange of data in a pipeline between senders and receivers, but as the construction of a shared meaning by people interpreting the signals in their social context (Mantovani, 1996).

The supply of *information* in our society is increasing rapidly, perhaps even exponentially. Pool et al. (1984) have assembled a large amount of data and research indicating an increase in information supply of some 8 to 10 per cent each year since 1950, while demand lags behind with about only 3 per cent. The increase in the amount of *knowledge* our society extracts from this information is much more moderate. Information supply overlaps and repeats itself many times, and in receiving information we have to deal with selective attention, selective perception and a surplus of information. The most astonishing and dramatic conclusion, however, is about the consequences of information. The impact of information in *affecting behaviour* (pragmatics) appears to be marginal: the activities of individuals and organizations are highly insensitive to information once a particular stage has been reached. Compared with 30 years ago, public institutions and companies turn out to be using more information to reach the same kind of decisions (Van Cuilenburg and Noomen, 1984: 51). According to these Dutch communication scientists, decision quality has not improved very much. Similarly, Dordick and Wang (1993) have referred to the well-known 'productivity paradox': information technology produces fewer productivity gains than expected, especially in the service sectors.

Information Use Lagging Behind Supply

How should one explain these daring and disturbing conclusions? They certainly do not mean that information technology is not working. On the contrary, they may indicate that the level of complexity of our societies, organizations and personal lives has grown so dramatically that we would no longer be able to handle that complexity without this technology. Imagine a present-day corporation or government department without it. They would get stuck in old types of bureaucracy. The best explanation might be the conjecture that information and communication technology are barely able to keep up with the complexity of social, economic and cultural life we have produced.

Information Overload

Anyway, the difference between the increase of information and knowledge on the hand and their application on the other produces *overinformation*: too much information is produced in relation to its use. Furthermore, it points to a phenomenon Van Cuilenburg and Noomen have called 'information dud' (1984: 52): an increasing amount of information does not offer answers to questions asked, but produces answers to questions that still have to be posed. Indeed, the production of information has partly become an autonomous, self-augmenting process. David Schenk (1997) calls these phenomena simply *data smog*. He claims our information supply is so contaminated with useless and redundant data that information is no longer valuable or empowering, but is overly abundant and is making us helpless. 'At a certain level of input, the law of diminishing returns takes effect; the glut of information no longer adds to our quality of life, but instead begins to cultivate stress, confusion and even ignorance' (1997: 15). For human minds, information overload is not a problem until we are forced by our environment to select information and knowledge from an overwhelming amount of data, for instance at school, at work or in an overfull leisure time programme. In all of these cases, information overload leads to stress. However, outside situations of this kind, people simply do not perceive the surplus of signals. Humans have several mental mechanisms to prevent signals coming into their minds, and these mechanisms will work even more strongly in times of stress – until they break down and nothing at all is recorded any more (see Milgram, 1970). Under normal circumstances, our cognition has all the filters necessary for perceiving and processing signals. They are intensified when there are too many signals to record. Another reaction is to spend less time on each input. Low-priority signals are ignored. In social exchange the problem is transferred to others: 'ask someone else', 'let others find out'. Signals are also rejected, by the recipient not responding or by putting on an unfriendly face. Finally, the things causing the damage – sources such as documents, tapes, files or programs – are simply ignored and not used any more.

Overcommunication?   Another question is whether we are also dealing with *overcommunication* and *communication duds*. After all, the quantity of mediated communication is increasing fast. This is most obvious in the case of mass communication (referring to the overabundance of broadcasting channels, for instance). Over the past decades, the amount of data communication and telecommunication has also increased strongly. Here the situation is different from mass communication, as supply is not able to exceed demand so easily. After all, telecommunication is a two-way process. Its capacities may increase, but this does not mean they will be used. Large corporations, for example, make extensive use of data communication, but households use it very little, at least not compared with telephony. This fundamental difference between information and communication relieves the potential discrepancy between the growth of communication, the amount of knowledge derived and the effects on behaviour as compared with information. We might say that by the late 1990s only the communication supply in particular mass media had reached a point of overcommunication. An increasing number of radio and television channels offering the same (kind of) programmes is accompanied by decreasing average numbers of viewers and listeners for each of them. The results are fragmentation and redistribution of the market. Supply continues to expand, driven by the revenues from commercials. Here 'communication duds' may arise: general interest channels with broadly the same content are created, but with few viewers and listeners.

Demand for data communication and telecommunication in the late 1990s was still exceeding supply. There is no question of overabundance here. However, here we are also confronted with 'data smog'. It is getting harder to extract relevant data from an ever growing supply. The Internet, for instance, has a problem of abundance, supplying innumerable sites and pages and offering an unmanageable number of sources as a result of using search engines. In the use of electronic mail, fax and answering machines, we are dealing with phenomena like 'junk mail' or 'spam' (unsolicited e-mail) and simply too many messages in general.

Another phenomenon, which might become very important in the future, is much harder to call a general problem. There is a problem of 'communication overload' for those people trying to protect themselves from being reachable at any time and place as a result of digital and cellular telephony. In general, these new kinds of telephony provoke a huge number of messages that subsequently appear redundant or valueless.

Information Agents as a Solution

Technical solutions to both information and communication overabundance are being developed and introduced rapidly. All kinds of personal or information agents, systems to filter all incoming information and messages, and search engines are offered. These techniques will become essential in the information and network society. A matter of decisive importance, however, will be the extent to which we use these means. We should not rely on them completely, as three great risks with fundamental consequences are associated with them.

Risks

The first of these risks is to *rely too much on their intelligence* and to allow one's own ability to judge to remain weak. Systems do get smarter, but their users might become stupider. In fact, these systems possess all the pros and cons of artificial intelligence (see the next chapter). Intelligent systems are able to adapt to changing user preferences. However, people's standards, values and emotions are changing much faster. And what is more, they differ depending on innumerable contexts. They cannot be entirely (pre-)programmed.

A second threat is that by continuously using these information devices, people might cut themselves off from new and surprising impressions and contacts. People may even lock themselves up in a personal 'information prison' (Schenk, 1997: 120). We may settle down in environments that are as safe and controllable as they are limited. We may create a personal subculture locked away from the rest of the world or society, perhaps not in principle but very often in reality.

The final risk is a threat to the *privacy* of users who increasingly entrust their personal preferences and characteristics to systems of registration. In the twenty-first century, your information agent will inform your contacts who you are. Authorities and corporations will be very interested, without doubt.

So, it is necessary to use these systems critically and in a selective manner and to retain control over all important steps and judgements.

Better quality?

To a certain extent the appreciation of information and communication quality is an arbitrary affair. Therefore we need to develop particular criteria for the quality of information and communication. This last section will consider quality criteria in terms of substance and pragmatics.

Substantial Quality

According to standards concerning the *substance* of information and communication, the huge quantities supplied in the new media do not necessarily lead to better quality. The so-called pyramid of knowledge is often presented to clarify this statement. A better term would be the

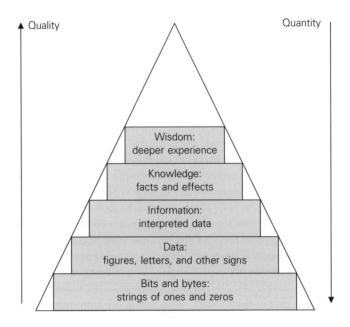

FIGURE 7.1   The pyramid of information processing

pyramid of information processing, for knowledge is only one of the results of processing information mentally and technically (see Figure 7.1).

In the process of digitalization, at the base of the pyramid, endless amounts of *bits and bytes* are produced. Subsequently, every digital zero and one can be translated technically into certain *data* by means of computer machine language. These data can be letters, images or other tokens. Then humans are able to mentally translate these data into *information*. For information merely consists of data being interpreted: they are tokens bearing a particular meaning. Data are not interpreted when humans do not consider them relevant. In turn, information is often only temporarily important, or is even trivial. A relatively small amount of information has a lasting importance: this is what we call *knowledge*. Knowledge consists of facts (describing reality) and relations of cause and effect that explain how things work and how we can use them. A specific type of knowledge is called scientific knowledge. Finally, the top of the pyramid contains the most rare result of human information processing: *wisdom*. This rather vague term represents the deeper experience to be gained by associating specific types of knowledge over time, putting them in a context, offering explanations about backgrounds, and connecting them with the values and standards important to humans.

So, information processing using ICT increases the quantity of information as one descends the pyramid toward the base of bits and bytes, while decreasing its quality. In the opposite direction, as one ascends the pyramid towards wisdom, using ICT will improve quality. However, ascending the pyramid gets harder and harder as one approaches the top. More and more data smog or information overload has to be disposed of to reach the next step. So, the use of ICT as such is no guarantee of higher information quality. It does provide us with more opportunities, but we can only use them by making more and better selections simultaneously.

A similar balance can be drawn up for the quality of *communication* contents. The new media are a considerable improvement for fast communication over long distances. More, better and faster channels for communication are being constructed. This does not mean an improvement of communication in all respects. Kubicek and Rolf (1985: 367) once said that modern relations of communication are spatially global but limited in content, while traditional relations are spatially limited but comprehensive in content. In this chapter we have noted the selective enhancement *and* limitation of communication contents. The improvement of channels of communication might mean they are used for shallower and more ephemeral types of communication. Think about most 'chatting' on the Internet and about many conversations on the mobile phone: the simplicity of the connection promotes 'small talk'. And communication might be limited by the capacities of the new channels, as will be explained in the social-psychological section of the next chapter.

Pragmatic Quality An assessment of the *pragmatic* quality of information and communication implies, among other things, questions about their efficiency. What is the relation between costs and yields? Van Cuilenburg and Noomen (1984: 49ff.) state that information involves diminishing returns. At a particular moment the point of satiation is reached: then human actions become highly insensitive to more information. Does such a relation exist in connection with increasing communication? Yes – and no. The essential difference with information is that the initial costs of mediated communication are much higher than the returns, because a costly infrastructure has to be constructed. After some period, the costs of the investment are recovered. Then the marginal returns increase strongly. So, efficiency would seem to be the most important characteristic of improved communication facilities.

However, it would be wrong to think that time and capacity are no longer important. On the contrary, they become more important, particularly in economic transactions. The construction of an on-line connection between international stock markets, for instance, was a great improvement. However, once these were introduced, transmission times between these markets could never be fast enough. Fractions of a second are vital. Huge investments have had to be made to increase transmission speed, while the size of financial transfers grows simultaneously. The same applies to connection and processing times in data communication between companies. After some period the law of diminishing returns applies to communication connections as well. This phenomenon will also appear in the contents of communications. The need to be 'within reach at any time and place' will lead to various forms of 'overcommunication' (see earlier): the telephone or a similar device is picked up too readily, and too much talking takes place. No one saves on messages. Subsequently, a lot of communication turns out to have served no purpose, or could have been much shorter. In these cases communication appears to be inefficient, though it may have served an important emotional and informal need.

PSYCHOLOGY

8

In the psychology of perception and mass communication science, increasing attention is paid to the characteristics of mediated perception. On this subject, television has been investigated the most of all the media. Perception in the new media has not yet been the subject of extensive research. So, a large part of the following account is based on assumptions derived from the characteristics of the new media described earlier, and from research into the perception of images, sounds, text and data in the old media which are now to be combined in new media. In the next section the centre of attention will shift to the processing of perceptions by the human brain. We will deal with the question of new media stimulating some thought processes and inhibiting others. The third section is about learning with the new media. The fourth section concerns social-psychological aspects. Here we are able to present more results from empirical research. The social-psychological differences and similarities between face-to-face communication and communication by telephone, by electronic mail and by computer, audio and video conferencing have been fairly well examined. The final section is dedicated to the question of a potential change of human personality by new media use in the long run. This will be the most speculative part of this book.

From direct experience to mediated perception

In all mediated communication some kind of entity is present between human beings and their experience of reality. In allocution we are dealing with a medium–human monologue. In consultation and registration the patterns shift to a medium–human dialogue. In the pattern of conversation, this is turned into a human–medium–human dialogue or polylogue. In all of these cases direct *experience* is replaced by mediated and technically supported or affected *perception*. Direct human experience has always been an observation of reality involving all the senses *simultaneously*. **Restrictions of** This consists not only of *knowledge*, but also of *skills* (for instance mental, **Mediated** social and communicative skills), *values*, *feelings* and *abstractions*. **Communication** Compared with this, mediated communications always involve *particular* *restrictions*. Here the use of all senses is impossible. Some types of knowledge can be gained, others cannot. Specific skills are used. One medium is suitable for a transfer of feelings, values or abstractions, while another is absolutely incapable of doing this.

In opposition to all the restrictions of the old and new media in relation to direct experience, these media also offer *additions* to experience, of course. Media are the extensions of man, according to a famous expression of McLuhan. To an increasing extent they help us to overcome the limitations of space, time and lack of information. These forms of help cannot compensate for all limitations, but for many purposes, for instance formal and business communication, this does not have to be a problem. Moreover, the creative human mind is able to fill the gaps, as will be argued below.

Pre-programming   A second aspect of the transition from direct experience to mediated perception is a partial *pre-programming* of perception and experience in using media. With respect to allocution this is obvious. It explains the large number of studies about the influence of television. In consultation and registration, perception is also pre-programmed to some extent. In mediated conversation, it is either restricted or enhanced by the communication capacities and the practical applications of the medium concerned.

Therefore, aspects of comprehensiveness, freedom and the individual's own initiative are at stake in the shift to mediated perception.

From learning by action to learning by symbol systems and visual models

Bruner and Olson (1973: 213ff.) hold that three *modes of experience* fit three *types of learning*:

1   the *enactive* mode fits learning by direct action;
2   the *iconic* mode fits learning by the observation of visual models;
3   the *symbolic* mode fits learning through symbol systems (for instance languages).

With the transition from direct experience to mediated perception, the first of these automatically shifts to the other two types of learning. On the one hand we could say this does not make any difference. All these types of learning are able to provide the same basic structure of knowledge (1973: 220). On the other hand, knowledge gained in a particular mode cannot be gained in another mode. Symbol systems (such as languages) merely enable us to process knowledge we have gained in other modes: 'Instruction through language is limited to rearranging, ordering and differentiating knowledge or information that the listener already has available from other sources such as modeling or through his own direct experiences' (1973: 220). A similar point applies to learning through visual models:

'Complex acts cannot be simply imitated unless the performer already knows how to carry out the act' (1973: 218). A person cannot imitate completely unknown behaviour. In the end, knowledge is always tied to personal experience (1973: 225). Furthermore, learning through language and models always requires particular skills to be acquired first.

The new media offer new possibilities for all three modes of experience and types of learning, but this applies much more to the iconic and symbolic modes than to the enactive mode. The former modes are aided by all kinds of facilities such as slow motion, rewind, fast forward or searching, and by new ways of presenting information using menus, windows, graphs, figures and other images. Furthermore, the combination of images, sounds, text and data enables easier usage of several languages/codes at the same time. Research carried out by Heuvelman (1989), for instance, has demonstrated how schemes (images) and accompanying commentary of text or speech stimulate more focused attention, mental processing and remembering of television programmes than separate realistic images. This is so as long as the commentary is supplied at the right time and does not lead to information overload. In the same manner, new media will only support learning by action in an artificial way, leaning on the other two modes of experience (iconic and symbolic). This is done in simulations or pre-programmed instruction and practice.

Reduction in Learning by Direct Action
On the whole, however, the use of new media will reduce learning by direct action even more than the old media did. As direct action remains the basis of human experience, heavy use of the new media could lead to a decay of this type of learning. Some examples will help to explain this statement. Testing a product in a shop will give you a better impression of the product than reading about its specifications on the Internet. For a long time to come, physical examinations by a doctor will not be replaced in a satisfactory way by medical diagnostic systems. In general, iconic and symbolic modes of experience do not stimulate *active* engagement with the media concerned. A *comparably* passive mode of perception will prevail: far more is read than written, more is listened to than spoken, more is viewed than depicted, and more use is made of a device/program than of calculation or measurement. The new media will continue this development, which had already been started by the old media. Even though these media offer more opportunities for active inputs and choices by local units, they primarily enlarge the 'weight' and complexity of the medium itself. A lot of viewing, reading, listening and operating has to be done before any active input can be realized. An overload of information and instructions do not stimulate such input.

Shifts in the modes of symbolic communication and mental skills required

Gross (1973) has made a distinction between the *linguistic*, the *social-gestural* (non-verbal), the *iconic*, the *logico-mathematical* and the *musical*

modes of symbolic communication. In the course of human history, many alterations have occurred in these general modes of communication and their specifications. The linguistic mode, for instance, has an oral, a written and an audiovisual variant. They were the dominant ones in this particular order. Several modes of communication, or their variants, have become more important in the first and in the second communications revolutions, and others have become less important. The relative importance of the oral-linguistic and the social-gestural modes of communication, which every human being learns as a child, has decreased in Western cultures. The written-linguistic mode and subsequently the audiovisual-linguistic, the logico-mathematical and the iconic modes (photography, film and all sorts of visual signs and designs) have come to the fore.

In the new media, shifts occur once again. Within the linguistic mode, the audiovisual variant (texts accompanied by images and sounds) is gaining importance at the expense of the oral and written variants. This includes the rise of the iconic mode in the shape of film, photographs, figures, graphs, windows and other pictures and images. This reveals the central position of the screen and the rise of a culture of images. The logico-mathematical mode is also becoming more important. Computer operations dominate not only data processing, but all kinds of software and operating instructions in consultation, registration and mediated conversation. In the new media, the role of the musical mode is not decreasing in comparison with the old media, but it operates on its own. Increasingly, music is accompanied by images. And radio music is downgraded to serve as a background for other activities.

The non-verbal (social-gestural) mode is receiving the least attention in the new media. It even disappears where mediated communication using only speech, text or data replaces face-to-face communication. The intelligentsia's ceaseless mourning of the decline of printed text should not conceal the fact that in the new media, the verbal or linguistic modes of communication will continue to gain importance. The overview in Table 8.1 of the modes used in the new media clarifies this statement. It can be seen that spoken and printed words have growing audiovisual and iconic support in the new media.

Integration of Modes of Communication

However, the most basic trend in the modes of communication used in the new media is their advancing *integration*. With the combination of images, sounds, texts and data in a single medium, the modes of communication are also integrating (see Table 8.1). The resultant multimedia combinations acquire a power of communication unprecedented in human history. They will have a (largely unpredictable) influence on human perception and cognition. However, a number of assumptions can be derived from changes to be expected in the modes of communication in the new media. We will discuss this on the basis of known psychological implications of these modes of communication.

Symbol Systems

In his extremely important book *Interaction of Media, Cognition and Learning*, Gavriel Salomon (1979) has explained the psychological differences between 'symbol systems'. This term is comparable to the concept of

TABLE 8.1   Composition of modes of communication in a number of new media, 1990–2000

	Type of data (order of importance)	Mode of communication (order of importance)
Pay TV Video/audio on demand Electronic press	1 Images 2 Sound 3 Text	1 Linguistic (audiovisual/written) 2 Iconic 3 Musical 4 Non-verbal (limited) 5 Logico-mathematical
Videotex Databanks	1 Text 2 Data 3 Images	1 Linguistic (written/ audiovisual) 2 Iconic 3 Logico-mathematical (limited)
Computer networks	1 Data 2 Text	1 Logico-mathematical 2 Linguistic (written) 3 Iconic (graphics)
Electronic mail	1 Text 2 Data	1 Linguistic (written) 2 Iconic (limited)
Videophone Video conferencing	1 Images 2 Sound	1 Linguistic (audiovisual) 2 Iconic 3 Non-verbal (limited)
Integrated networks	1 Images 2 Sound 3 Text 4 Data	1 Linguistic 2 Iconic 3 Logico-mathematical 4 Musical 5 Non-verbal

modes of (symbolic) communication used above. It is taken from the work of Goodman (1968). (Others prefer the term 'sign systems', since some signals in communications are not symbols, for instance realistic images.) Salomon distinguishes the following four differences to be related to the mental effects of new media use.

Differences of content and complexity of processing   Each symbol system or mode of communication is particularly suitable for the transfer of a specific type of content. For instance the linguistic mode is used for explanations, the iconic mode for portrayals or expressions and the non-verbal mode for emotions. Abstract notions, arguments and all the things important in a dialogue can be best explained in words. Mediated images are pre-eminently suitable for giving a direct view of reality or for clarifying things usually not visible to the human eye with the aid of a particular visual language.

Notational and Non-notational Systems   Symbol systems or modes of communication are either *notational* or *non-notational*. They contain a set of notations for the clearly identifiable, specific matters they are referring to, or they contain signs not unambiguously referring to a particular thing or matter, for instance all kinds of images with their varied and mostly ambiguous contents (Salomon, 1979:

33). The logico-mathematical mode and the musical mode (represented by stave notation) are notational systems, while the iconic and non-verbal modes are non-notational. The linguistic mode is partly notational, since several interpretations of spoken and written words are possible. In the new media, especially multimedia, the linguistic mode becomes less ambiguous under the influence of strict notational computer language and the advancing integration of texts, images, sounds and data. In multimedia the iconic mode is joined with the audiovisual linguistic mode. *All in all, the notational symbol systems or modes appear to be intensified in the new media*. This will have important consequences. Mental processing in notational systems is known to be more complex than in non-notational ones. The appropriate codes have to be learned and subsequently applied over and over again. In non-notational systems, the distance between symbols and representations (for instance images) in a person's mind is shorter (1979: 73–4).

Mental Development

Mental skills required The notational linguistic, logico-mathematical and musical-written modes of communication are primarily processed mentally in the left half of the brain, and the non-notational non-verbal, iconic and musical-auditive modes are primarily but not exclusively processed in the right half of the brain (Ivry and Robertson, 1998). So, in general the new media will appeal relatively more to the left half of the brain. However, the expectation of a much stronger simultaneous appeal of integrated new media (multimedia) to both halves of the brain is far more important. An intense dialogue between both halves through their cross-connections is required. This requires all-round mental development. *The ability to benefit fully from all the opportunities of the new media demands a full-grown visual, auditive, verbal, logical and analytical mental development.* Of course this will increase the complexity of the mental activities required. But the level of this complexity depends on three other crucial factors (Salomon, 1979: 71–2):

1 the cognitive development of individuals, being related to age, education and experience;
2 individual cognitive preferences in perceiving texts, images, sounds or data;
3 the tasks to be performed, being more or less demanding: study, information retrieval, conversation or amusement.

In conclusion: an *optimum* use of the new media requires full-grown and versatile mental development and a multifunctional use of their capacities.

Variations in Meaning

Differences in the construction of meaning Various (types of) modes of communication can cause different meanings to be ascribed to one and the same content. Listening to a sound recording of a speech will result in meanings other than those obtained by reading its literal transcription (1979: 78). This is caused not by the contents themselves, for they are (almost) entirely the same, but by the skills of the receiver. In their turn these depend upon two factors: the basic knowledge of the receiver and the novelty of the information.

The broader the basic knowledge of the receiver, the less sensitive this person will be to the (type of) mode of communication offered (1979: 79ff.). This means that less educated people depend more on the mode of communication concerned than do better educated people. This must be very relevant to any introduction of the new media because, in theory, the range of options in choosing modes of communication is increased.

The newer the information offered, the more important is the choice of mode of communication (1979: 80ff.). New information requires more adaptation in mental frameworks; information that is 'too new' may even be rejected (see Neisser, 1976). This must also be relevant to all multi-media information supplied in patterns of allocution and consultation, revealing new shapes and contents in their presentations.

In spite of all the myths about the stultifying impact of modern visual culture, almost all psychological research shows that reading in general has a more *compelling* but not necessarily greater appeal to our mental efforts than perceiving audiovisual messages. Conceptual thinking, required by reading, goes beyond perceptual thinking (Peters, 1989). On the basis of these statements we might expect (new) media containing audiovisual presentations to be more easily accessible to less educated people than the (new) media mainly using texts and data. At the same time, they would be less instructive for them than they are for better educated people, for the latter are less dependent upon the particular mode of communication offered and they profit more from the increasing elements of text and data.

Dual Nature of *A differential cultivation of mental skills* The (types of) modes of communica-
Mental tion not only appeal differently to mental skills, but also help to develop
Requirements them differently. In order to do so, they have to be demanding and they must force receivers to develop their skills (Salomon, 1979: 82). However, there are several modes of communication, particularly the non-notational types, that allow the receiver to choose the line of least resistance. 'The pictorial system of television *allows* (but does not require) shallower processing than a written story or a verbally told one. To generalize, some symbol systems may *allow* shallower mental processing and others may *demand* deeper mental elaboration' (1979: 223, final italic added). 'Notational symbol systems require crystallized ability, based on verbal skills, and non-notational symbol systems require mainly fluid ability, based on spatial and perceptual skills' (1979: 224).

All this has relevance to the new media. In theory they can help to develop mental skills better than most old media as they integrate a multitude of modes of communication. In practice they require full-grown mental capacities and a multifunctional usage. The problem is they do not have to be used optimally. The integration of modes of communication in the new media can also be accessed separately and enable a much shallower use. The strength of the audiovisual and the iconic modes offers potential uses that do not stimulate the mental skills required for notational symbol systems. 'The employment of charts, graphs or pictures could save mental effort and make the acquisition of knowledge more effective, but it will impede skill development' (1979: 83). The transition from the (audio)phone to the videophone is a good example. The latter gives more cues and therefore requires less mental skill to understand the conversation (see later in this chapter). People who have to rely on one or two modes of communication must develop the appropriate skills, no matter how one-sided these skills may be. The best case of this until now has been the written linguistic mode.

So, a paradoxical situation arises. On the one hand the new media (can) make human perception and cognition more complicated and on the other hand they (can) facilitate and simplify them. This means that the goal and the task of the user will determine what happens. Experiments have shown that children learn more from watching television, for instance 'Sesame Street' (1979: 225), when they are guided by their parents or by courses for achieving educational goals. Since people with high education in general will be willing to 'do' more with the new media than people with low education, the former will benefit more and will increase their mental advantage. This is the most fundamental psychological cause of the usage gap described in Chapter 6.

COGNITION AND THE NEW MEDIA

In the new media, people are offered greater, possibly more varied quantities of information. Furthermore, they are able to communicate with an increasing number of people in a variety of ways. On many occasions they have to be reachable at any time and place, and the technology enables them to do this. These opportunities offer the mental counterpart of the social aspect of scale extension enabled by the new media. But here also, scale extension is accompanied by scale reduction as, increasingly, individuals have to rely upon their own resources in processing the enormous amount of different kinds of information. This does not refer to individual watching of television or listening to radio or audio, or to consuming data on computer screens by oneself. This is a real tendency we can see happening as a result of individualization in living conditions and isolation in working conditions, but it should not be exaggerated (see McQuail, 1987: 228–9). Some older media were also primarily used individually (for instance reading and listening to recorded music), whereas some newer media encourage collective uses (for instance watching rented videos, playing in MUDs (computer games), using electronic billboards, chatting and holding teleconferences).

Mental Combination and Integration No, we are mainly concerned with the problems caused by having to *mentally combine an ever growing quantity and heterogeneity of information and to mentally integrate mediated and face- to-face communica-*

tions. Chapter 6 referred to the particular problems of individuals in managing dense and diffuse social networks or organic and virtual communities. In parallel, people are faced with an unprecedented arsenal of old and new media with several combinations of the patterns of allocution, consultation, registration and conversation. There are no fixed limits to the human capacity to handle information (Neisser: 1976: 97ff.); it is very 'elastic'. For this reason, the effect of phenomena like information overload and 'overcommunication' should not be exaggerated. However, problems arise *whenever we begin to combine tasks that have no natural relationship to each other* (1976: 101). In the new media, human communication and the handling of data are more and more accompanied by and sometimes even taken over by data processing and computer-mediated communication. The key questions then become whether these forms of processing and communication look alike and whether they are able to develop a natural relationship to each other. If the answers to these two questions are primarily positive, there is no reason to worry about any special problems in mentally dealing with the new media. These media will become very useful tools. When, on the other hand, the answer is primarily negative, problems are bound to arise. In the latter case communication between human beings and media/computers will meet limitations and complications. Then the tool might transform into a burden on or a substitute for 'natural' human cognition and communication.

Human–Computer Similarities
    The *similarities* and possible relationships between processing and communication performed by human beings on the one hand and by media/computers on the other are evident. Computers are used as a metaphor (image) for the description of the human mind, and for good reasons. Terms derived from this source, such as information, processor and memory, play a key role in computer jargon. The same goes for terms derived from communication between human beings, like interaction, interface, dialogue, sign and command. In media technology jargon, terms derived from human perception, symbolization and representation of reality, prevail. Media and computers may be considered an extension or even a means of human perception, mental processing and communication. They span time and space and they decrease the effects of the limits our body and mind impose upon us.

Human–Computer Differences
    In answering the two questions posed earlier, a discussion of the *differences* and the possible malfunctions in processing and communication by humans and by media/computers is more important. Critics of the new technologies and the accompanying computer culture and visual culture often phrase these differences in philosophic, humanistic and romantic terms. Human beings, they claim, differ from computers, because they have a broader range of experience, associations, intuition, feelings and emotions at their disposal. Well-known critics are J. Weizenbaum, Th. Roszak, J. Searle and H. Dreyfus. Usually, their reactions are much too defensive. This leaves them no option other than to stand by and watch how the fifth, sixth and later generations of computers seem to be clearing away one difference after the other. Devoting oneself to modern psychology, and even

TABLE 8.2 Basic differences between human and computer/medium processing

Human processing (cognition)	Computer/medium processing
Situation-bound	Context-free
Total experience	Separate and successive perception and cognition
Flexible schemata	Fixed schemata
Operant and intelligent learning	'Intelligent' learning
Processing through social communication	Processing through technical communication

to so-called cognitive psychology, which actually uses the computer as the most important model of the human mind, would be a wiser thing to do. Additionally, one should take note of empirical studies about the ways humans really use computer hardware and software and one should observe attempts to make designs that take into account the psychology of the user. After all these efforts, at least five differences will continue to exist (see Table 8.2).

Direct Intentionality *Situation-bound versus context-free processing* The most basic difference can be attributed to the fact that human perception and cognition are *situated physically* in a tangible world. A human being has an active and autonomous relationship to its environment. This is of crucial importance to the versatile perception and cognition in the so-called 'perceptual cycle' (Neisser, 1976). The basic principles of this perceptual cycle are perceptual activities which are controlled by continuously changing mental schemata. This is caused by the *direct intentionality* of the human mind. Intentionality is inspired by the needs and values of human beings as biological and social beings in a particular environment.

This is the basic principle used by neurobiologist Gerald Edelman and his Neurosciences Institute. Edelman's work, summarized and popularized in his book *Bright Air, Brilliant Fire: On the Matter of the Mind* (1991), firmly supports the five differences dealt with in this section. Edelman rejects the principle of most cognitive psychologists that the human brain can be compared to a computer or to a power plant of neurones. He claims it is more like an organic jungle of continuously changing groups and connections of neurons which are unique for every human being. They are only partly specified by genes. The needs every human being appears to have in their ongoing interaction with the environment cause a continuous *selection* of neurons in the Darwinian sense, changing the human brain ceaselessly. A process of *trial and error* produced by these needs shapes the brain. The workings of the human brain should not be separated into the functioning of hardware (brain) and software (mind), like most cognitive psychologists do. According to Edelman the complete human brain/mind, but obviously not particular thoughts, can be explained by neurobiology.

Derived Intentionality Perception and processing in computers or other media, on the other hand, can only start with some kind of *derived intentionality*. They are programmed by others and only reproduce or present programs. 'For a computer to have intentional states, it would have to be a robot of some kind', is how one of today's most important cognitive psychologists, Jerry Fodor (1986: 103) phrased the prime difference between man and computer in an interview. The principle of computer processing is programmed *instruction* following algorithms, not neural *selection* as in mental processing (Edelman, 1991).

Situated Action   Computers and media are programmed for various purposes and environments. So to some extent they are *context-free and abstract*. They are intended (instructed by a command) and they follow a rational planning model of the human mind. In her book *Plans and Situated Actions*, Lucy Suchman (1987) has severely criticized this model. In her empirical, anthropological study of the ways people use modern electronic equipment in everyday life, she came to the conclusion that people do not use this equipment according to a certain plan, the way developers of this equipment expect them to do. Planning models of human action and thinking do not match the reality of 'situated action', which Edelman claims is inspired by neural selection following needs. Suchman feels plans are merely an anticipation and a reconstruction of action. They are a way of thinking, not a real-life representation of action. 'Situated action is an emergent property of moment-by-moment interactions between actors and between actors and the environments of their action' (1987: 179). This interaction has four features which go substantially beyond the three levels of interactivity that computers and media have been capable of supporting so far (two-way communications, synchronicity and, to some extent, control from both sides: see Chapter 1). In fact, these features are an interpretation of the fourth and highest level of interactivity distinguished in Chapter 1 (1987: 180):

1 Ordinary interaction between people presupposes *mutual intelligibility* of the parties involved. This understanding is effected during intense cooperation and communication in *fully fledged environments*.
2 General communicative practices that people have learned in these environments are designed to *maximize sensitivity to particular partners and occasions of interaction*.
3 The use of face-to-face communication includes *resources for detecting and remedying difficulties in understanding*.
4 Human communication is embedded in and makes use of *a background of experiences and circumstances*.

Human–Computer   Opposed to this, interaction between humans and computers/media is char-
Interaction   acterized by the following problems. A human being usually understands only partially what the equipment/software 'intends' (its derived intentionality) and why this is the case. Equipment and software 'understand' even less of the user's motives (his/her direct intentionality). Equipment/ software works according to general schemata that are relatively insensitive to special users and circumstances. Communication malfunctioning will often not be noticed by equipment, let alone solved. Ultimately, the background knowledge programmed in computers/media is not broad and

profound enough to fully support the broad range of potential situated (inter)actions.

In a general sense this applies not only to computers, but also to media of allocution, consultation and registration and their software/programs. Think of the problem of messages meaning something for the sender (coding) which is different from how the receiver (decoder) understands it. And think of the limitations of social presence and information richness in the capacities of particular media (see Chapter 1).

Of course, developers of software and pioneers in artificial intelligence have been trying to solve these problems for many years now. Some try to make hardware and software more transparent for users (see Norman and Draper, 1986; Norman 1991; 1993). Others want to give users the means to involve their social environment, for instance colleagues, in solving problems of human–computer/medium interaction (see for instance Bannon, 1986: 433ff.). Furthermore, all sorts of 'intelligent' tutor systems and user models are available which are built through 'observation' of the users' successive input. With these systems the computer should be able to devine the user's knowledge and misconceptions to a certain extent (see Suchman, 1987: 181ff.). Finally, computers are increasingly equipped with 'scripts' of concrete situations of a standard appearance which enable them to 'interpret' specific situations. In hardware, developers try to offer human cognition more context as well. The integration of types of data and modes of communication in multimedia creates (virtual) environments which are harder to distinguish from reality than in the old media, for instance TV (Kubey and Csikszentmihalyi, 1990; Bryant and Zillman, 1991). This applies in particular to the media of virtual reality created to simulate artificial environments, immersing users (almost) completely. The huge problems met by these advanced designs perfectly reflect the essential differences between human interaction and interaction between humans and computers or other media (Norman, 1991; Biocca, 1992).

Holistic Experience

'Total' experience versus separate perception and cognition Being physically present in a tangible reality is largely responsible for human experience as well. In a way this can be called 'holistic'. From a varied and active relationship with their environment, from the use of many senses simultaneously and from a whole series of special mental schemata and general conceptual models (among them representations of space and time), people develop a comprehensive view of reality. When we take into account the associations between these schemata or models and the needs, drives and emotions also affecting them, because their neural selection processes all contribute to shaping this comprehensive view, we get the 'total' experience of human beings. Of course this experience is selective, but this is how human beings observe and process objects all at once. Human perception and processing is not a step-by-step process and does not happen linearly. 'Because of their physical condition, human beings first observe the whole with all its internal relations before getting to the specification of aspects. . . . That is how we recognize the face of an

acquaintance before noticing certain details in the person's countenance, such as the eyes' (Coolen, 1996: 144, my translation from the Dutch).

Instructional Processing

Computers and other digital media operate the other way around, namely according to the principle of instruction. They work with an atomizing perception of one piece of information after another (in the shape of digital bits). Then a piecemeal transmission of these data will lead to step-by-step processing by means of algorithms. So, perception and cognition are separated. It is a sequential and linear process unhindered by indefinite associations, drives and emotions that one cannot program. These fundamental differences in perception and cognition are responsible for the innumerable problems in the interaction between humans and computers or other media and in the attempts to let computers handle human language. For the time being they will be solved only partially. This even applies to computers working with numerous parallel processors (the so-called fifth generation) and to present neural networks and future neural computers superficially resembling the workings of the human brain.

Changing Contexts

'Total' experience also means perception, interpretation and interaction in continually changing *contexts* (see above). Most attempts by software developers and AI experts to solve the problems just described are aimed at creating some sort of context in the programs and the presentation on a screen. Traditional languages using only commands have been partly replaced by visual overviews – menus from which to choose with the click of a mouse button. The second step was to display several windows on a single screen. Each window is a separate context. It may connect to another window, integrate another window or (partly) overlap. As a result, interaction with computers and other media using screens could be improved (Reichman, 1986). However, it will be far more difficult to create contexts by trying to make devices and software that fit or connect better to natural human language and senses. There has been considerable progress in speech recognition (using the human voice as an input and output medium), in visual presentation techniques and in pre-programmed scripts describing contexts for the interpretation of human language.

All these means are useful, but they will not help to overcome the difficulties completely. Present-day window systems consist of independently operating windows. In this way contextualization does not live up to expectations. Users still work in poor and isolated environments (Reichman, 1986). Programming contexts in scripts will always prove to be incomplete: 'The number of relevant facts needed to completely define a context in theory is unlimited. . . . On the one side you always need a broader context, or you will never be able to distinguish relevant from irrelevant data. On the other side you need a final context which needs no further interpretation, otherwise an infinite regression of contexts will occur and you would never be able to start formalizing relevant data' (Coolen, 1997: 137–8). In some fields, computers and other media considerably exceed the performance of human perception and cognition. (For instance, a camera can see/show much more than the human eye is able to do.) But these devices will never be able to replace fully the 'total' experience of humans and their face-to-face communications.

Flexible versus fixed schemata   Human cognition is controlled by a series of *continuously* changing schemata referred to as mental maps by Edelman (1991). 'The schema accepts information as it becomes available at sensory surfaces and is changed by that information; it directs movements and exploratory activities that make more information available, by which it is further modified' (Neisser, 1976: 54). So, schemata are stable to a certain extent without being fixed. This is what makes humans capable of learning and of creative thinking. (See Neisser, 1976 for the schemata and Edelman, 1991 for the concrete neural processes involved.) On the other hand, computer programs, and to some extent other media programs, are relatively fixed. The number of states that the human nervous system is able to adopt is almost infinite, whereas the number in computers is by definition limited (Edelman, 1991). The basis of computer programs is the idea that all human knowledge can be formalized. 'Everything . . . can be presented in a structure consisting of unambiguous terms linked by formal-logical or mathematical relations' (Coolen, 1997: 134). Fixed forms are the basis. Subsequently they have to be turned into more or less flexible programs. However, formalization, standardization and all sorts of automatization remain present in a prominent way. This is what causes the inevitable communication breakdowns in human–computer/medium interaction. 'The process of achieving mutual intelligibility in face-to-face human communication rests on detection and repair of misunderstandings through the use of a variety of linguistic, contextual and cognitive resources – a capability that current interactive systems crucially lack' (Brown, 1986: 476).

Developers of software and AI experts try to compensate for this inflexibility by creating programs able to 'learn' from communication breakdowns and (user) errors (Brown, 1986: 464ff.; Suchman, 1987: 181ff.; Norman, 1991; 1993). These 'intelligent' programs are not designed for a more flexible communication between computer/medium and users or for avoiding errors, but for mutual 'learning' from mistakes and problems deemed to be inevitable.

Another way of compensating for inflexibility is to enlarge the learning capability of the user by increasing the levels of interaction and integration typical of the new media. Extensive psychological research shows how people can learn better and more quickly by using interactive (multi)media and programs. (The next section will be dedicated to this issue.) However, these programs will never be as flexible as the schemata of the human mind, for the reasons explained earlier in this section.

Operant and intelligent learning versus 'intelligent' learning   One of the reasons for the difference in flexibility is the structure of the human brain. According to several psychological theorists (for example see Koestler, 1967; Maclean, 1978; Ornstein, 1986) the 'triune' human brain is a not

Computer Formalization *(margin note)*

Compensating for Inflexibility *(margin note)*

fully integrated whole of three parts accumulated in a long evolutionary process. These parts are the brainstem with its instincts and reflexes ('the reptile brain'), the limbic system as the source of emotions ('the mammal brain') and the neocortex as the source of intelligence ('the typical human brain'). Computers are designed to come close to the last of these three parts only. In these devices, developers try to simulate intelligent learning. The previous exposition of the differences has shown they have succeeded only partially. All human learning is based on neural *processes of selection* driven by concrete needs and values. Simulation of intelligent learning by computers, however, results from abstract, programmed *instruction*. Furthermore, the human brain is not entirely driven by intelligent learning. Instincts and emotions are essential. Recently, neurobiologists have demonstrated that humans cannot even think without emotions. The classical Cartesian dividing line between reason and emotion is based on a misconception (see Damasio, 1995). Operant learning*, a capability of all mammals, in practice often dominates intelligent learning by humans. Operant learning happens when rewarded behaviour is repeated, and punished behaviour is not displayed again. It concerns direct consequences and immediate reactions. It is short-term learning. Intelligent learning, on the other hand, is drawing conclusions from consequences in the long run. This is the basis for planning. Intelligent learning by humans is often influenced by, is competing with and is often even defeated by much more direct types of operant learning and by the remains of ancient instincts and reflexes. And most of the time this is not a disadvantage. It enables human beings to respond rapidly (to danger for instance) and yet adequately as seen from the person's needs.

Simulation of Intelligent Learning

Obviously, classical commentary on computer culture (claiming humans are capable of having emotions, contrary to computers and suchlike) is related to this fourth difference, though it is not based on the psychology concerned. From the hypothesis of the triune brain mentioned above (and the psychological experiments concerned), better explanations can be derived for a large number of phenomena in contacts between humans and computers/media. An instance is Suchman's finding that humans do not use this equipment in a planned way. Furthermore, all kinds of ergonomic observations in psychology become clear: physical signs of stress and even panic if there is a problem, reflexes in the operation of a keyboard, energy-consuming response times, and so forth. In addition, numerous social-psychological phenomena in the contacts of humans with media and networks – see the fourth section – can be explained by the theories developed by Koestler, Maclean and others: for instance, the uninhibited nature of computer-mediated communication resulting from the absence of non-verbal cues and immediate sanctions.

Of course software developers have taken this fourth difference into consideration. Interactive programs are pre-eminently capable of incorporating elements of operant learning. They provide direct output after a particular input, such as error messages. However, this important didactic principle does not help to remove the ergonomic phenomena mentioned above (like stress in case of malfunctions or error messages) and the problems occurring in the integration of intelligent and operant learning (the problem of not understanding an error message, for instance).

Social communication versus technically mediated communication   Human cogni-
tion requires communication with other people by using language. Without it, mutual understanding would be hard to accomplish. It makes a great difference, however, whether natural language is used or a (partly) arti-

Artificial Language ficial, technically mediated language programmed and transferred by computers and other media. Developers have still not been able to relate artificial languages to natural languages adequately and satisfactorily. The fundamental reasons have been explained earlier in this section. In fact, it is wrong to speak of 'communication' and 'dialogue' in human–computer/medium interaction. However, humans have tried to improve the conditions of their natural social communication by using media. In the course of human history, natural types of social communication have been supplemented with and partially or completely replaced by technically mediated communication. This means that one or more parts of the communication process are shaped technically. This can be the sender, the message, the medium, the channel and the receiver. This technical *design* can have great influence on the *contents* of the communication process and on the mental processing of information produced in it. The number of cues for mental processing can not only increase but also decrease. When using face-to-face communication as a normative reference point, this will be the case almost by definition. However, this may be called the bias of face-to-face communication, as the comparisons made are not fair. In fact this kind of communication has many disadvantages as well, which may be removed in technically mediated communication. A fair comparison means a study of the decrease *and* increase of cues that the technical parts of a communication process bring about.

LEARNING WITH THE NEW MEDIA

An increase of cues is partly responsible for new potentialities of learning with the help of new media. They can make a great contribution to the improvement of education in general and didactics in particular. These opportunities are derived from the two distinguishing characteristics of the new media: interactivity and integration. The following summary shows a sizeable potential (see Issing and Strebkowsi, 1995 for elaborations).

Interactivity of   The *interactivity* of the new media enables a more active and more
New Media independent way of learning than we are used to. Interacting with and through these media, the superior type of enactive learning (see the first section in this chapter) is *simulated*, not equalled. In this way the three modes of learning – enactive, iconic and symbolic – can be combined, as all three of them now use media. With these means, students are enabled to

Independent Studying study independently and teachers are gaining another role. Until now, teachers have mainly passed on large amounts of information (allocution). In the future they will mainly be tutors of students studying independently and sitting in front of a terminal in a computer classroom or at home using the means developed for distance education. This will result in a complete, unprecedented transformation of our educational system. This transformation will take at least one and probably two or three generations to complete. The following five opportunities of interactive learning can be summarized:

1   Students will be able to *manipulate subject matter themselves*. The order, the speed and even the complete contents do not have to be determined in advance. Thus, with enough additional and stimulating guidance from their tutors, they will be able to determine their own course, style and speed of studying.

2   Making use of the many choices available in multimedia course material, students are able to *learn by exploring and experimenting* in open environments. Extensive research in education and psychology proves that self-directed and exploratory learning can be highly motivating.

3   Students may *choose from several types of presentation*, each with the same contents. These contents may take the form of texts, data (such as figures, graphs and models), (moving) images and sounds. Thus, students with special preferences for reading texts or with special capacities for auditive and visual learning may all be served according to their abilities.

4   Course material used in multimedia education is extremely suitable for *visualizing, modelling and simulating* information. 'Playing' with this material proves to be a very valuable experience. It helps to clarify and understand abstract matters.

5   Finally, interactivity enables the student to start a *direct dialogue* with a program in a device. This combination of hardware and software is called 'intelligent'. Students receive direct feedback and immediately know what they are doing wrong.

Integration in Studying The *integration* offered by the new media, particularly multimedia, mainly has consequences for the perception and cognition of students, as discussed in the previous two sections. Three of those consequences can be repeated and renamed in the following way.

1   The *addition of new data types*, such as images and speech, to the traditional ones of text and numbers increases the chances of more attention being paid to the subject, more intensive processing and better remembering. The same applies to the addition of audiovisual linguistic, iconic and logico-mathematical modes of communication.

2   These chances can be improved even more when the types and modes mentioned are combined in a didactically appropriate way to allow them to be *integrated cognitively* by students.

3 This integration enables perhaps the most basic transformation in education. This is the transition from *linear learning to learning by association*. Traditional memorizing of a string of words, facts or figures is an expression of linear learning: trying to bang knowledge into the student's head in bits and pieces. This is an extremely poor and ineffective way of learning. It achieves some result with young people only. The larger part of our brain capacity is not used in this process. Associative learning is a quite different mental activity. (Inter)actively dealing with parts of the course material, which can be not only chopped into pieces but also recombined, has much more effect. Neuro-psychological research shows that the right half of the brain is used more and interacts better with the left half in associative learning, among other things with the help of visual cognition.

Shortcomings in At the time of writing, these opportunities are barely used in educational
Education systems, not even when a school has sufficient new media and computers at its disposal. A lot of preliminary work has to be done first. New course material will have to be made and adapted to the didactical concepts outlined above. Furthermore, a lot of didactical and psychological research will have to be conducted. Only good new course material and an improvement in teaching methods will convince teachers of the potential benefits of multimedia education and motivate them to learn and explore it. Large-scale retraining will be necessary. These are merely the most important conditions. The next chapter contains policy perspectives.

SOCIAL-PSYCHOLOGICAL ASPECTS OF THE NEW MEDIA

Conversation is the most important pattern for social psychology. We may consider to what extent communication in mediated conversation is either naturally shaped or technically realized and designed (see above). Here the sender and receiver are both humans communicating through a technical medium. The question is how much room this will offer for natural communication and for the cues produced in that kind of communication. This depends on the type of medium (transmission and reception), the type of message (images, sounds, texts, data) and the social or usage context (work, education, leisure). Most new media research in social psychology is about the consequences of these differences in the channels used and the messages produced for conversation by groups and pairs. We will take a closer look at these consequences by dealing with the following five aspects:

1 technical pressure in electronic conversation;
2 extensions and limitations of electronic conversation;

3 coordination of electronic conversation;
4 participation in and influence on electronic conversation;
5 standards in electronic conversation.

Technical pressure

___

Vulnerability of Networks

In using media, conversation becomes dependent on technology. This applies even more to the new media than to the old. In Chapter 4, we discussed the *vulnerability* of networks in great detail. Computer meetings, video conferencing, electronic mail and videophony are obviously more vulnerable than traditional mail and telephony. The more use is made of computers, complicated switches and video media, the bigger the chances of a partial or even complete technical failure of the conversation. It only takes a defective microphone or camera, a wrong communication protocol or a slow switching/processing unit to cause great damage to the entire conversation process. Though such malfunctions do not occur very often, they are always unexpected and hard to repair.

Lower Adaptive Ability

A second aspect of technical pressure on mediated conversation is a lower capacity of adaptation to the environment. In traditional meetings, participants are able to repair bad conditions for conversation immediately, for instance by altering the pitch of the conversation and by repositioning furniture, changing seats, closing doors or windows and so forth. In electronic meetings, most conditions are fixed. Participants are tied to their equipment in all sorts of ways (see Johansen et al., 1979: 24). A third aspect is the pressure of 'having to be available at any given place and time', caused by the new conversation media. This causes an increase

Pressure of Availability

not only in *time pressure*, but also in the *pressure to communicate* as a matter of course. The availability of these media increases expectations. In computer meetings, for instance, quick and well-considered answers are expected (Kiesler et al., 1984: 1125). However, the people and devices involved often do not meet these expectations.

Reduced Responsibility

Finally we can point out the *lower sense of responsibility* of groups for a communication process that is so much determined by technology. The burden of taking the initiative of starting and maintaining the communication is left to the technical medium much more than would happen in face-to-face communication (Johansen et al., 1979: 24).

Extensions and limitations

___

Extension in New Media

Technical mediation of parts of the communication process causes the following *extension* of facilities being perfected in the new media (Weingarten and Fieheer, 1988: 59–60):

1 Communication partners do not have to be present in the same location.
2 They do not have to communicate at the same time (synchronously).
3 Computers or media can partially or completely replace humans as conversation partners.
4 The mental processing required for conversation can be replaced (partially) by information processing devices.

The last facility enables users to involve external sources (knowledge, advice) in the conversation process. Users no longer depend on their communication partners' direct knowledge. Teleconferences can receive the assistance of databanks and knowledge systems.

When the new media turn to broadband transmission for a simultaneous transfer of images, sounds, texts and data, they can open up communication channels more widely than ever before. The extension of communication channels involves not only quantitative improvements, but also extensions of width.

Limitations in New Media Compared with face-to-face communication, each new medium imposes its own *limitations* on communication channels. As we have seen, some modes of communication are given room, others are not. The non-verbal mode of communication, body language in particular, is restricted most. This mode is transferred only in video conferencing and in videophony, be it in a limited and altered form. Here kinetic communication is very limited. It has been known for a long time from experimental research that small images of, for instance, faces in videophony give very few more cues than sound telephony; much larger images, on the other hand, will increase cues (Midorikawa et al., 1975). Sign language on a screen comes across differently: it is emphasized and gestures may appear undesirably aggressive (Johansen et al., 1979: 56).

The absence of one or more modes of communication in the new media has consequences already explored by American and Japanese experimental research in the 1970s (see Johansen et al., 1979: 140ff. for an overview).

In general, face-to-face meetings are valued more highly than teleconferences and electronic mail. The latter are considered to be too impersonal. In spite of the on-line connection, users feel they are detached and are taking part in some unrealistic process (Short et al., 1976).

These limitations make it hard to build a good relationship with and confidence in conversation partners. Furthermore, time and again difficulties arise in attempts to agree on definitions, and misunderstandings arise as a result (Johansen et al., 1979: 22). Teleconferences and electronic mail are not suitable for getting to know people or for problematic conversations (for instance in case of a conflict). They serve best when the participants already know each other and have a good (business or personal) understanding. Computer meetings (synchronous) and electronic mail (asynchronous) are suitable for the exchange of information, opinions and orders, for asking questions, maintaining existing contacts and generating ideas (Vallee,

1978). Furthermore, audio meetings help to solve relatively simple problems and differences of opinion and to take decisions (Johansen et al., 1979). Conducting negotiations is a possibility, but participants should realize the situation is most advantageous to those with the strongest substantial arguments (1979: 104, 156). Apart from face-to-face meetings, video conferencing is the most suitable medium for complex communication tasks in interpersonal communication. However, high-quality channels for video conferencing are very costly and rarely available. Most often only a small number of groups with a limited size can take part, and not all participants can be seen simultaneously. For most business purposes, electronic mail and audio meetings are a better and much cheaper alternative.

Compensation for Limitations

The consequences of these limitations need to be qualified in three ways. In the first place, it is remarkable how well people are capable of compensating for missing cues in images, sounds, texts and data by using other cues. In a telephone conversation, most people prove capable of compensating for the lack of visual and non-verbal signs by making subtle adaptations to their conversation style (Fielding and Hartley, 1987). Fielding and Hartley draw the conclusion that ordinary human communication is much more flexible and robust than is expected by most people. It can cope with considerable decline in quality before normal patterns of communication break down (1987: 121). After all, we are dealing with the *totality* of cues people derive from information, even when it is only partial. As far as the absence of visual cues is concerned, this is much more about being cut off from *seeing* the complex of expressions, gestures and behaviour than from *looking*, for instance through eye contact (see Rutter, 1984).

The second qualification is connected to the first. In their comment on the approaches of 'social presence' and 'reduced social context cues' (see Chapter 1), Spears and Lea (1992) have claimed that users involve all of their social, cultural and personal identities in participating in computer-mediated communication. Mantovani has put it this way: 'The social world is not only outside but also inside people, as part of their individuality, and functions even when they sit – physically alone – in front of their computer screens' (1996: 99). Limitations are to be compensated for by the use and amplification of *available* cues. If this is true, the social identity of individuals and groups is more likely to be stressed than to be reduced in electronic communication.

A third important qualification is the fact that limitations of communication channels are not by definition a disadvantage. They enable the user to gain more control. (Conversely, a lack of privacy and control is one of the reasons for the failing acceptance of the videophone until now.) A cause of the enormous success of the (audio) telephone is the limitation of this medium. It enables users to have a more or less personal conversation without exposing themselves completely to the other person. Computer conferences and electronic mail enable anonymous communication. In these media, business conversation can be carried out without social obligations or distractions. Furthermore, a limitation to one or two types of data enables concentrated mental processing. In computer conferences and electronic mail, participants can concentrate fully on the texts and the data, and they are able to consider these things for longer when communication runs asynchronously. In all audio media the participants are forced to listen carefully. In video conferencing, visual impressions appear to be more powerful than ordinary observation in face-to-face meetings.

Coordination

In comparison with face-to-face meetings, conversation in the new media is usually at a disadvantage when it comes to coordinating communication. In the first place, participants contribute much more as they can 'talk' simultaneously. A second reason is the lack of non-verbal cues. The communication process is extremely vulnerable in its technical mediation.

> Electronic communication can be inefficient when it comes to solving problems concerning coordination, such as letting someone who is explaining something to you, know you already have this information. . . . Terminals and electronic signals offer less historic, contextual and non-verbal cues. Electronic media do not effectively transfer nuances concerning meanings and frames of reference. (Kiesler et al., 1984: 1125–6)

Coordinating Communication This applies in particular to computer conferencing and electronic mail, especially when they are used asynchronously. Direct feedback is greatly missed. In audio or video conferencing or in a conversation by telephone, these deficiencies are partly overcome spontaneously. Ending the contribution and taking turns is accomplished in extremely subtle ways. In some applications of digital telephony these possibilities are not available because communication takes place through answering machines and the like, making it asynchronous again. Answering machines break up the dialogue into two monologues. Negotiations and coordination prove to be a great problem here (see Schmale, 1988). Callers get the feeling they are losing control over the 'conversation'. They usually consider such a call a failure (see Fielding and Hartley, 1987: 116); according to some estimations about half of the people calling answering machines disconnect prematurely (Gumpert, 1987: 135).

Coordination problems are different for each medium, but they do have some general consequences. People need more time to build and maintain group organization (Weston et al., 1975). Natural leadership is created far **Leadership** less easily in mediated conversations (Kiesler et al., 1984). This is one of the reasons why much more time is needed to reach mutual understanding (see below).

In electronic media of conversation, coordination and leadership have to be introduced artificially. The chairmanship and technical organization of teleconferences has to meet many more demands than in face-to-face meetings. Moreover, many teleconferences are controlled by programs, otherwise all sorts of subjects and lines of discussion get mixed up. In digital telephony services a growing number of instructions have to be followed.

For all these reasons, communication in the new conversation media, with the exception of more individual media like electronic mail or billboards and completely informal media like electronic chatting, is more orderly than in face-to-face meetings (Johansen et al., 1979: 23). Even so, contributions made by the participants are less inhibited. Uncontrolled outbursts take place regularly. This is called *flaming*. It runs the risk of prematurely ending the conversation by argument or by participant drop-out (Johansen et al., 1979; Kiesler et al., 1984).

Participation and influence

Until the 1990s most social psychologists were convinced that status, power and prestige have a smaller chance of affecting computer-mediated communication (CMC) than traditional communication. The more limited a communication channel, the more the necessary context cues and non-verbal behaviour cues are lost (Edinger and Patterson, 1983) and the more the remaining cues become important (Lea, 1992). Taking this into account, it is no surprise that participation in well-organized mediated group conversations appeared to be more equal than in (similar) face-to-face conversations in laboratory contexts. This opinion was backed by extensive experimentation (see for instance Finholt and Sproull, 1987; Johansen et al., 1979; Kiesler et al., 1984; Vallee et al., 1975). This appeared to apply most to computer conferences and electronic mail, and less to audio conferences and still less to video conferencing, but in all cases participation turned out to be divided more equally (Johansen et al., 1979: 114). Also, in video conferencing experiments, less internal group structure and hierarchy developed than in face-to-face meetings (Strickland et al., 1975).

Reduced Conversation Barriers

It is well known that face-to-face meetings with a particular task in organizational contexts are often dominated by one person or a few people. In contrast, it turned out that people who usually keep quiet contribute more to electronic group conversations (see Finholt and Sproull, 1987: 221 for instance). And research also indicated that women are more forthcoming in electronic meetings, particularly in meetings mediated by computers (Turoff, 1989: 115).

The barrier for people to join and participate in groups shaped by electronic mail, computer networks and other electronic conversation is not a very high one. It can be crossed as soon as the technical knowledge and devices required are available (Finholt and Sproull, 1987; Huff et al., 1987: 198). Moreover, participants can leave the group with little problem.

Emphasis on Contents

The result of this removal of traditional barriers in electronic conversation is held to represent an equalization of participation and influence in discussions. The presumed key for it is the *emphasis on contents*, as the lack of cues prevents all kinds of (status) distractions.

This potential equalization of electronic participation in organizations has not been appreciated by everyone (see Zuboff, 1988). Some managers considered it to be a threat (Turoff, 1989: 115). Superiors were assumed to fear the loss of verbal and non-verbal power and status. Johansen et al. (1979: 146) referred to earlier observations by Dickson and Bowers (1974) of people with high status preferring to use the videophone to contact their subordinates, while these subordinates preferred to contact their superiors by ordinary telephone.

Internet Discussions

This common view among psychologists in the 1970s and 1980s was countered by a clearly different situation outside the laboratory in less organized large-scale Internet conversations. In discussion lists or electronic chatting groups on the Internet, everyone could observe a lack of participation and equality among the unlimited number of potential members addressed and a lack of central moderation of discussion, leading to anarchy and the rule of the hard core instead of democracy. The dominant practice is that a relatively small core of people dominate the discussion, while the majority contribute only once in a while or just read the contributions of others (e.g. Rojo and Ragsdale, 1997).

Doubts on Equalization

The practice of Internet discussions and electronic mail, collaboration and discussion in real organizational settings outside the laboratory has cast doubt on the presumed equalizing effects of electronic conversation. Bikson et al. (1989) tried to show that CMC generally tends to strengthen existing patterns of hierarchy, status and interaction in organizations instead of creating new ones. Rice (1998) even expressed the view that CMC increased rather than decreased status differences in real organizational contexts. Research by Saunders et al. (1994) on the use of teleconferences in health care and research by Scott and Easton (1996) on the equality of participation in group decision support systems revealed a persistence and even a reinforcement of status barriers. Smith et al. (1988) showed that the vast majority of e-mail messages in the organization they investigated were addressed within the same divisions and hierarchical levels. The same conclusion was reached by Lux Wigand (1998) 10 years later when e-mail had become a widespread medium inside organizations.

The most important reasons given for these remaining or increasing status barriers are the lack of accessibility and usability of computer networking and the organizational rules and authorities reinforced by the control of computer programming. Spears (1994) even expressed the view that the apparent freedom of CMC conceals the hidden power of management opposing the privacy and autonomy of employees.

Power is Internalized

Mantovani (1996) reaches the conclusion that on most occasions electronic democracy in organizations is a myth and that the actual use of CMC is determined by decisive social and organizational contexts. He questions the validity of the laboratory experiments, mainly on American students, of Sproull, Kiesler and others. Spears and Lea cast doubt on the individualistic assumptions behind their approach. According to Spears and Lea, social power does not come only from outside the individual. Individuals will not be released from group and organizational power in electronic environments. Power is a relational affair and it is internalized in the self and the group identities of individuals. When status cues are lacking, people will attach more importance to the remaining cues and to the identities they bring with them in electronic conversations (Spears and Lea, 1992; Postmes and Spears, 1998).

We may conclude that the evidence of more equal participation and influence in electronic conversations is contradictory. Actual social and organizational contexts and the use of particular conversation media (from closed and regulated organizational networks to open and free Internet discussions) appear to be decisive.

Standards

Conversation in the new media has not yet developed accepted standards. No socially accepted codes of conduct apply. So, we must be very cautious in generalizing the findings discussed in this section. The limitations of conversation in the new media are not conducive to the creation of group structures with clearly defined standards of behaviour. In computer meetings and in electronic mail, formal and informal, public and intimate messages run side by side (Kiesler et al., 1984: 1126). People do not yet know how to exchange greetings and other courtesies. The right mixture of politeness and efficiency (speed) is not easily achieved.

Undeveloped Standards

Groups not having a close mutual understanding prior to the mediated exchange run the risk of adopting an apparently conflictive and aggressive style. So, one should always ask oneself whether an electronic meeting really is the most effective means. 'In order to be effective, instead of objective, groups may need personal relations, a division in status which helps in choosing between several targets, and a hierarchy which determines possible influence, even if this behaviour obstructs "good" decision-making' (1984: 1127).

This does not mean that there are no standards in electronic conversations. They are not widely known and accepted, however, and they are always strongly determined by specific contexts (Spears and Lea, 1992). After some time, groups develop their own standards and language systems, such as so-called *netiquette* for behaviour on the net and *smileys* as a paralanguage – certain key combinations indicating emotions, such as ☺. Group identity and personalities are able to grow in electronic meetings (Walther, 1992; 1996). Sometimes participants even fight over identities (Finholt and Sproull, 1987: 18). In organizations, new media are often used for less formal communication. They seem to serve as a safety valve for emotions (Finholt and Sproull, 1987). Paradoxically, in these cases it is the impersonality of the medium that enables intimate communication (see Rice and Love, 1987) – a phenomenon with which we are already familiar in sex lines, electronic personal adverts and suchlike. In the next section, we will try to resolve this apparent contradiction.

CHANGES IN HUMAN PERSONALITY?

Several authors expect interaction with computers and other media to change human personality in the long run. They might be right. Still, their expectations are extremely speculative, though they are supported by some empirical research. The best known example is the interviews Sherry Turkle (1984) conducted with 400 computer users, 50 per cent of them adults, the other 50 per cent children. The results were used for her book *The Second Self: Computers and the Human Spirit*. Other examples can be found in social-psychological research. Such research shows, for instance, how people with certain personality characteristics are attracted to mediated communication. Finally we can refer to research on mass communication, which has always been engaged in establishing the influence of media on the human spirit.

Anthropomorphosis of Technology The main starting point in this section is the universal approach of information and communication technology in using names derived from the human mind and human communication. This anthropomorphization (humanization) of technology can easily lead to technical influences on humans and their personalities. It is well known that people tend to approach computers as if they are partners instead of devices. Reeves and Nass (1996) have published a large number of experimental cases indicating the *media equation* that media experience equals real life, as people treat media like real people and places. People consider contact with a computer to be a dialogue, and technically mediated interaction with and through other media to be full human communication. This anthropomorphization of computers and media is very understandable. At least three fundamental reasons can be given (Turkle, 1984: 281ff.; Suchman, 1987: 10ff.; Brown, 1986: 459ff.):

1 The technologies concerned are *non-transparent*. Computers are like closed black boxes. Large-scale networks are opaque to most people. Even if one sees through the structure of these technical complexes (something far more difficult in micro-electronic devices than in mechanical ones), this still does not clarify their functions. For computers and other new media are reprogrammable and multifunctional. So, these new technologies cannot be compared with the old ones to serve as a basis for insight.

2 These technologies appear as *autonomous units responding to questions and commands*. The tendency to talk about devices and

even to devices (such as cars and cameras) using terms derived from communication with humans is intensified.

3 These technologies respond as *intelligent equipment/software*. They are *logical* units operating with a *linguistic* mode of communication. They work with languages themselves, and interact with humans. It is no surprise that humans get the impression they are dealing with units similar to the human mind. This impression will be strongly reinforced as soon as speech recognition enters the world of computer technology on a mass scale.

Humanization of The result is a humanization of the *relationship* between humans and
Human–Computer computers or other new media. Three phenomena are observed over and
Relations over again (see Turkle, 1984; Reeves and Nass, 1996):

1 The relationship is *personalized*. People handle computers as if they are other humans. Consulting help utilities or information services gives the impression of a dialogue with a human service provider. During an electronic conversation people unconsciously compensate for the limitations and impersonality of communication taking place. Media personalization is such a strong phenomenon that it can even be found in relationships with allocutive media like television. Think about the personalization of mass communication as described by Beniger (see Chapter 6).

2 The relation becomes *binding, fascinating or even addictive* to humans, because they have far greater *control* over these relations than over relationships with other humans. A whole series of psychological needs can be fulfilled (to be discussed later). The binding and sometimes even addictive relationships of humans with computers and existing mass media are well-known phenomena.

3 A *partnership* develops between humans and computer/media. People consider computers to be partners fulfilling several psychological and social needs. A computer is a powerful projective medium (cf. Turkle, 1984): it is a second self, it can be used by humans to project a (desirable) other identity onto it. Subsequently they are able to communicate with this safe environment created by themselves. A related characteristic of computers and other media like radio and television is their well-known social function of serving as a substitute for company.

In humanizing their relationships with information and communication technologies, humans submit themselves to technology without knowing
Changes in it. This is most obvious in *language*. We are referring not only to the
Language increasing use of technical jargon, but also to changes in 'normal' language. In human–computer interaction and in conversations of electronic mail and computer conferences, the number of words used decreases, the sentence structure becomes more rigid, the number of abbreviations, stopgaps and half-finished sentences increases, and the expressions of emotions become

less rich and varied (see Volpert, 1985: 83). Other examples are to be found in word processing appearing to have a fragmenting effect on messages (Heim, 1987).

Social Contacts   The consequences are most severe in processes of making *social contacts*. Technology allows strong control in making contacts and turn-taking in ensuing communication. These processes can be planned more than ever before. A likely consequence is a reduction in the number of chance meetings in and by the media of network society. Of course, surfing on the Internet and clicking or responding to hyperlinks and addresses still offer opportunities for surprise, chance and adventure, in the same way that people previously ran into unexpected programs and contents in the overwhelming supply of the old media of allocation and consultation. However, one is not forced to pay attention. The supply is overabundant and there is absolutely no social pressure prompting people to do so. Therefore, future uses of personal information agents will block unexpected and unselected contacts and contents. The most likely result will be that social relations will become more pragmatic, businesslike and rationalized. Another effect might be a decay of traditional social skills, such as responding flexibly to chance meetings in the public sphere.

John Naisbitt (1982) once stated that human needs and opportunities for social contact will increase as technology develops further. He used the expression 'high tech, high touch'. The problem is, however, that communication technology can serve not only as a mediator, but also as a substitute

Loneliness   for social contact. Apparently this technology relieves loneliness. How can loneliness survive 'in a world where the choice of media contacts with another person is always possible' (Gumpert, 1987: 189)? In order to answer such a big question one must realize that the initiative in making contacts is placed increasingly on the individual in modern society. The individual will have to negotiate about continuing communication. Some will succeed; others will fail. Perhaps this (partly) explains the astonishing fact of increasing loneliness in modern Western society, according to countless social surveys, while the number of media at the disposal of this society grows and grows. Mediated communication with familiar people and with strangers is often no satisfactory substitute, as it produces a gnawing feeling of remoteness and asynchronicity of communication (1987: 186). It seems to be detached and impersonal. In spite of the advantages of instantaneous network communication with everybody at large distances, modern Western humans continue to long for small-scale face-to-face communication in dense social networks and close-knit communities (1987: 167ff.).

Personality   The impact of technology on human language and communication may
Changes   lead to personality changes in the long term. At best the increase of opportunities for information and communication will contribute to *a universally developed personality*. In the worst case, these changes may lead to the following four related personality types.

Rigid Personality   The first will be called the *rigid or formalistic personality*. People working frequently with computers or other media and, in doing so, being constantly confronted with the changes in language and (coarsening)

manners described above, may start to make the same demands on natural communication with their fellow humans as they do on technically mediated communication. For instance, they might get annoyed with vague, ambiguous and incomplete, in other words normal, human language. They could become irritated by chatter and communication with no clear direction or goal. In the end they might only be satisfied by the quick and clear answers they are used to receiving from their computers or information services (see Kubicek and Rolf, 1985: 259 for these speculations). In interpersonal communications these people might desire the same extent of control they have gained over their relationship with computers/media. If the other person does not wish to meet the demands made, the rigid personality will withdraw and return to the safe, self-created environment of his 'second self':

> But if the sense of self becomes defined in terms of those things over which one can exert perfect control, the world of safe things becomes severely limited – because those things tend to be things, not people. Mastery can cease be a growing force in individual development and take on another face. It becomes a way of masking fears about the self and the complexities of the world beyond. People can become trapped. (Turkle, 1984: 124).

Computerized Personality   A second type, often combined with the first, could be called the *computerized personality*. When the popular comparison between the human brain and the computer is taken too literally, some people may start considering the human brain to be a series of parallel connected processors and the personality to be programmed and reprogrammable software. In her research among the first generation of computer users, Sherry Turkle found several indications pointing in this direction. Users defined their personalities in terms of the differences and similarities with computers (and computer programs).

Unsocial Personality   A third type could be called *the unsocial personality*. Computers and other media serve as a safe substitute for direct human company. This applies in particular to all those people who, for some reason or other, are afraid of intimacy, or rather, who want to gain more control over it.

> Terrified of being alone, yet afraid of intimacy, we experience widespread feelings of emptiness, of disconnection, of the unreality of self. And here the computer, a companion without emotional demands, offers a compromise. You can be a loner, but never alone. You can interact, but never feel vulnerable to another person. (1984: 320).

Turkle (1984: 216–17) also observed computer hackers, particularly male hackers, fleeing from direct contact with other humans. In electronic mail and during computer conferences, the more silent, introverted participants appear to come out very well (Kiesler et al., 1984; Turoff, 1989). One can only guess at the types of personality among people calling sex lines or practising some kind of erotic conversation on the Internet. In any case, the new media offer a lot of opportunities for 'intimate strangers'.

Multiple Personality

Our final speculative type is the *multiple personality*. The Internet and many computer games enable us to play several roles and to assume several other identities by taking on pseudonyms. A game or simulation, such as a multi-user dungeon or domain (MUD) is based on these opportunities. Seriously playing with identities is a typical activity of modern society. Here, for the first time in history, people are not simply offered a fixed personality, but have to partly shape their own personalities (Giddens, 1991b). Coolen (1997) claims the use of several identities on the Internet holds a mirror to our eyes. In this mirror a modern view of people and the world is projected. This reality is not merely counterfeit, for modern identities are not fixed in advance.

Sherry Turkle (1995; 1996a; 1996b) believes the positive side of MUDs and all kinds of role playing on the Internet is the chance to experiment with our identities, as much as we like, and to find an answer to the question: who am I? Adolescents in particular could benefit from this. The negative side of this play for the construction of one's identity is the fact that it does not help us very much in real life. Habitual searching for one's identity already causes existential doubt (Giddens, 1991b). The problem with these Internet creations and games lies in the fact that *this reality does not offer any resistance* (Coolen, 1997). It offers safe environments (see above). Users are not corrected and they can assume another identity when they want to. For people with personality disorders, frequent visits to MUDs and the like are usually not a solution and may even lead to problems (Turkle, 1995; 1996a; 1996b).

Cyborgs

A continuing development of these personality types and the advance of the technical capabilities of ICT and biotechnology may turn humans into some sort of *cyborgs*. This term links *cyber*netics with the human *organism*. This combination results in a system of human and technical components increasingly regulating itself within the environment and constituting a new whole. Little by little this technology is taken out of the sphere of science fiction and films such as *Robocop* and *Blade Runner* and adopted in reality (see Featherstone and Burrows, 1996; Thomas, 1996). Cyborgs are humans integrated in technology and technologies integrated in humans. It is a fact that people are more and more often equipped with artificial limbs and other technical devices, carrying them around everywhere and even inside their bodies. On the previous pages the potential consequences of humanizing technology and of technology taking over ever more functions from humans have been described. The influence of ICT on humans must be greater than that of any other instrument. After all, it is an 'intelligent' technology having a direct impact on the human mind. Thus the means of ICT come closer and closer to the human brain. In the future, ICT devices will be located not only in front of us, but also on and even inside our heads or bodies. Try to imagine what the mental consequences might be if, in 50 years' time, humans carry around a miniature but extremely powerful multimedia computer in the shape of a head installation for 24 hours a day.

A simple oral command processed by voice recognition would suffice to literally see each image or piece of information desired projected in front of their eyes (through glasses) or perhaps even directly on the retina through an implant chip. This extremely personal computer would serve not only as a second self, but also become a part of our 'first self', increasingly entering our deepest and most intimate personalities. When this time comes, we humans have to know who we are, what makes us different from machines such as computers, and, even more importantly, who we want to be. Otherwise one of our strongest capabilities, the ability to adapt quickly to our environment, will turn into a submission to a technology we would at present call inhuman.

CONCLUSIONS AND POLICY PERSPECTIVES

Network Society Defined

In Chapter 1 network society was defined as a form of society increasingly organizing its relationships in media networks which are gradually replacing or complementing the social networks of face-to-face communication. This means that social and media networks are shaping the prime *mode of organization* and the most important *structures* of modern society. They are not the whole *substance* of society, as they are in the exaggeration of Manuel Castells (1996; 1997; 1998; see van Dijk, 1999). Society still consists of individuals, pairs, groups and organizations. Of course, they establish external and internal relations, but these relations do not equal society. The organic and material properties of individuals, pairs, groups and organizations with all their rules and resources cannot be cut out of society in order to return it to a set of essential relationships. Even a totally mediated society where all relations are fully realized by and substantiated in media networks, where social and media networks equal each other, would still be based on bodies, minds, rules and resources of all kinds.

Transition of Mass to Network Society

Now, the first conclusion of this book is that modern society is *in a process of becoming* a network society, just as it is developing into an information society, a related concept. It is in a transition from mass to network society. In the preceding chapters we were able to identify a network structure in the economy (within and between corporations and on the global electronic market), in politics (the political system) and in society at large (in a combination of unity and fragmentation, inclusion and exclusion, organic and virtual community). A network structure not only pervades these spheres, but increasingly connects them as well: the metaphor of a nervous system of society was seen to be appropriate. For example, global economic networks undermine the central role of the national state in the political system. Virtual communities are a new market in electronic commerce. The selectivity of global electronic networks in the economy aggravates social exclusion.

Network Structure Pervades Society

Finally, a network structure connects all levels of society, usually called the micro-, meso- and macro-level or the private and the public spheres. It was noticed that the dividing lines between these abstractions are blurring in reality. On the Internet, interpersonal, organizational and mass communication come together. Using this medium we bring the 'whole world' into our homes and workplaces. However, the public computer networks used are intruding into our personal privacy here as well. Conversely, the personal autonomy of network users might increase through opportunities of individual choice never previously known in history. The blurring of traditional dividing lines does not result in their disappearance. On the contrary, it means both more integration and more differentiation, as has been observed in several chapters. This is a feature of rising complexity in society.

The Dual Structure of Networks

The second of our main conclusions is that the network structure is a *dual structure*. A combination of scale extension and scale reduction marks all applications of the new media in the economy, politics, culture and personal experience. This combination is the prime advantage and attractiveness of these media. It explains their fast adoption in what was considered to be a communications revolution. A dual structure results in several oppositions explained in the previous chapters: centralization and decentralization, central control and local autonomy, unity and fragmentation, socialization and individualization. To claim that these opposites form a whole and may be observed in both the causes and the effects of new media usage is not the easy assertion of an indecisive author. It is a prime characteristic of network structure itself. Networks both connect and disconnect. They have centres, nodes and relations between them. At these points we find human beings who participate and decide differently and who are central or marginalized, included or excluded.

Network Structures are Defining and Enabling

The dual structure of network use leads to a third main conclusion. This structure should not be reified to the status of an autonomous existence. Structure, action and consciousness or mental states are a dialectic unity, such as that explained in the theory of structuration, for example (see Giddens, 1984). Structures appear in communicative action. This leaves room for agency and consciousness. Dual structures are not natural necessities but they are both defining and enabling. They offer choices within particular limits. This is the reason why the duality of centralization and decentralization, central control and local autonomy, enables both more and less freedom in using networks and both more and less choice in all kinds of affairs. This is why it is claimed here that the views presented in this book are neither pessimistic nor optimistic. In the context of the huge euphoria accompanying the hypes about the Internet and other new media in the 1990s they might seem pessimistic, stressing the dark sides of the technology concerned. In fact, a balanced view is intended. When new media like the Internet gradually appear as 'normal media' in the first decade of the twenty-first century, because they are used by ever larger sections of the population and by vested interests in the economy, politics and culture, a balanced view might be accepted more easily.

The Bias of Vested Interests

There is another reason why vested interests should receive major attention anyway. Despite the duality stressed, it must be admitted that there is a certain bias in the uses and effects of ICT. The main actors designing and introducing this advanced and expensive technology are at the top of corporations and governments. They are the investors, the commissioners and the decision-makers. It is to be expected they are using it to strengthen central control, be it in flexible forms, and to limit personal autonomy and free choices at the bottom of the organization which do not match their interests. In this book it has been noted several times that ICT is more advantageous for advanced and intelligent forms of central control than old technologies. It is a matter of social and organizational struggle whether the (other) opportunities of ICT to spread decision-making will be utilized.

Media Networks as New Social Environments

The pervasiveness of network structures in modern society is enforced by combinations of social and media networks. Media networks are not simply channels or conduits of communication: they are becoming social environments themselves (Meyrowitz, 1985; 1997). They are settings for social interaction, bridging the individual settings or environments of numerous people acting at their nodes and terminals. Media have their own particular characteristics, which are called communication capacities in this book, but we cannot understand how they work out in practice if we do not learn about the social context of their use and their users. This contextual approach explains the attention to the relationship between mediated and face-to-face communication in this book. The central conclusion is that media networks and mediated communication do not replace social networks and face-to-face communication, but are added to them. They become interwoven, and both will benefit if their strong characteristics are utilized.

Organic and Virtual Reality are Linked

The emphasis on context, environment or embeddedness in the analysis of network use has yet another consequence. Popular views about the irrelevance of fundamental dimensions of existence like time and place in new media networks are not taken for granted. On the contrary, the physical, biological, mental and material conditions of their users and usage are expected to retain their causal effects. Their relevance will even grow as the new media offer better chances to select and confront directly the different conditions, needs and opinions of their users. Organic and virtual reality will link up to each other, hopefully to the benefit of both.

Evolutionary Change

A last conclusion concerns the overall effect of the new media on modern society. Will they have revolutionary implications for society, will they transform society only gradually, or will they have no substantial effect? To put it otherwise: will the network society be an altogether different type of society? The answers to these questions in this book are that changes will be evolutionary rather than revolutionary and that the network society will not be an altogether different type of society. Both answers are for the short and medium term. Nobody is able to predict the long-term total effect of the extremely wide-ranging aspects linked to information and communication technology, at least as long as one is not a technological determinist.

New Media Reinforce Existing Trends

These answers are not opposed to the acceptance of the concept of the communications revolution in Chapters 1 and 3. This is a revolution at the level of media development itself. It is not a concept of revolutionary effects of media on society. On the contrary, the first communications revolution at the turn of the nineteenth to the twentieth century as described by Beniger was a *consequence* of a revolution, the industrial revolution. In this book we have frequently observed that the new media intensify trends which have already appeared and reinforce existing social relationships in modern society. This comes close to the picture presented by Brian Winston in his *Media Technology and Society* (1998). In a detailed overview of media history from the telegraph to the Internet he contends that modern media's most important contribution is the so-called 'law of the suppression of radical potential'. New media technologies, which at first have a revolutionary promise, are later moulded to existing social processes. According to Winston we should not forget that these processes both promote and hinder the adoption of new technologies. It would be interesting to test this 'law' in the development of the Internet from its revolutionary promise in the 1990s to its 'normalization' in the first part of the twenty-first century.

However impressive and wide-ranging the potential social consequences of the new media as described in this book, they will not change the foundation of present developed societies, let alone developing societies. Perhaps ICT has made a contribution to the collapse of the Soviet Union and other communist states, as this technology does not fit traditional bureaucratic authority and planning (see Castells, 1998). However, capitalism is here to stay. It is likely to be reinforced or reinvigorated by the new media in a more effective, flexible and socially harsher shape. Patriarchy may be in crisis in large parts of the world (Castells, 1997), but it will take a very long time before it withers away, and the new media will have only a small if any part in that process. Nor will ecological destruction be halted by the new media. At the most these media contribute to a dematerialization of the economy and to higher efficiency and effectiveness in helping to save natural resources. The globalization of the economy is not caused by but is intensified by ICT. It is to be observed that the national state and sovereignty are undermined by the new media, but they will not disappear. Moreover, a concentration of politics in a surveillance state, party state or infocratic state is a possibility as well (see Chapter 4). Rising social and information inequalities are not caused by ICT, but they might be increased by an exclusive appropriation of its opportunities by a relatively minor part of the population. We could carry on in this vein. It seems wiser to continue describing the diverging ways modern societies have tried to fit the advent of this new technology to their existing policies.

THE INFORMATION SUPERHIGHWAY IN AMERICA, EUROPE, EASTERN ASIA AND THE THIRD WORLD

In the year 1993 the American presidential team of Clinton and Gore acted as a catalyst to nascent policy perspectives on computers and networks, launching the idea of an information superhighway and a national information infrastructure (Catinat, 1997). It was the beginning of a global upsurge in attention to these perspectives and a boost to the hype about the Internet. One can observe a number of striking similarities to these policy perspectives in all interested countries. One can also find some differences that tended to grow in the ensuing years. The similarities will be listed first.

In all policy perspectives adopted by national governments and international bodies and conferences after 1993, it is clear they are a matter of *promotional action*. The technology concerned was developing for decades and nothing special happened at the beginning of the 1990s. In fact, the Internet and other new media meant nothing to the vast majority of Americans, Europeans and other populations at that time. Launching the information superhighway or a national infrastructure was a matter of raising awareness among corporations and citizens about things to come. Almost every developed country in the world adopted an action plan to support the construction, regulation and promotion of this new infrastructure.

The things to come were presented in *grand visions* of the immense potential benefits of this technology to the societies and economies concerned. The opportunities were emphasized rather than the risks. The information revolution would produce economic growth, new jobs, better education, a higher quality of life, environmental protection by savings on travelling and energy and a boost to more direct types of democracy. Approaching the risks was a matter of courage and of regulatory protection of universal access, safety, privacy and intellectual property rights.

A third similarity is the nature of national initiatives and action plans: they were essentially *economic projects*. The predominant intention was to improve nations' positions on the global markets of the future. Clearly, it was part of the economic race between North America, Western Europe and Eastern Asia. This means that the economic aspects always came first and the social aspects second or nowhere at all.

A related point of agreement was the *technological determinist nature* of the perspectives and the *supply-side orientation* of the economics concerned. The focus was on infrastructure rather than on the content and the services that the new media were supposed to deliver. The fast diffusion of ICT, and in its wake the information society, were seen as inevitable. The opportunities were simply too attractive to be refused by corporate and household consumers. They just had to adopt the new media. These expectations were backed by a series of hypes following one after another: first the Internet in general, then virtual reality and virtual community, to be followed by the Intranet and electronic commerce.

A last similarity, and by far the most important for its real and lasting impact, is the historic decision to invite *market forces to take the lead* and construct the nervous system of our future societies. In this age of liberalization and privatization, governments have acquired the role of catalyst and protector of social and legal conditions in the construction of the information superhighway. Building the highway itself and defining all its

(margin note) **Similarities in Policy Perspectives**

opportunities and effects was left to business enterprise. This goes for the policy of every country, from the complete dominance of corporate interests in the United States, though the somewhat stronger public–private partnership in Europe, to the strong stimulus of the developmental states in Eastern Asia (to be explained below). In all information superhighway action plans the role of government is to:

1   activate (serve as a catalyst and propagandist);
2   subsidize research and development and pay for education;
3   care for safeguards (public access and security);
4   adapt legislation and remove obstacles, putting an end to public monopolies in telecommunications and broadcasting;
5   set a good example by itself introducing ICT in government, democracy and education.

In this time of cuts in public expenditure, the level of economic investment by governments themselves is low. Most often they do not even have a plan or vision about the shape and nature of a coherent information infrastructure. Therefore business corporations construct this infrastructure according to their own interests and expectations (see Brown, 1997). The governments, perhaps, correct afterwards by enforcing competition, interconnection and common standards.

Changes in Policy Perspectives   The first of these similarities was worded in the past tense. Between 1993 and 1998 propaganda and wild expectations gradually gave way to a more sober view of the information society. In these years the new media slowly entered social and economic life, producing real problems requiring solutions that were different from the early expectations. In fact, age-old differences between countries with regard to their economic, social and political systems and cultures drifted to the surface again. After the euphoric launch of the National Information Infrastructure Task Force by Clinton and Gore in 1993, the Bangemann Report for the EU in 1994 and the Japanese Technopolis and Teletopia programmes of 1994, differences started to appear between these countries and others. We will deal with them briefly, taking each country or region in turn.

United States   The United States reveals the similarities just described in the clearest way. It is the guiding country in the design of information highway plans, products and services. Presumably, it will be the first to be a real information and network society. The country is the main centre of ICT on the global market and it dominates the Internet with about half of the hosts and connections in 1998. It is leading the market in hardware, software and services.

So, it is no surprise that the centrality of business interest and private initiative with regard to the new media is the strongest in the US. Catinat calls it 'an American bias which too often privileges the business power to the detriment of the general public interest, technology to the detriment of law and unilateral domestic interest to the detriment of the international one' (1997: 8). Others will say that both American business and American communities at least do not wait for governments to take action, as in Europe or Asia, but take their own initiatives in adopting the opportunities of the new media.

The centrality of business interest in the US has led to the growing part played by private corporations in the provision of public services. The US has a policy of extending the principles of universal service to the new media environment. However, as universal service in computer networks does not seem to be a realistic goal in the short term, public service replaces it. Instead of the obligation to connect everyone in the whole country on an equal basis, American common carriers are asked to connect schools, libraries and community centres. In this way universal service in computer networking is 'bought off', as it were, and the carriers acquire complete freedom to construct the American information infrastructure as they wish. As new media health and education services are increasingly offered by private enterprise as well, it is to be expected that a much bigger part of health and education will be supplied on a private basis in the twenty-first century than in the twentieth.

Corporate economic freedoms in the construction of the information superhighway are not matched by comparable cultural and economic freedoms for its users in the US. On the contrary, the US record of restricting these freedoms in the name of national security and the fight against crime is impressive: the Communications Decency Act, the discouragement or ban of encryption, the proposals of key escrow, a clipper chip and a violence chip, and copyright protection in the interests of producers instead of users, are clear examples which were described in Chapter 5.

A related distinction of the US design of the information superhighway is that it has no strong civil rights orientation (Miller, 1996; Catinat, 1997). People claiming these rights often lose their case in the courts against business interests and government security. This is mainly due to legal shortcomings: one has to make an appeal either to one of the many specific acts or to the very general constitution (see Chapter 5). A fragmentary legislation full of holes benefits parties with the best lawyers or well-organized interest and pressure groups. There is no comprehensive legislation for computer networks or other new media covering privacy and freedom rights, among others.

Canada Compared with the US, the other Northern American state, Canada, has produced more safeguards against the effects of corporate dominance, for instance in public information supply and privacy legislation (Magder, 1996). In this way Canada reveals aspects of the European model.

European Union In Europe we have to make a distinction between the European Union of 15 member states in the north, west and south of the continent and the formerly communist Eastern Europe. For the EU the development of the information society is a matter of the highest priority. The EU risks losing the battle of competition on the global information market with Northern America and Eastern Asia. It lags behind in hardware production, except for telecommunication equipment, in software and in audiovisual productions. It takes a prime position only in the production of local services and so-called multimedia content because of its alleged rich cultural heritage.

In the EU every policy is subordinate to the task of creating a common market between member states. Information society projects are excellent opportunities for the European Commission and Council of Ministers and central directorates to unify Europe with a new mission, to strengthen Europe's position on the world market and to legitimize their own role as coordinating powers of the Union (see Garnham, 1997).

So, in the EU, constructing the information superhighway is an economic project from the start as well. However, the attempts to create a single market imply a bigger role for European governments and institutions than in the US. Each year the EU spends several billion ECUs on information society projects. The legislation of the member states is adapted and harmonized to create a stronger economic position. The role of government is greater in Europe for yet another reason: the heritage of the tradition of being welfare states. This leads to policies of consensus building between all social partners engaged in information society projects and to policies of public–private partnership in their execution. Let there be no mistake: business enterprise is supposed to take the lead as well. However, the socially and legally protective role of the state is stronger than in the US.

After the so-called Bangemann Report (1994) which revealed all the similarities described above, one can observe a shift to a more social or societal view of the information society in Europe. The social sustainability of the information society conditioned by access for all Europeans has become a first priority. The titles of policy documents like *Living and Working in the Information Society: Putting People First* (European Commission, 1996b), *Building the Information Society for Us All* (High Level Expert Group, 1996) and *Building Networks for People and their Communities* (Information Society Forum, 1996) speak for themselves. Of course, the insight that a broad participation of consumers, employees and SMEs in the information society is a necessary condition for a sufficiently large European market in ICT is the prime motivation behind this shift. The number of people and enterprises with access to computers and networks in the EU clearly lags behind North America and there are huge differences of access between northern and southern Europe. However, there is growth. It is the first sign of a European model of the information society becoming visible (van Dijk, 1998).

One of the (other) signs is a comparatively greater civil rights orientation in the information society policy of the EU as compared with the US and, much more clearly, Eastern Asia. The EU has adopted a comprehensive Privacy Directive; it has attempted relatively few restrictions on information and communication freedom; and it is friendly towards encryption and the right to anonymity of communication on the Internet. However, concerning intellectual property rights it has adopted roughly the same position as the US, benefiting the copyright industry and harming the public interests of users, libraries and educational institutions. See Chapter 5 for these differences and similarities.

A stronger role of government, both European and national, has enabled the EU to emphasize interconnection and open standards and to confront new monopolistic tendencies on the private market (see European Commission, 1995; 1996a). In 1998 there were six US standards for mobile telephony as compared with one in the EU. Competition and a free market have not prevented the surge of strong monopolies or oligopolies like Microsoft and Intel. At the time of writing the United States is trying to proceed in court against Microsoft concerning the integration of its browser Microsoft Explorer into Windows 1998. Here proceedings are an action taken afterwards, when perhaps it is too late. In the EU there is a greater tendency to act in advance, as the Union did, for example, in the ban on a common pay TV system proposed by the media giants Bertelsmann and Kirch in 1997.

Eastern Europe   Eastern Europe lags behind the EU in the diffusion and development of ICT, even compared with southern Europe. EU policies are exemplary policies here, as these ex-communist states aspire to EU membership. The Eastern European countries keep large state bureaucracies, and invite a wild type of capitalism which is no longer present in the EU. As the bankrupt states in these countries lack the means for investment in new technologies, transnational media and telephone companies jump into the gap and offer commercial broadcasting and mobile telephony. The initial results decrease rather than increase access to information channels for the populations concerned, first of all in Russia (Vartanova, 1998). The causes are rising social inequality and the low quality of the sensational or street forms of new commercial media offered. Former state provisions in mass media have been dropped. Though they were censored and their quality was rather low, they at least provided information for everybody.

Very small minorities of the Eastern European populations have access to the new media. Often they even lack basic telephony (Konvit, 1998). The distribution of computers and network connections is extremely uneven and the gap between major cities and the countryside is growing (Konvit, 1998; Vartanova, 1998).

Eastern Asia   Eastern Asia (Japan, China, Taiwan, Hong Kong, South Korea, Malaysia and Singapore) is the second largest actor on the global market of information technology after the US. It is particularly strong in hardware production. In software and international services it is much weaker. The most conspicuous characteristic of Eastern Asia concerning the information and network society is the large role of the state, which is called a *developmental state* by Castells (1998). In Japan the powerful MITI ministry introduced the Technopolis programme, trying to imitate Silicon Valley in several regions, and the Teletopia programme to install 63 digital cities. In Malaysia the government paid for the start of the Multimedia Super Corridor Project and in Singapore the government heavily subsidized Singapore One, a nation-wide high-speed multimedia network. These large public works are unique in the world, with the exception of the French Teletel or Minitel Project in the 1980s. And we should not forget the indispensable investment in and construction of the

ARPANET as the precursor of the Internet by the American Ministries of Defence and Education.

The Eastern Asian developmental state is not some kind of socialist planning agency. This kind of state accepts the rules of global capitalism and just aims to transform the economic order in the interest of the nation, neglecting or repressing all other interests like information and communication freedoms in civil society (1998: 271). It makes strategic and selective interventions in the economy to promote and sustain development, but it leaves the execution to private enterprise. It guides and coordinates the process of industrialization, sets up the necessary infrastructure, attracts foreign capital and decides on priorities for strategic investment (1998: 256).

This role of the state might be very beneficial to the expansion of information superhighways in newly developing or industrializing countries. However, its biggest problem is the relationship between the developmental state and the private institutions (banks, enterprises) which have to execute economic policy. Here the logic of this state and of the international market might collide, which actually is the case in Eastern Asia for social and cultural reasons. Family networks and personal relationships organize business enterprise, the state institutions and the links between them. Personal and state protection prevent unfavourable conditions in industry and bad bank loans from resulting in immediate punishment by the market, or independent control and supervision by financial authorities. This works until one link breaks in the chain connected to the international system of free capital movement. The problem is not too much protection by the state and financial supervisors but wrong protection, biased by particular interests.

The second problem is the growing conflict between the developmental state and the information or network society it has brought to life (1998: 236). The conservative and bureaucratic character of this state does not fit with the continuous innovation, flexibility and openness (debate to improve things) required in a network society. Many local experts complain about the bureaucratic nature of educational institutions in Eastern Asia (Aizu, 1998; see also Fransman, 1998). At the time of writing, ICT development is stagnating in Eastern Asia. The step to the production of multimedia content and Internet or other network services poses difficulties (Aizu, 1998; Fransman, 1998). Hardware production is becoming even more important, but its margins of profitability are shrinking or are based on the lower costs produced by the crisis.

The lack of openness and innovation capacity in developing computer networks is partly caused by restrictions on communication freedom and even outright censorship of the Internet (Wang, 1998). This especially goes for the so-called Asian tigers (Singapore, Malaysia, Hong Kong, Taiwan and South Korea) and the communist dictatorship of China. Singapore and China reveal the strongest violations of freedom and privacy on the net at the time of writing. Here, the government is able to look into any user's activity on networks, including any attempted access, message exchanges and business and financial transactions in the name of the law or public security (1998: 7). Restrictions on the circulation of pornographic, politically undesirable and other contents are attempted, and blacklisted sites are blocked by providers, compelled to do so by the police and security agencies. These kinds of restrictions are also to be found in South Korea and Malaysia (Yang, 1997). The restrictions and blocks are far from effective and are not always stringently enforced (Wang, 1998). However, new content selection software like Net Shepherd and Cyber Patrol might give the authorities the means to solve their basic dilemma: stimulating economic activity while engaging in content control.

Third World   The connection of Third World countries to the global information superhighway is a clear case of combined and uneven development. It is *combined* because any country in the world has connections to the international telephone system, global broadcasting and data networks and almost all of them to the Internet. In all countries there is a small elite with new media access and experience. The pronoun 'small' is relative, as the elite can consist of hundreds of thousands of people, as is estimated to be the case in India (see Kumar, 1995). This elite is working in the few cities and nodes in their countries which are connected to global networks. Most of the nodes are business and government research centres, financial markets, branches of transnational corporations, software programming departments and defence or security agencies.

However, the development is *uneven* as well, and increasingly so, because the overwhelming majority of the population does not participate at all. It is lagging behind compared with the diffusion of new media in the nodes of their own countries, and even more compared with distribution in the developed countries. This majority has little access even to old media like the telephone, radio, television and the press and to essential services like electricity.

A consequence of this combined and uneven development is a subordination of the organic development required in poor countries to the dynamics of the global economy and its networks. The few computers and network connections in developing countries are barely used for applications in agriculture, health, education, public works, water resources, public transportation, public information, population planning, rural and urban land development or public utilities. Instead, they are used by the military, executive branches of government, transnational corporations, banks, major universities and research centres (Sussman, 1997: 248).

There are a number of praiseworthy but rather naive or too technologically oriented projects to advance connections of the developing countries to the global information infrastructure (Hudson, 1997; 1998). Connecting these countries might be very important for emergency and health services or for research in development, but one can seriously doubt the high priority of connecting countries or regions with extremely low literacy, absent or failing electricity and one or two telephone lines per hundred inhabitants. The diffusion of (reliable) electricity and old media (telephone, broadcasting), and the improvement of literacy by traditional means, must have a much higher priority for the organic development and for any future prospects of an information society in these parts of the world.

SOCIAL VALUES AND POLICY PERSPECTIVES

Welfare

We can start with two relevant questions, simply put. What is the use of these new media? Will they improve our welfare? Welfare comprises both material and intangible aspects. The latter, among other things, give an indication of the quantity and quality of social and interpersonal communication and the richness of the human mind which might be influenced by new communication technology. These aspects will be discussed later.

Economic Welfare   As far as material welfare is concerned, the new communication technology seems to have a positive effect in both the short and the long run. We have already noted that it helps solve bottlenecks of a general nature in economy and society: bureaucratic organization; a jamming and polluting infrastructure of transportation and regional planning; and a continuing lack of communication in an increasingly differentiated, fragmented and individualized society. In the short term, the powerful communication capacities of the new media (speed, few restrictions on place and time, large storage and processing potential, accuracy and interactivity) will cause an increase in the effectiveness and efficiency of production and distribution processes and office work. These capacities are crucial to the process innovations we have summarized in the term 'flow economy'. These innovations could very well be the most important mechanisms for the partial recovery following the economic crisis of the 1970s and 1980s. Apart from improving effectiveness and efficiency, they also help to save on production factors, amongst them the use of energy and materials. So, they might have a role to play in environmental protection. Furthermore, control of production processes as a whole will increase. Media networks have become indispensable in controlling widespread chains of companies and other organizations and in the increasing division of labour within these organizations.

Regional Policy   Networks are capable of fulfilling all these tasks because they help to replace a geography of fixed places by a geography of flexible flows in management, coordination and transportation tasks. This will have far-reaching effects on every regional and even national economic policy. Policy-makers believe companies can be persuaded by local authorities to come to their region, and this will have positive effects on activities in the entire region/state. However, increasingly the conclusion will have to be drawn that international companies determine their own priorities and preferences on a global scale. They are indifferent to the general organic development of a particular region/state and contribute to one specific economic field of activity only. These specific assets of regions and states will be of far greater importance in the future. This will result in uneven development barely controlled by local authorities, except perhaps by stressing the region's strong assets. The problem of uneven development can be solved only in the long run by strengthening international political and economic bodies and regulatory agreements.

Employment On balance, few jobs are created by information and communication technology. In the network sector itself, the new services, transport, operations and the manufacture of equipment cannot balance the loss of jobs in old services and the declining labour costs of support and maintenance of new infrastructures and equipment, primarily in telephony and cable networks. On the other hand, the network sector does cause the reduction of a lot of existing activities in production, distribution and administration, mainly through labour-saving data communications. Yet existing authorities have no real option of refusing to stimulate this technology. To an increasing extent network technology is the backbone of any technological innovation held to be necessary for lasting economic growth. Virtually every government on earth realizes it must strongly stimulate ICT in its economic policy. The European Union has made ICT the central issue in its economic and technological policies, hoping to catch up finally with the US. Northern America and Eastern Asia have developed comparable policies and other countries of the world are trying to follow – at a considerable distance (see the previous section). Their latest insight is that the largest part of the long-term growth in employment as a result of ICT is to be expected in so-called 'services of content'. In the future, only advanced knowledge economies will be able to ensure sufficient employment, at least in the developed countries. This means government authorities will have to invest in knowledge infrastructures (first of all education). Making investments in technological infrastructure (hardware) will be left mainly to the business world. Yet government investment in this field may be important too, as is shown by the Internet and the French Teletel service, both mainly designed and constructed with government funds. However, a 'technology push' from above will have no chance of being successful.

Labour Productivity The growth in labour productivity, caused by streamlining processes of production, distribution, administration and management in networks, will make room for a further reduction of annual working hours, for all kinds of advanced services and for environmental protection, initially in the developed countries. A dark side of the picture, however, is an increase in the gap between developed and developing countries, caused by the same technology. Differences in labour productivity and in organizational efficiency will increase. The employment created by transnational corporations in developing countries is one-sided and polluting. They mainly serve the interests of the central command and capital funds of these corporations, most often located in the developed world.

Producers Push Consumers Another dark side of the picture is the discrepancy between the role of manufacturers and consumers in the introduction of network technology. All initiative lies with companies and public administrations. Consumers, at least individual consumers, experience an unprecedented 'technology push'. So, it is very possible they will have to pay for the infrastructure of future information superhighways from which the corporate world and government will benefit most. Most often the new products are designed, constructed and offered from a technical standpoint (their facilities), much less from the standpoints of economic rationality and the needs of individual consumers and organizations. Organizations of users and consumers are hardly ever involved in the technical development of a new medium in advance. Usually they are not even involved in the introduction of a medium onto the market. In this way, the success of a new medium becomes a matter of trial and error with insufficient learning from success and failure.

Safety

Alarm and Security

Networks may help to increase the safety of humans, organizations and society as a whole. Alarm and security systems may prove to be a great improvement for the ill, the handicapped and the elderly. Monitoring and registration systems can help to protect the safety of organizations in general and production processes in particular. Internal and external state security is improved by all sorts of registration systems. In certain respects we are heading for a society free of risks (Beck, 1992). Risks are reduced at all levels. States will face less surprise (for instance rebellion) because they will know more about the mood and the conduct of their subjects. Individual companies will be confronted less with overproduction because they will have greater registration of their stocks and the daily demand of their customers. Finally, individuals will need to communicate less with strangers and unwanted callers or writers because they will have greater control over their contacts.

Risk Society

In other respects, the risks for society, organizations and individuals are increased by the use of network technology. The preconditions of human (co)existence in general become both more extensive and more complex. They are ever harder to control. We are referring to unsustainable burdens placed on the environment, uncontrolled population growth, international capital flows and largely unplanned technological development. Networks belong to the last two examples. In their usage, networks prove to be a very vulnerable technology. After a more or less forced choice for the construction of and connection to a network, a social unit becomes dependent on a technology full of risks. The pressure of technology on communication processes may increase as well. Sometimes, if there is a malfunction, vital functions cannot be performed any more. We have seen that security often has contradictory effects. Yet we reached the conclusion that most security is offered by a connection which is as 'empty' as possible and which has most of its intelligence stored in the terminals. These are interchangeable and can be controlled locally. The same applies to small-scale networks, which can be interconnected, instead of large-scale networks.

Centralizing and Decentralizing Effects of Networks

Almost every chapter has indicated that medium networks can result in both centralization and decentralization. This applies to decision-making as well. However, as the initiative for the development and introduction of networks is usually taken entirely by central management, and since network technology is very suitable for central registration and control, the centralizing effect of networks at first is stronger than the decentralizing effect. Nevertheless, large organizational units have soon met the limits of central control. Furthermore, it is well known that employee motivation is stimulated by local execution with wider margins. This is why all kinds of flexible control and controlled or guided decentralization are gaining popularity in business organizations and political systems. Many variants are possible. Increasing decentralization and room for local decisions usually have to be fought for by employees or have to be supported by legislation or self-regulation (such as more authority for works councils).

Economic Democracy

Economic democracy is not only involved in the (de)centralization of decision-making and control in companies. Centralization of strategic corporate power and decentralization of production internationally enable the avoidance of laws, regulations and taxes by (at least more or less democratic) national authorities. This also applies to the 'communication sector' itself. In these times of deregulation and privatization, when public monopolies are being dismantled, one can observe the rise of large private oligopolies in tele-, data and mass communication (as we have done in Chapter 3). Obviously, natural monopolies are organized in one way or another. The technical convergence of tele-, data and mass communication is a stimulus to corporate concentration within and between these three sectors. Very soon, fewer than 10 companies will dominate the world market in each of them. They will obtain a disproportionate grip on the communication policies of countries, companies and households. From a democratic point of view, this does not mean progress. The public monopolies at least were under some sort of democratic control.

Political Democracy

Political democracy is immediately at issue in political decision-making and in the relation between government and citizens. We have explained why the new information and communication technologies are a lethal threat to traditional totalitarian rule. Unfortunately, more ingenious ways to exercise control, to rule and to supervise are possible, enabling states to gain great control over citizens by coupling all kinds of registration networks. On the other hand, networks can be used by citizens themselves to ask for better information and to become involved in processes of decision-making. It is important to safeguard the accessibility of services for citizens with low income or the inability to work with new media. A drastic commercialization of public services would work against that. When suggestions are made for involving citizens in processes of decision-making by means of new media, one should not immediately think of plebiscites or referenda (teledemocracy). For the time being, the formation of citizenship (information and education in two directions, that is towards both citizens and governments) and open electronic discussions about social and political affairs are better alternatives. But first, one has to realize that new technological opportunities do not automatically bring solutions to deeply entrenched problems of democracy in political systems and communities. One of the reasons for this sober conclusion is the observation that the use of these opportunities remains a matter of political will among both governors and citizens. Political activity will not suddenly become more attractive when people are enabled to express opinions and decisions through these media.

Social equality

Social Democracy Social democracy will be at issue from the moment the new media create a new information gap between social groups or widen existing gaps. We have shown that this danger is a real one. It does not mean that the level of information and communication among social categories with fewer opportunities will decrease in absolute terms, though there is a possibility of total exclusion for people with minimum wages and benefits who are relatively often deprived of old media, such as the telephone. The relative distance between these categories will be of most concern. The higher social classes appear to benefit more from the new media than do the lower ones – a phenomenon we have called a usage gap. This will offer them even greater control over social decision-making. There is a chance of an
Information Elite, existing *information elite* strengthening their position in society, while
Included and certain other social groups are excluded. In the latter case, 10, 20, 30 or
Excluded perhaps even 40 per cent of the population, even in the developed world, will participate only marginally in network society, if at all. As stated before, we are not dealing here with a simple division into two groups. On the contrary, the whole spectrum of social positions is becoming more extended and complicated. Therefore, we should not seek to avoid any increase in information inequality as such, but should try to prevent unequal distributions becoming permanent structures of society. In such a situation, some people would take all the decisions in society, while others would not have part in any decision at all. This would be a real threat to democracy. The following means may help to avoid this situation (van Dijk, 1997b).
Ways to Prevent In the first place, all legal inhabitants of a particular (network) society
Structural Inequality must have access to the following basic facilities:

1 *Basic connections* of private and public communication and information. This is a necessary condition for participation in society. In the late 1990s, public mail, telephone and broadcasting systems mainly took care of this. Now the right of access to electronic mail and

interactive broadcast services is being put on the agenda. This means new claims on universal and public service.

2 *Public information and communication contents.* This is about provisions from governments and public administrations and from public broadcasting or other public information services. Information and communication from governments and public administrations to citizens, and vice versa, are a condition of participation in a democratic society. Each citizen is supposed to know the law and other rules. Increasingly, existing means will be supplemented with electronic ones. All public documents will also have to appear in electronic form, either for free or for the cost of access only. Moreover, citizens must be enabled to respond electronically. In the case of public broadcasting and information services, receivers must retain or obtain access to a diverse range of sources and opinions. This diversity might be threatened by pay TV and by a segmentation of audiences, in practice offering less choice for some segments.

3 *Communication and information in health services.* It is evident people are entitled to alarm facilities and to basic electronic health information.

4 *Communication and information in compulsory education.* The requirement of electronic educational tools for all students in an information society is a logical consequence of compulsory education in this society. This means that, in the long run, all students must have at their disposal a computer, appropriate software and expert supervision.

Apart from the sources mentioned, in the second but definitely not the last place, *basic skills* are needed to handle them. And being able to *convert them into useful opportunities* for one's own daily practices of work, education and leisure time is an important capacity as well. It is evident one must know how to handle the appropriate hardware and software. Yet, even this is not the most important skill: that is being able to *search, select and process information and communication sources* from a growing supply of information and media. These skills are probably least equally divided among the population. But they are of decisive importance in being able to live and work in the information or network society. Subjects at school, such as courses of information and communication or media education, can only partially fulfil this need. Unfortunately these subjects are marginal compared with subjects such as mathematics and language. These subjects have to substantially change as well. Mathematics must partially shift to digital data processing and language must give much more attention to searching, selecting and processing information. Moreover, language subjects should pay much more attention to audiovisual language and contents. It may be considered a missed opportunity when no attention at all is paid at school to the most important reality of experience and learning for children in contemporary society: television and computer games.

Finally, changes will have to be made in the organization of labour. After all, in Chapter 6 it was pointed out that regular education cannot do enough to decrease the widening gap in the usage of ICT. In the organization of labour, room must be made for permanent education, parental and sabbatical leave, career mobility, task circulation, task extension and task enrichment for as many employees as possible. In this way employees will get more chances in learning to use multifunctional applications of the new media.

Personal autonomy

Because of their systemic character, networks automatically take away part of the autonomy of those connected. Citizens, employees, clients and consumers as individuals usually have little choice as to whether they are to be connected to such a network or not. And once they are connected, they have little control over its usage. One way to solve this problem is to

Freedom of Choice increase the choice opportunities of users. Another is to grant the bodies representing these individuals more control and to extend the area in which they have a say. In particular this applies to organizations of employees. Networks will be a structuring part of any organization, not merely a technical instrument. They have far-reaching effects on existing organizational practices. Concerning public networking, citizens' representatives should start a discussion about the design, construction and use of public networks on every relevant occasion. So far this hardly ever happens. Politicians and civil servants are often accused of lagging behind when it comes to personal experience in the usage of new media such as the Internet. But this is not the main problem. It is their incompetence in evaluating the opportunities and risks of ICT for society in general and for law and politics in particular. They usually lack vision into the 'nervous system' of our future society.

When organizations of employees are allowed to interfere in fields of network technology they have little knowledge of issues such as organization structure, management strategy and information control. Consumer organizations will have to comment not only on final products and prices, but also on the design of these products and on the remaining availability of non-electronic alternatives.

Privacy Protection The introduction of networks implies a greater threat to the informational and relational privacy of individuals than preceding information and communication techniques. The threat comes from the coupling and the integration of files and the traceability of individuals' daily routines. The last threat is a new one. Before long an important value will be realized by the new communication technology: being reachable at any given time and place. This value also has a counter-value: individuals will be traceable into the deepest crevices of society – and, what is much more important, they will have to justify to their relatives and superiors their choice to be left alone. So, technical blocking options are not sufficient in daily social practice. Relational privacy is hardly at issue yet. Legislation and other regulations on this subject are far from adequate. Unfortunately this also applies to informational privacy in general, which has been an issue for a long time now. The vast majority of countries in the world have no comprehensive (informational) privacy law. The countries of the European Union do have one, but it remains to be seen what it will mean in practice. Network traffic remains elusive. This applies in particular to the Internet, which crosses every border and is barely regulated. When legal options do not offer adequate solutions, forms of individual and collective self-regulation and technical options of protection will come to the fore. The self-regulation of codes of conduct and (privacy) rating systems should be stimulated, and research programmes dealing with new techniques of encryption and digital anonymity should be funded. However, we have argued that a combination of legal, self-regulatory and technical solutions remains the only viable alternative in the long run.

Legality

The far-reaching consequences of networks, and the uncontrollability and opacity of data flows circulating through these networks, demand new measures of legal protection. Instead, existing law is undermined by the use of networks. Since no social value has resulted from the practice of using this technology yet, legislation is not up to date. We have advocated the draft of and discussion about general framework legislation. It should not start from the extremely time-sensitive features of technology, but from basic legal principles like those in constitutions and from basic principles of information and communication like the traffic patterns described in this book.

Framework Legislation Required

The use of networks intensifies the process of socialization of knowledge and information. Intellectual property rights will be harder and harder to protect. A forced protection of these rights by strict copyright laws and extensive tolling on the information superhighway will clash with rights of information freedom and privacy. Legislation will have to balance these rights.

Considering the increasingly difficult enforcement of these laws, one has to realize that criminal law and prohibitions in general will easily lose their effectiveness. The protection of material property rights and other vital economic rights will be difficult enough. For many other, more intangible rights, network technology itself might be too intangible and too spread across jurisdictions. International treaties and declarations of rights have to fill the gaps for decades to come. In the meantime all kinds of public stimulation, funding and self-regulation might offer better opportunities in daily practice.

Strong and Weak Communication Capacities

Networks fulfil vital economic functions. They are needed in the coordination and management of increasingly complicated social systems. As has been mentioned before, they score well on communication capacities such as range, speed, accuracy, selectivity and storage capacity. This does not automatically imply that economic and political needs for these capacities are fulfilled. We have seen that the capacity of selectivity elicits growing demands in choosing categories of space and time. And it remains to be seen whether networks and new media can also fulfil social needs: in other words, can they add to our intangible welfare? They seem to intensify the rationalization and commodification of social relations, already characteristic of modern Western culture. They do not score too well on communication capacities such as interactivity (relatively low levels), stimuli richness (some sensorial decay compared with face-to-face communication, even in multimedia), complexity (of appropriate communication activities) and privacy (confidentiality and intimacy). The last of these capacities applies in particular in comparison with face-to-face communication. A comparison between mediated and face-to-face communication will be made with respect to ever more activities. It would be unjust to take face-to-face communication as a basic point of reference for these comparisons, and then conclude that mediated communication fails on aspects like those just mentioned. Face-to-face communication also has many disadvantages, which may be partly overcome by networks: being tied to place and time, inaccuracy, small processing and storage potential, inequalities of status, power, prestige, speaking skills and participation in group communications, and lack of orientation to the 'pure' content of arguments.

Face-to-face and Mediated Communication Add to Each Other

Many people consider the possibility of a mutual *completion* of mediated and face-to-face communication in a whole range of activities as an opportunity to completely *replace* face-to-face communication with mediated communication. We have seen that the opportunities for completely independent tele-activity are grossly overestimated. Technical possibilities do not automatically become new social realities. In making such an overestimation, one gravely underestimates or even ignores the significance of important social/human needs. Such needs include mobility, the shaping of daily rhythms and routines, a division in heterogeneous activities, informal and direct social contact on the one hand and individualization and personal autonomy on the other. Networks will lead not to extensive multifunctional uses of spaces, for instance the home, but to *universal connections* of spaces mainly used in a specialized way and enabling the connected system as a whole to become multifunctional. Tele-activities are a useful addition to activities bound to a particular place and to face-to-face communication. Mistakes occur when one tries to replace such activities and communications. We have seen why tele-activities hardly form a solution to the environmental problems caused by traditional transport. They may even worsen the situation when they stimulate new needs for mobility. It was also explained why virtual communities cannot restore vanishing organic communities. When their particular strengths are used, virtual and organic communities can mutually strengthen and enrich each other.

Quantity and Quality

Mediated communication replacing or dominating face-to-face communication is not a desirable option for the future. Increased mediated communications are very likely to cause an increase in the quantity of communication. At the same time, communication quality may decrease because there is too much technical pressure (distortion or restriction), or because it also comprises unnecessary communication ('overcommunication') and unwelcome contacts (risks to relational privacy).

Richness of the human mind

Enrichment and Impoverishment

The new media intensify the historical process replacing direct experience with mediated perception. The new media may enrich direct experience because they can help overcome barriers of distance, time and lack of information. On the other hand, they may also rob this experience of its 'total' character, its freedom and its ability to take own initiatives. For mediated perception also has limitations varying across media. In addition, perception is pre-programmed, and the medium itself acquires a disproportionate weight in perception, cognition and application. Together with direct action, the new media reduce the enactive mode of experience and learning. At best, they may be called a substitute. Instead they stimulate iconic and symbolic experience and learning by means of visual models and symbol systems. Since direct action and experience will remain the basis for human experience in general, excessive and one-sided use of the new media will result in a decay of human experience. This is all the more reason to combine their use with natural experience, learning and action and communication.

Optimum Use Requires Full Mental Development

The optimum use of new media capacities requires people to develop themselves visually, verbally, auditively, logically and analytically. For most people this is too much to ask. So, in fact the optimum use of the new media requires a varied mental development and a multifunctional use of their capacities. The truth is, they do not really have to be used optimally. Simple and superficial uses are often also possible. Thus the paradoxical situation may arise of new media making human perception and mental processing more complicated on the one hand, and simpler on the other. People with high education are most likely to use the first possibility, while people with low education will probably choose the latter. In doing so, well-educated people will increase their advantage. In general they tend to 'do' more with the (new) media than poorly educated people. This is the most important reason for the potential usage gap in new media practice, as has been explained in this book.

Improvements by Learning with New Media

In Chapter 8, we pointed out that the new media's interactivity and multimedia integration may enrich human learning considerably. Active and independent learning at one's own speed, using one's own style, and exploratory, associative learning instead of ineffective modes of traditional linear learning, are all among the possibilities. Actually using these possibilities will cause a revolution in our educational systems, which will take not one generation but most likely two or three generations to complete. Experience over 10 to 15 years has shown that introducing the new media in educational systems is very difficult. Almost all the effort goes into supplying schools with the necessary hardware such as computers, printers and network connections. Too little attention is being paid to teacher education and motivation, and even less to research and development into didactic innovations that really improve educational practices. Obviously, students cannot be taught to operate new media without having access to the necessary equipment. The priority, however, should lie with developing interactive and multimedia teaching courses and software. They should demonstrate considerable progress to convince teachers. These tasks will take several decades. In the meantime, computers in schools will not be used optimally.

Who Adapts: People or Technology?

If we ignore the fundamental differences between human cognition and computer or medium processing that we have discussed, the richness of the human mind will be at stake. This could happen if typical human perception and cognition are subjected to or adapted to the workings of hardware and software. Perhaps human beings will then even turn into cyborgs – creatures that are half computer and half man. Probably, or perhaps fortunately, this will not be a balanced unity. The differences between humans and computers or other new media most likely will remain and will cause friction in human–medium/computer interaction. Education, including media education, and experience at work should be directed towards learning how to handle such frictions, not denying them. People in the network society will have to learn how to mentally integrate the various impressions and relations offered by mediated and by face-to-face communication. Otherwise they will change into tragic personalities torn apart by their fragmented experiential and technological environment.

APPENDIX 1: NEW MEDIA IN 2000

ON-LINE (NETWORK SERVICES)

Allocution media

* Interactive broadcasting and press
* Video/audio on demand
* Distance education

Consultation media

* Videotex
* Audiotex
* Voice-response systems
* Public information systems
* Commercial information services

Registration media

* Teleshopping
* Telebanking
* Telereservation
* Telepolling

Conversation media

* Electronic mail
* Electronic data interchange (EDI)
* Video telephony
* Teleconferencing (video conferencing, computer conferencing)

Integrated networks

- ISDN
- Internet
- Intranet
- Local area networks

OFF-LINE (MULTIMEDIA)

- Traditional PC
- Multimedia PC
- Multimedia CD (CD-ROM, CD-I, CD-R,CD-RW, DVD)
- Personal digital assistants (palmtop computers)
- Virtual reality devices

COMBINATIONS (MULTIMEDIA NETWORKS)

- Intelligent networks and high-speed networks
- Internet-2
- Virtual reality networks
- Information superhighways

APPENDIX 2: GLOSSARY

access provider Organization offering access to the Internet by direct (modem) connections, e-mail addresses and mailboxes.

ADSL Asymmetrical digital subscriber loop. A digital connection into the home at the end of a telephone line.

allocution See p. 12.

analogue Through direct and continuing creation or transmission of natural signals, for instance vibrations in the air.

ATM Asynchronous transfer mode: network protocol based on cell switching, dividing data into small equal cells of 53 bytes for the most efficient, that is not synchronous, transmission. Particularly suited for broadband networks as it is able to combine text, voice, video and data on high-speed channels. Future competitor of TCP/IP as a protocol for the Internet.

audiotex Interactive electronic information and communication system offering various audio services such as service numbers in telephony (free or paid for), voice mail and recorded music on the Internet.

bit Binary digit: smallest unit of information in digital data (a 1 or a 0). Series of eight bits is a byte.

broadband/wideband Property of a communication channel offering high-frequency space for fast transmission, generally 1 million bits per second (Mb/s) or more; high-quality moving pictures require 2 Mb/s.

browser Program to move through electronic channels such as Internet sites and pages or channels of interactive TV.

bus structure See p. 35.

CD-I Compact disk–interactive: optical readable disk for the storage, reading or presentation and interactive use of all data kinds, mainly designed for the consumer market; surpassed by CD-ROM and DVD.

CD-R, CD-RW Compact disk for one-time recording (CD–recordable) or recording many times (CD–rewritable) of all data kinds.

circuit switching See p. 35.

communication (social) Transfer and/or exchange of symbolic information by senders with interpretation of its meaningful context and with attention to the presence of receivers.

communication capacity Desired characteristic of a communication kind. Nine new media communication capacities are given in Chapter 1.

communication kind/type Communication with a common character, filled with communication modes and shaped by data kinds. Examples: face-to-face communication, telecommunication, data communication and mass communication.

communication mode Way of communication using particular signs or symbols (words, images, speech acts, gestures, formulas etc.). Alternative terms: symbol systems and sign systems. Examples: linguistic, iconic, musical, gestural.

communication network Network, the main function of which is to supply facilities of communication; the most important information traffic patterns are allocution and conversation.

compression Technique condensing or compacting large amounts of data for bigger and faster storage or transmission.

consultation See p. 12.

conversation See p. 14.

cookie See p. 101.

CSCW Computer supported collaborative work: computer-programmed tools and working methods to support teamwork in organizations using computer networks.

cyberspace Term coined by the science fiction writer William Gibson to describe the 'consensual hallucination' of people working in computer networks; adopted by network users as a (vague) expression for the common virtual or abstract space created and experienced in computer networks.

data Numerical, alphanumerical and other notational signs or symbols rendered in bits and bytes and serving as the raw material for information.

databank Collection of data managed by a particular organization.

database Systematically composed and retrievable file of data in a computer (network).

data communication See p. 44.

data kind/type A form data can take by means of various notational signs or symbols. In this book: sound/speech, text, images and numerical data.

digital Through the creation, transmission or simulation of artificial signs in the form of binary digits (ones and zeros).

diode   Electron pipe with two electrodes.

distribution network   Point-to-multipoint connection from a central unit to local units unable to connect among each other (e.g. broadcasting).

DVD   Digital video/versatile disk: compact disk with high capacity and high-quality images; able to contain movie pictures of two hours; likely successor of the videotape and recorder (DVD player) and the CD-ROM; in its first design only able to read, not write.

electronic billboard   Central file or medium storing and forwarding messages of electronic mail to be retrieved at any time; also called bulletin board system (BBS).

electronic commerce   Formal transaction of buying and selling goods and services on proprietary or open networks like the Internet.

electronic data interchange (EDI)   Standardized electronic exchange of data between computers, most often in proprietary business networks; used for business-to-business electronic commerce.

electronic mail   Conversation with (mainly) messages of text, asynchronously sent and received in computer networks and stored in an electronic mailbox on a computer (server).

electronic town hall   Electronic space for political conversation and local community building.

encryption   Encoding of messages to protect them from unwanted access; to be decoded for reception by a legitimate user.

fax (facsimile)   Photocopying at a distance by means of electronic signals on telephone lines.

fibre-optic cable   See p. 30.

Fordism   Economic mode of production based on a conveyor belt system and mass production, distribution and consumption.

full service network (FSN)   Integrated network for consumers offering all kinds of services of communication, information, transaction and entertainment, designed as a prototype of the information superhighway in a number of American cities from 1994 onwards.

GSM   Global system for mobile communications. European-made standard for digital mobile communications using personal codes for better security.

HDTV   High definition television: television system with digital sound and wide screens offering high-resolution images, advanced colour rendition and quality sound.

HTML   HyperText Markup Language: graphic code to edit WWW pages.

hybrid media   Combination of heterogeneous media, not actually belonging to one another.

hypertext/hypermedia   Text and other contents edited and to be received and read in a non-linear way, jumping from one source, page, image etc. to another; typical way to design and consume multimedia content.

IBCN   Integrated broadband communications network: broadband digital network for various applications (integrated); projected in the 1980s to be the successor of ISDN; actually a synonym for information superhighway.

information   Data and other signals interpreted by humans and animals with sufficient capacities of perception and cognition.

information network   Network, the main function of which is to supply facilities of information retrieval; the most important information traffic patterns are consultation and registration.

information richness   Extent of information a medium is able to process and transmit objectively; contained in the concept of communication capacity.

information society   Society in which information has become the dominant source of productivity, wealth, employment and power.

information superhighway   Projected future communication network(s) with a broadband capacity high enough to integrate current networks of tele-, data and mass communication; also see IBCN.

innovation   See p. 7.

integrated network   Network characterized by an integration of infrastructure and/ or transport, management, services, kinds of data.

integration   Accomplishing a unity; here in the field of infrastructure, transport, management and services of media networks and the kinds of communication called tele-, data and mass communication.

interactive television   Television channels and programmes offering viewers the chance to react to the source, ask questions, participate in discussions, quiz, game and talk shows, order products and fill in questionnaires.

interactivity   Sequence of action and reaction.

interactivity levels   (1) Two-way connection; (2) synchronicity; (3) mutual control (4) consciousness of interactions and their contexts. See pp. 11–12.

Internet   Global connection of hundreds of thousands of public and private computer networks by means of public exchanges, that is nodes, gateways and computer centres using the TCP/IP protocol. It is a narrowband exchange; broadband, high-speed pieces of it are called Internet-2.

ISDN Integrated services digital network: narrowband, digital network offering integrated services of (mainly) digital telephony (e.g. videophony), data communication (file transfer) and relatively fast Internet connections, to be used alongside each other as the network is based on two lines to the subscriber; with improving capacity one gets broadband ISDN (B-ISDN).

local area network (LAN) See p. 34.

logistics Principles of the most logical and efficient (di)versions, connections, structures, divisions etc. in a given situation.

mass communication See p. 37.

media network Connection between senders and receivers made of material means of transmission.

mesh structure See p. 31.

microwave Electromagnetic (short) wave of length 0.1 mm to 1.0 cm, used in air connections and cooking devices.

modem Modulator and demodulator: a device connecting a digital computer to analogue media like the traditional telephone.

multimedia Used with two meanings: (1) a connection or system of a number of devices (media); (2) a single device integrating several functions formerly used separately, like a multimedia PC (computer, VCR, audio, photo-editing and telephone in a single machine).

multi-user network Network in which a multitude of local units (workstations) use the same central facilities (servers, programs etc.).

narrowband Property of a communication channel offering low-frequency space, generally less than 1 Mb/ps and often even less than 64,000 bit/s; sufficient for speech telephony, low amounts of data and text and low-quality images.

net-PC Personal computer with limited own storage and other capacities included in a computer network.

network See p. 28.

network computer (NC) Computer terminal included in and completely dependent upon network distributing programs and storage or processing capacities.

network society Society in which social and media networks are shaping its prime mode of organization and most important structures.

neural network Network consisting of several processors switched in parallel (hardware) and working with unifying programs (software). In its structure resembling a primitive nervous system; mainly used for pattern recognition (vision) and as an alternative for single-expert systems.

new medium Medium at the turn of the millennium integrating infrastructures, transport, management, services and kinds of data in tele-, data and mass communications and being interactive at a particular level.

open system interconnection (OSI) Network designed in such a way that it can be easily connected to or integrated in another network. Internationally accepted standard (protocol) for the hardware and software of networks enabling open systems and interconnectivity. Standard protocol consists of seven functional network layers.

organic (community etc.) Tied to a particular time, place and physical reality.

packet switching See p. 35.

pay-per-view Commercial supply of television and video programmes, paid for by the piece, whole programme or unit of time: also *see* video/audio on demand.

registration See p. 14.

relay Electrical switch opening or closing with a weak current and a stronger circuit.

resolution Resolving capacity of a screen; increases as the screen contains more picture lines or points.

ring structure See p. 35.

set-top box Device connecting a television and a broadcasting centre (to demand particular channels or programmes) or connecting to another network of tele- and data communication.

social presence Attention to the presence of communication partners in media use; contained in the concept of communication capacity.

social network Connection between social units made of interactions.

star structure See p. 31.

switching network Point-to-point connection between local units made by central switching of connections (e.g. telephony).

symbol system See communication mode.

technology assessment See p. 3.

Taylorism Referring to a labour organization with far-reaching division of tasks, first separating executive tasks and management or conceptual tasks, subsequently dividing them 'endlessly'.

TCP/IP Network protocol based on packet switching, most often used in narrow-band networks like the Internet.

tele-CD Device connecting a CD player to a network.

telecommunication See p. 31.

teledemocracy See p. 86.

telematics Fusion of telecommunications and informatics.

teletex Automatic exchange of messages between the memories of computers via tele- and data communication networks.

teletext Information service transmitting pages with text and simple standing images together with broadcasting signals.

telex Teleprinter exchange: oldest form of electronic mail, first using telegraph lines, then telephone lines.

time–space distantiation See p. 20.

tree structure See p. 35.

two-way cable TV Cable connection with feedback channel to be used for interactive TV or video/audio on demand.

value-added network (VAN)

video/audio on demand Service offering viewers and listeners separate programmes, films and music according to their own choice as a pay-per-view using a set-top box.

videotex Interactive electronic information and communication system offering various services; data kinds are text, data and images. In transmission, use can be made of tele-, data and mass communication networks. In the 1990s gradually replaced by the Internet, leaving only advanced information services (business, finance) for this medium.

virtual Not tied to a particular place and time and not directly to a physical reality.

virtual reality media Multimedia switched in parallel creating three-dimensional artificial environments to be perceived and experienced with a plurality of senses and offering the opportunity to interact with this simulated and pre-programmed environment.

voicemail box See p. 33.

webcasting Broadcasting information and television channels on the Internet (e.g. receiving TV on a multimedia PC).

webportal Opening menu of an Internet access or service provider or a search engine offering a variety of daily services (news, entertainment, shopping etc.).

web TV   Broadcasting Internet sources/sites on a television using a set-top box as a switch between a telephone or cable TV line and a television device offering interactive services from the Internet; one of the steps on the way to interactive television.

wide area network (WAN)   See p. 34.

World Wide Web (WWW)   Collection of graphically designed Internet sites and pages, at the end of the 1990s mainly using HTML.

REFERENCES

Abrahamson, J.B., Arterton, F. and Orren, G. (1988) *The Electronic Commonwealth: the Impact of New Technologies upon Democratic Politics*. New York: Basic Books.

Aglietta, M. (1979) *A Theory of Capitalist Regulation: the US Experience*. London: Verso.

Aizu, Izumi (1998) 'The impact of economic crisis on IT and the Internet industry in Asia. Or: can IT and the Internet help recover from the damage?' Paper presented at Beyond Convergence: ITS-98 Conference: Stockholm, Sweden, 14–21 June. www.ITS98.org/conference.

Anderson, P. (1983) *Imagined Communities*. London: Verso.

Anderson, R., Bikson, T., Law, S.-A. and Mitchell, B. (eds) (1995) *Universal Access to e-mail: Feasibility and Societal Implications*. Santa Monica, CA: Rand. http://www.rand.org/publications/MR/MR650.

Ang, Ien (1991) *Desperately Seeking the Audience*. London: Routledge.

Arterton, Christopher F. (1987) *Teledemocracy: Can Technology Protect Democracy?* Newbury Park, CA: Sage.

Asteroff, J.F. (1987) 'Paralanguage in electronic mail: a case study'. Doctoral dissertation, Columbia University, New York.

Auletta, Ken (1997) *The Highwaymen: Warriors of the Information Superhighway*. New York: Random House.

Balance, R.H. and Sinclair, S.W. (1983) *Collapse and Survival: Industry Strategies in a Changing World*. London: Allen and Unwin.

Baldwin, T., McVoy, D. and Steinfield, C. (1996) *Convergence: Integrating Media, Information and Communication*. Thousand Oaks, CA: Sage.

Bangemann Report (1994) *Europe and the Global Information Society: Recommendations to the European Commission*. Brussels. www.ispo.cec.be.

Banisar, David (1995) 'U.S. State Department reports worldwide privacy abuses', on Privacy International website. www.pi/reports/1995_hranalysis.html.

Bannon, L.J. (1986) 'Computer-mediated communication', in D.A. Norman and S. Draper (eds), *User Centered System Design: New Perspectives on Human–Computer Interaction*. Hillsdale, NJ: Erlbaum.

Barber, B.J. (1984) *Strong Democracy: Participatory Politics for a New Age*. Berkeley, CA: University of California Press.

Barber, Benjamin (1996) *Jihad versus McWorld: How the Planet is both Falling Apart and Coming Together*. New York: Ballantine.

Barnett, G.A., Salisbury, J., Kim, C.W. and Langhorne, L. (1998) 'Globalization and international communication: an examination of monetary, telecommunications and trade networks'. Paper presented to International Communication Association, Annual Conference, Jerusalem, 20–24 July.

Beck, Ulrich (1992) *Risk Society: Towards a New Modernity*. London: Sage,

Becker, T.L. (1981) 'Teledemocracy: bringing power back to the people', *Futurist*, 15 (6): 6–9.

Benedict, M. (1991) 'Cyberspace: some proposals', in M. Benedict (ed.), *Cyberspace: First Steps*. Cambridge, MA: MIT Press.

Beniger, J.R. (1986) *The Control Revolution: Technological and Economic Origins of the Information Society*. Cambridge, MA: Harvester.

Beniger, J.R. (1987) 'Personalization of mass media and the growth of pseudo-community', *Communications Research*, 14 (3): 352–71.

Beniger, J.R. (1996) 'Who shall control cyberspace?', in L. Strate, R. Jacobson and S. Gibson (eds), *Communication and Cyberspace*. Cresskill, NJ: Hampton. pp. 49–58.

Benjamin, Walther (1968) 'The work of art in an age of mechanical reproduction', in W. Benjamin (ed.), *Illuminations*. London: Fontana.

Bikson, T.K., Eveland, J. and Gutek, B. (1989) 'Flexible interactive technologies for multi-person tasks: current problems and future prospects', in M.H. Olson (ed.), *Technological Support for Work Group Collaboration*. Hillsdale, NJ: Erlbaum.

Biocca, Frank (1992) 'Communication within virtual reality: creating a space for research', *Journal of Communication*, 42 (4): 5–22.

Bolter, J.D. (1984) *Turing's Man: Western Culture in the Computer Age*. Chapel Hill, NC: University of North Carolina Press.

Bordewijk, J.L. and Van Kaam, B. (1982) *Allocutie: Enkele gedachten over communicatievrijheid in een bekabeld land*. Baarn: Bosch and Keuning.

Bordewijk, J.L. and Van Kaam, B. (1984) 'Informatiestromen: openbaar of particulier vervoer?' *Informatie en Informatiebeleid*, 7.

Bordewijk, J.L. and Van Kaam, B. (1986) 'Towards a new classification of tele-information services', *Intermedia*, 14 (1): 16–21.

Brenner, Robert (1998) 'Uneven development and the long downturn: the advanced capitalist economies from boom to stagnation, 1950–1998, *New Left Review*, 229, May/June: 1–264.

Brown, D. (1997) *Cybertrends: Chaos, Power and Accountability in the Information Age*. London: Viking.

Brown, J.S. (1986) 'From cognitive to social ergonomics and beyond', in D.A. Norman and S. Draper (eds), *User Centered System Design: New Perspectives on Human–Computer Interaction*. Hillsdale, NJ: Erlbaum.

Bruner, J.S. and Olson, D.R. (1973) 'Learning through experience and learning through media', in G. Gerbner, L. Gross and W. Melody (eds), *Communications Technology and Social Policy*. New York: Wiley.

Brunn, S. and Leinbach, T. (eds) (1991) *Collapsing Space and Time: Geographic Aspects of Information and Communication*. London: Harper Collins.

Bryant, J. and Zillman, D. (eds) (1991) *Responding to the Screen*. Hillsdale, NJ: Erlbaum

Burgers, J. (1988) *De Schaal van Solidariteit: Een studie naar de sociale constructie van de omgeving*. Leuven: Acco.

Burnham, D. (1983) *The Rise of the Computer State*. London: Weidenfeld and Nicolson.

Castells, Manuel (ed.) (1985) *High Technology, Space and Society*. London: Sage.

Castells, Manuel (1989) *The Informational City: Information Technology, Economic Restructuring, and the Urban–Regional Process*. Oxford: Blackwell.

Castells, Manuel (1994) 'European cities, the informational society and the global economy', *New Left Review*, 204: 18–32.

Castells, Manuel (1996) *The Information Age: Economy, Society and Culture. Vol. I: The Rise of the Network Society*. Oxford: Blackwell.

Castells, Manuel (1997) *The Information Age: Economy, Society and Culture. Vol. II: The Power of Identity*. Oxford: Blackwell.

Castells, Manuel (1998) *The Information Age: Economy, Society and Culture. Vol. III: End of Millennium.* Oxford: Blackwell.

Catinat, Michel (1997) *The 'National Information Infrastructure Initiative' in the US: Policy or Non-Policy?* Cambridge, MA: Harvard University, Center for International Affairs.

Chaum, David (1992) 'Achieving electronic privacy', *Scientific American*, August: 96–8.

Chaum, David (1994) 'Towards an open and secure payment system'. Speech at the 16th International Conference on Data Protection, 6 September, The Hague.

CommerceNet and Nielsen Media Research (1996) *Internet Demographics Survey.* http://www.nielsenmedia.com/whatsnew/execsum2.html.

Coolen, Maarten (1996) 'Artificiële Intelligentie als de metafysica van onze tijd', in P. Hagoort and R. Maessen (eds), *Geest, Computer, Kunst.* Amsterdam: Stichting Grafiet.

Coolen, Maarten (1997) 'Totaal verknoopt', in Ymke deBoer and J. Vorstenbosch (eds.), *Virtueel Verbonden: Filosoferen over cyberspace.* Amsterdam: Parrèsia.

Cyberatlas (1996) *Internet Demographics: Usage Patterns.* http://www.cyberatlas.com/demographics.html en . . . . ./usage_patterns.html.

Daft, R.L. and Lengel, R.H. (1984) 'Information richness: a new approach to managerial behavior and organization design', in L. Cummings and B. Staw (eds), *Research in Organizational Behavior. Vol. 6*, pp. 191–233.

Damasio, Antonio (1995) *Descartes' Error: Emotion, Reason and the Human Brain.* New York: Avon.

Datamation (1998) 'The Datamation Global 100, Calendar Year 1997', www.datamation.com

Davidow, W.H. and Malone, M.S. (1992) *The Virtual Corporation.* New York: Harper Collins.

Davies, A. (1994) *Telecommunications and Politics: the Decentralized Alternative.* London: Pinter.

Davies, Simon G. (1994) 'Touching big brother: how biometric technology will fuse flesh and machine', *Information, Technology and People*, 7 (4).

De Sitter, L.U. (1994) *Simple Organizations, Complex Tasks: the Dutch Sociotechnical Approach.* Maastricht: MERIT.

Debord, G. (1996) *The Society of the Spectacle.* London: Verso.

Dickson, E.M. and Bowers, R. (1974) *The Video Telephone: Impact of a New Era in Telecommunications.* New York: Praeger.

Doets, C. and Huisman, T. (1997) *Digital Skills: the State of the Art in the Netherlands.* 's-Hertogenbosch: CINOP. http://www.cinop.nl (summary).

Dordick, H. and Wang, G. (1993) *The Information Society: A Retrospective View.* Newbury Park, London, New Delhi: Sage.

Dyson, Esther (1995) 'Intellectual value', *Wired*, July: 136–41, 182–4.

Dyson, Esther (1997) *Release 2.0: a Design for Living in the Digital Age.* New York: Broadway.

Edelman, Gerald (1991) *Bright Air, Brilliant Fire: On the Matter of the Mind.* New York: Basic Books.

Edinger, J.A. and Patterson, M. (1983) 'Non-verbal involvement and social control', *Psychological Bulletin*, 93: 30–56.

Ellul, J. (1964) *The Technological Society.* New York: Vintage.

Elton, M.C.J. (ed.) (1991) *Integrated Broadband Networks: the Public Policy Issues.* Amsterdam: North-Holland.

Eurich, C. (1985) *Computerkinder: Wie die Computerwelt das Kindsein zerstört.* Reinbek bei Hamburg: Rowohlt.

European Commission (1992) *Pluralism and Media Concentration in the Internal*

Market: Assessment of the Need for Community Action. Green Paper. COM(92) 480 final. Brussels: Office for Official Publications of the European Communities. www.ispo.cec.be.

European Commission (1995) *The Protection of Individuals with Regard to the Processing of Personal Data and the Free Movement of Such Data*. Directive. Brussels: Official Journal no. L 281, 23/11/1995. www.ispo.cec.be.

European Commission (1996a) *On Standardisation and the Global Information Society: The European Approach*. COM (96) 359. Brussels: Office for Official Publications of the European Communities. www.ispo.cec.be.

European Commission (1996b) *Living and Working in the Information Society: Putting People First*. Green Paper. COM (96) 389 final. Brussels: Office for Official Publications of the European Communities. www.ispo.cec.be.

European Commission. (1997a) *On the Harmonization of Certain Aspects of Copyright and Related Rights in the Information Society: Proposal for a European Parliament and Council Directive*. COM (97) 628. Brussels: Office for Official Publications of the European Communities. www.ispo.cec.be.

European Commission (1997b) *Ensuring Security and Trust in Electronic Communication: Towards a European Framework for Digital Signatures and Encryption*. Draft communication to the European Parliament. COM (97) 503. Brussels: Office for Official Publications of the European Communities. www.ispo.cec.be.

Featherstone, J.M. (1990) *Global Culture*. London: Sage.

Featherstone, M. and Burrows, R. (eds) (1996) Introduction to *Cyberspace/Cyberbodies/Cyberpunk: Cultures of Technological Embodiment*. London: Sage.

Featherstone, M., Lash, S. and Robertson, R. (1995) *Global Modernities*. London: Sage.

Ferguson, M. (1990) 'Electronic media and the redefining of time and space', in M. Ferguson (ed.), *Public Communication: the New Imperatives*. London: Sage.

Fidler, Roger (1997) *Mediamorphosis: Understanding New Media*. Thousand Oaks, CA: Pine Forge Press/Sage.

Fielding, G. and Hartley, P. (1987) 'The telephone: a neglected medium', in A. Cashdan and M. Jordin (eds), *Studies in Communication*. Oxford: Basil Blackwell.

Finholt, T. and Sproull, L. (1987) 'Electronic groups at work'. Research Paper, Carnegie Mellon University.

Fiske, John (1987) *Television Culture*. London: Routledge.

Fodor, J. (1986) 'Minds, machines and modules: an interview of Brown, C., Hagoort, P. and Maessen, R. with J. Fodor', in P. Hagoort and R. Maessen (eds), *Geest, Computer, Kunst*. Amsterdam: Stichting Grafiet.

Fransman, Martin (1998) 'Convergence, the Internet, multimedia and the implications for Japanese and Asian tiger companies and national systems'. Paper presented at Beyond Convergence: ITS-98 Conference, Stockholm, Sweden, 14–21 June. www.ITS98.org/conference.

Fraunhofer Institut (für Software und Systemtechnik) (1994) *Bedingungen erfolgreicher Telekooperation: Ein Erfahrungsbericht* ISST-berichte 22. Berlin: Fraunhofer Institut (ISST).

Freese, J. (1979) *International Data Flow*. Lund: Studentliteratur (Swedish University of Lund edition).

Frissen, P.H.A. (1989) *Bureaucratische cultuur en informatisering: Een studie naar de betekenis van informatisering voor de cultuur van een overheidsorganisatie*. Contains a summary in English. The Hague: SDU.

Frissen, P.H.A. (1999) *Politics, Government, Technology: a Postmodern Narrative on the Virtual State*. London: Elgar.

Fulk, J. and Steinfield, C. (1990) *Organizations and Communication Technology*. Newbury Park, London, New Delhi: Sage.

Fulk, J., Steinfield, C., Schmitz, J. and Power, J.G. (1987) 'A social information processing model of media use in organizations', *Communication Research*, 14 (5): 529–52.

Gandy, Oscar (1994) *The Panoptic Society*. Boulder, CO: Westview.

Garnham, N. (1990) *Capitalism and Communication*. London: Sage.

Garnham, N. (1997) 'Europe and the global information society: the history of a troubled relationship', *Telematics and Informatics*, 14 (4): 323–7.

Gates, Bill (1995) *The Road Ahead*. New York: Viking Penguin.

Gershuny, J. and Miles, I. (1983) *The New Service Economy: the Transformation of Employment in Industrial Societies*. London: Pinter.

Giddens, A. (1979) *Central Problems in Social Theory*. London: Macmillan.

Giddens, A. (1984) *The Constitution of Society: Outline of the Theory of Structuration*. Cambridge: Polity.

Giddens, A. (1991a) *The Consequences of Modernity*. Stanford, CA: Stanford University Press.

Giddens, A. (1991b) *Modernity and Self-Identity: Self and Society in the Late Modern Age*. Cambridge: Polity.

Goodman, N. (1968) *Languages of Art*. Indianapolis: Hacket.

Graham, A. and Davies, G. (1997) *Broadcasting, Society and Policy in the Multimedia Age*. Luton: John Libbey Media.

Greiff, I. (ed.) (1988) *Computer Supported Co-operative Work: a Book of Readings*. Cambridge, MA: Kaufmann.

Gross, L.P. (1973) 'Modes of communication and the acquisition of symbolic competence', in G. Gerbner, L.P. Gross and W. Melody (eds), *Communications Technology and Social Policy*. New York: Wiley.

Guéhenno, Jean-Marie (1993) *La Fin de la Démocratie*. Paris: Flammarion. Translation: *The End of the Nation State*. Minneapolis: University of Minnesota Press, 1995.

Gumpert, G. (1987) *Talking Tombstones and Other Tales of the Media Age*. New York: Oxford University Press.

GVU Center (1994–8) *GVU's 1st–9th WWW User Surveys*. Georgia University. http://www.gvu.gatech.edu/user_surveys.

Habermas, J. (1981) *Theorie des kommunikativen Handelns. Vols I and II*. Frankfurt: Suhrkamp.

Hacker, K. and van Dijk, J. (eds) (forthcoming) *Digital Democracy: Issues of Theory and Practice*. London: Sage.

Hagel, H. and Armstrong, A. (1997) *Net Gain: Expanding Markets through Virtual Communities*. Boston, MA: Harvard Business School Press.

Hamelink, C. (1994) *The Politics of World Communication*. London: Sage.

Harrison, Bennett (1994) *Lean and Mean: the Changing Landscape of Corporate Power in the Age of Flexibility*. New York: Guilford.

Harvey, D. (1989) *The Condition of Postmodernity: an Enquiry into the Origins of Cultural Change*. Oxford: Polity.

Hawryskiewicz, I. (1996) *Designing the Networked Enterprise*. Norwood, MA: Artech.

Heim, M. (1987) *Electric Language: a Philosophical Study of Word Processing*. New Haven, CT: Yale University Press.

Heim, M. (1991) 'The erotic ontology of cyberspace', in M. Benedict (ed.), *Cyberspace: First Steps*. Cambridge, MA: MIT Press.

Held, David (1987) *Models of Democracy*. Cambridge UK: Polity Press.

Heuvelman, A. (1989) 'Buiten Beeld'. Dissertation, Technical University Twente. Contains a summary in English. Amsterdam: Swets en Zeitlinger.

High Level Expert Group (1996) *Building the Information Society for Us All, Final Report*. Brussels: ISPO. http://www.cec.be/hleg/building.html.

Hiltz, S.R. (1984) *Online Communities: a Case Study of the Office of the Future*. Norwood, NJ: Ablex.

Hiltz, S.R. and Turoff, M. (1978) *The Network Nation: Human Communication via Computer*. Reading, MA: Addison-Wesley.

Hirschkorn, L. (1984) *Beyond Mechanization*. Cambridge, MA: MIT Press.

Holmes, Robert (1995) 'Privacy: philosophical foundations and moral dilemmas', in P. Ippel, G. de Heij and B. Crouwers (eds), *Privacy Disputed*. The Hague: SDU.

Hudson, Heather E. (1997) *Global Connections: International Telecommunications Infrastructure and Policy*. New York: Van Nostrand Reinhold.

Hudson, Heather E. (1998) 'Global information infrastructure: the development connection'. Paper presented at Beyond Convergence: ITS-98 Conference, Stockholm, Sweden, 14–21 June. www.ITS98.org/conference.

Huff, C., Sproull, L. and Kiesler, S. (1987) 'Computer communication and organizational commitment'. Paper, Department of Social and Decision Sciences, Carnegie Mellon University.

Huijgen, F. and Pot, F. (1988) 'Recent onderzoek naar automatisering en arbeids-organisatie in Nederland', in *The Elfder Ure*, 41: 290–310.

IDC (1996) *Telework and Mobile Computing 1996–2000*. Amsterdam: IDC-Benelux.

Information Society Forum (1996) *Building Networks for People and their Communities*. First annual report, June. Brussels: ISPO. http://www/cec.be/infoforum/pub/inrep1/html.

Issing, L. and Strebkowski, R. (1995) 'Lernen mit Multimedia', *Empirischen Medienpsychologie*, 4: 115–35.

Ivry, R. and Robertson, L. (1998) *The Two Sides of Perception*. Cambridge, MA: MIT Press.

Jerome, H. (1934) *Mechanization in Industry*. New York: Publications of the National Bureau of Economic Research.

Johansen, R., Vallee, J. and Spanger, K. (1979) *Electronic Meetings: Technical Alternatives and Social Choices*. Reading, MA: Addison-Wesley.

Johansen, R., Vallee, J. and Spanger, K. (1988) 'Teleconferencing: electronic group communication', in R.S. Cathcart and L.A. Samover (eds), *Small Group Communication: a Reader*. Dubeque, IA.

Kamata, S. (1986) *Japan in the Passing Lane*. New York: Pantheon.

Katz, James E. (1997) 'Social and organizational consequences of wireless communications: a selective analysis of residential and business sectors in the US', *Telematics and Informatics*, 14 (3): 233–56.

Katz, Jon (1997) *Media Rants: Postpolitics in a Digital Nation*. Hardwired.

Keane, J. (1995) 'Structural Transformations of the Public Sphere', *The Communication Review*, 1 (1): 1–22.

Khandwalla, P.N. (1977) *The Design of Organizations*. New York: Harcourt Brace.

Kiesler, S. and Sproull, L. (1992) 'Group decision making and communication tech-nology', *Organizational Behavior and Human Decision Processes*, 6: 96–123.

Kiesler, S., Siegel, J. and McGuire, T. (1984) 'Social-sychological aspects of computer-mediated communication', *The American Psychologist*, 39 (10).

Koestler, A. (1967) *The Ghost in the Machine*. London: Hutchinson.

Konvit, M. (1998) 'Regulatory strategies in Central and Eastern – Europe and the former Soviet Union'. Paper presented at Beyond Convergence: ITS-98 Conference, Stockholm, Sweden, 14–21 June. www.ITS98.org/conference.

KPMG (1996) *Public Policy Issues Arising from Telecommunications and Audiovisual Convergence*. Report for the European Commission. Brussels: European Commission.

Kubey, R. and Csikszentmihalyi, M. (1990) *Television and the Quality of Life: How Viewing Shapes Everyday Experience*. Hillsdale, NJ: Erlbaum.

Kubicek, H. (1988) 'Telematische Integration: Zurück in die Sozialstructuren des Früh-Kapitalismus?', in W. Steinmüller (ed.), *Verdatet und Vernetzt Sozialökologische Handlungsspielraüme in der Informationsgesellschaft*. Frankfurt: Fischer.

Kubicek, H. and Rolf, A. (1985) *Mikropolis, mit Computernetzen in die 'Informationsgesellschaft'*. Hamburg: VSA.

Kumar, K. (1978) *Prophecy and Progress: the Sociology of Industrial and Post-Industrial Society*. Harmondsworth: Penguin.

Kumar, K. (1995) 'Telecommunications and new information technologies in India: social and cultural implications', *Gazette*, 54 (3): 267–77.

Lasch, C. (1977) *Heaven in a Heartless World*. New York: Basic Books.

Lash, S. and Urry, J. (1994) *Economies of Signs and Space*. London: Sage.

Lea, M. (ed.) (1992) *Contexts of Computer-Mediated Communication*. New York: Harvester.

Leeuwis, Cees (1996) 'Communication technologies for information-based services: experiences and implications', in N. Jankowski and L. Hanssen (eds), *The Contours of Multimedia*. Luton: John Libbey Media.

Loudon, K. (1986) *The Dossier Society: Comments on Democracy in an Information Society*. New York: Columbia University Press.

Lux Wigand, Dianne (1998) 'Information technology, organization structure, people, and tasks'. Paper presented to International Communication Association, Annual Conference, Jerusalem, 20–24 July.

Lyon, D. (1995) *The Electronic Eye: the Rise of the Surveillance Society*. Cambridge: Polity.

Maclean, P. (1978) 'A mind of three minds: educating the triune brain', in National Society for the Study of Education, *Education and the Brain*. Chicago.

Magder, T. (1996) 'The information superhighway in Canada'. Paper presented at Virtual Democracy: 9th Colloquium on Communication and Culture of the European Institute for Communication and Culture, 'Virtual Democracy', Piran, 10–14 April.

Mansell, Robin (1993) *The New Telecommunications: a Political Economy of Network Evolution*. London: Sage.

Mantovani, Guiseppe (1996) *New Communication Environments: from Everyday to Virtual*. London: Taylor and Francis.

Martin, James (1978) *The Wired Society*. Englewood Cliffs, NJ: Prentice-Hall.

McLuhan, M. (1966) *Understanding Media: the Extensions of Man*. New York: Signet.

McQuail, D. (1987) *Mass Communication Theory: an Introduction*, 2nd edn. London: Sage.

Mellors, C. and Pollitt, D. (1986) 'Policing the communications revolution: a case-study of data protection legislation', *West European Politics*, 4: 196.

Metcalfe, S. (1986) 'Information and some economics of the information revolution', in M. Ferguson (ed.), *New Communications Technologies and the Public Interest*. Beverly Hills, CA: Sage.

Meyrowitz, J. (1985) *No Sense of Place: the Impact of Electronic Media on Social Behavior*. New York: Oxford University Press.

Meyrowitz, J. (1997) 'Shifting worlds of strangers: medium theory and changes in "Them" versus "Us"', *Sociological Inquiry*, 67 (1): 59–71.

Meyrowitz, J. and Maguire, J. (1993) 'Media, place and multiculturalism', *Society*, 30 (5): 41–8.

Midorikawa, M. et al. (1975) 'TV conference system', *Review of the Electrical Communication Laboratories*, 23: 5–6.

Milgram, Stanley (1970) 'The experience of living in the cities', *Science*, 13 March: 1461–8.

Miller, J. and Schworz, M. (eds) (1998) *Speed-Visions of an Accelerated Age*. London: The Photographers Gallery.

Miller, S. (1996) *Civilizing Cyberspace: Policy, Power and the Information Superhighway*. New York: Addison-Wesley.

Mintzberg, H. (1979) *The Structuring of Organizations: a Synthesis of the Research*. Englewood Cliffs, NJ: Prentice-Hall.

Mintzberg, H. (1993) *Structure of Fives: Designing Effective Organizations*. Englewood Cliffs, NY: Prentice-Hall.

Moore, Barrington (1984) *Privacy: Studies in Social and Cultural History*. Armonk, NY: Sharpe.

Morley, D. (1986) *Family Television: Cultural Power and Domestic Leisure*. London: Conedia Publishing Group.

Mosco, Vincent (1996) *The Political Economy of Communication*. London: Sage.

Mowshowitz, A. (1992) 'Virtual feudalism: a vision of political organisation in the information age', in P. Frissen, A. Koers and I. Snellen (eds), *Orwell of Athene? Democratie en informetiesamenleving*. The Hague: NOTA/SDU, pp. 285–300.

Mowshowitz, A. (1994) 'Virtual organization: a vision of management in the information age', *The Information Society*, 10 (4): 267–88.

Mowshowitz, A. (1997) 'On the theory of virtual organization', *Systems Research*, 14 (4).

Moyal, A. (1992) 'The gendered use of the telephone: an Australian case study', *Media, Culture and Society*, 14: 51–72.

Mulgan, G.J. (1991) *Communication and Control: Networks and the New Economies of Communication*. Cambridge: Polity.

Murray, F. (1983) 'The decentralization of production: the decline of the mass-collective worker?', *Capital and Class*, 19: 74–99.

Nabben, P.F.P and van de Luytgaarden, H. (1996) *De Ultieme Vrijheid: Een rechtstheoretische analyse van het recht op privacy*. Deventer: Kluwer.

Naisbitt, J.R. (1982) *Megatrends: Ten New Directions Transforming Our Lives*. New York: Macdonald.

National Information Infrastructure Task Force (1995a) 'Intellectual Property and the NII', report of the Working Group on Intellectual Property Rights. NIITF: Washington, September 1995.

National Information Infrastructure Task Force (1995b) 'Privacy and the NII: Principles for Providing and Using Personal Information', report of the Privacy Working Group. NIITF: Washington, June 1995.

Negroponte, Nicholas (1995) *Being Digital*. New York: Knopf.

Neisser, Ulric (1976) *Cognition and Reality*. New York: Freeman.

Newman, B.I. (1994) *The Marketing of the President: Political Marketing as Campaign Strategy*. Thousand Oaks, CA: Sage.

Nicol, L. (1985) 'Communications technology: economic and spatial aspects', in M. Castells (ed.), *High Technology, Space and Society*. Beverley Hills, CA: Sage.

Nielsen Media Research (1996) *Home Technology Report*, July. New York: Nielsen Media Research Interactive Services. http://www.nielsenmedia.com/news/hotech-summary.html.

Noam, E. (1992) *Telecommunications in Europe*. London: Erlbaum.

Norman, D.A. (1991) 'Cognitive artifacts', in J.M. Carroll (ed.), *Designing Inter-*

face: Psychology of the Human–Computer Interface. Cambridge: Cambridge University Press, pp. 17–39.

Norman, D.A. (1993) *Things that Make Us Smart.* Reading, MA: Addison-Wesley.

Norman, D.A. and Draper, S. (1986) *User-centered System Design: New Perspectives on Human–Computer Interaction.* Hillsdale, NJ: Erlbaum.

OECD (1993) *Communications Outlook 1993.* Paris: OECD.

Ornstein, R.E. (1986) *The Psychology of Consciousness.* Harmondsworth: Penguin.

Palvia, S., Palvia, P. and Zigli, R. (eds) (1992) *The Global Issues of Information Technology Management.* Harrisburg, PA: Idea Group.

Perritt, Henry (1996, 1998) *Law and the Information Superhighway.* New York: Wiley.

Peters, Jean-Marie (1989) *Het Filmisch Denken.* Amersfoort: Acco.

Peters, Jean-Marie (1996) *Het beeld: Bouwstenen van een algemene iconologie.* Baarn: Hadewijch.

Piore, M. and Sabel, C. (1984) *The New Industrial Divide.* New York: Basic Books.

Pool, I. de Sola (1983) *Technologies of Freedom.* Harvard, MA: Belknap.

Pool, I. de Sola, Inose, H., Takasaki, N. and Hunwitz, R. (1984) *Communication Flows: a Census in the US and Japan.* Amsterdam: North-Holland.

Postmes, T. and Spears, R. (1998) 'Breaching or building social boundaries? Side-effects of computer-mediated communication'. Paper presented to International Communication Association, Annual Conference, Jerusalem, 20–24 July.

Preece, J. and Keller, L. (eds) (1990) *Human–Computer Interaction.* Hemel Hempstead: Prentice-Hall.

Rada, J. (1980) 'Micro-electronics, information technology and its effects on developing countries', in J. Berting, S. Mills and H. Winterberger (eds), *The Socio-Economic Impact of Micro-electronics.* Oxford: Oxford University Press.

Rafaeli, S. (1988) 'Interactivity: from new media to communication', in R.P. Hawkins, J. Wieman and S. Pingree (eds), *Advancing Communication Science: Merging Mass and Interpersonal Processes.* Newbury Park, CA: Sage.

Rash, Wayne (1997) *Politics on the Nets: Wiring the Political Process.* New York: Freeman.

Reagan, E.J. (1989) 'The strategic importance of telecommunications to banking', in M. Jussawalla, T. Okuma and T. Araki (eds), *Information Technology and Global Interdependence.* New York: Greenwood.

Reeves, B. and Nass, C. (1996) *The Media Equation.* Cambridge, MA: Cambridge University Press.

Reichman, R. (1986) 'Communication paradigms for a window system', in D.A. Norman, and S. Draper (eds), *User-Centered System Design: New Perspectives on Human–Computer Interaction.* Hillsdale, NJ: Erlbaum.

Rheingold, Howard (1993a) 'A slice of life in my virtual community', in L.M. Harasim (ed.), *Global Networks: Computers and International Communication.* Cambridge, MA: MIT Press, pp. 57–82.

Rheingold, Howard (1993b) *The Virtual Community: Homesteading on the Electronic Frontier.* Reading, MA: Addison-Wesley.

Rice, R.E. (1998) 'Computer-mediated communication and media preference', *Behaviour and Information Technology,* 17 (3): 164–74.

Rice, R.E. and Love, G. (1987) 'Electronic emotion: socio-emotional content in a computer-mediated communication network', *Communication Research,* 14: 85–108.

Rice, R.E. and Williams, F. (1984) 'Theories old and new: the study of the new media', in R.E. Rice and Associates (eds), *The New Media: Communication, Research and Technology.* Beverly Hills, CA: Sage.

Rifkin, J. (1987) *Time Wars.* New York: Holt.

Roberts, J.M. and Gregor, T. (1971) 'Privacy: a cultural view', in J.R. Pennock and J. Chapman (eds), *Privacy*. New York:

Rogers, E. and Picot, A. (1985) 'The impact of new communication technologies', in E. Rogers and F. Balle (eds), *The Media Revolution in America and Western Europe*. Norwood, NJ: Ablex.

Rojo, A. and Ragsdale, R. (1997) 'Participation in electronic forums', *Telematics and Informatics*, 13 (1): 83–96.

Roszak, T. (1986) *The Cult of Information: the Folklore of Computers and the True Art of Thinking*. New York: Pantheon.

Rothfelder, J. (1992) *Privacy for Sale*. New York: Simon and Schuster.

Rutter, D.R. (1984) *Looking and Seeing: the Role of Visual Communication in Social Interaction*. Chichester: Wiley.

Sabbah, F. (1985) 'The new media', in M. Castells (ed.), *High Technology, Space and Society*. Beverly Hills, CA: Sage.

Salomon, G. (1979) *Interaction of Media, Cognition and Learning*. San Francisco: Jossey-Bass.

Samuelson, Pamela (1996) 'Intellectual property, at your expense', *Wired*, January: 135–8, 188–91.

Samuelson, Pamela (1997) 'Maximum copyright, minimum use', *Wired*, March: 45.

Saunders, C.S., Robey, D. and Vaverek, K. (1994) 'The persistence of status differences in computer conferencing', *Human Communication Research*, 20 (4): 443–72.

Saunders, R.J. and Warford, G. (1983) *Telecommunications and Economic Development*. Baltimore, MD: World Bank and Johns Hopkins University Press.

Sayer, A. (1986) 'New developments in manufacturing: the just-in-time system', *Capital and Class*, 30: 43–72.

Schenk, David (1997) *Data Smog: Surviving the Information Glut*. New York: HarperEdge.

Schmale, G. (1998) 'Telefonische Kommunikation-technisch übertregene oder technisierte kommunikation?', in R. Weingarten and R; Fiehler (eds), (Technisierte Kommunikation). Opladen: Westdentscher Verlag.

Schoonmaker, S. (1993) 'Trading on-line: information flows in advanced capitalism', *Information Society*, 9 (1): 39–49.

Scott, C. and Easton, A. (1996) 'Examining equality of influence in group decision support system interaction', *Small Group Research*, 37 (3): 360–82.

Selnow, G.W. (1994) *High-Tech Campaigns: Computer Technology in Political Communication*. Westport, CT: Praeger.

Sennett, R. (1974) *The Fall of Public Man: on the Social Psychology of Capitalism*. New York: Vintage.

Shils, E. (1975) *Center and Periphery: Essays in Macro-sociology*. Chicago: University of Chicago Press.

Short, J., Williams, E. and Christie, B. (1976) *The Social Psychology of Telecommunications*. New York: Wiley.

Silverstone, R. (1991) 'From audiences to consumers: the household and the consumption of communication and information technologies', *European Journal of Communication*, 6 (2): 135–54.

Silverstone, R. (1994) *Television and Everyday Life*. London: Routledge.

Silverstone, R. and Hadden, J. (1996) 'Design and domestication', in R. Mansell and R. Silverstone (eds), *Communication by Design*. Oxford: Oxford University Press.

Smith, N., Bizot, E. and Hill, T. (1988) *Use of Electronic Mail in the Research and Development Organization*. Tulsa, OK: University of Tulsa Press.

Snellen, I. and van de Donk, W. (1987) 'Some dialectical developments of information in public administration'. Contribution to the Conference on New Technologies in Public Administration, Zagreb, 13–15 November.

Spears, R. (1994) 'Panacea or panopticon? The hidden power of computer-mediated communication', *Communication Research*, 21 (4): 427–59.

Spears, R. and Lea, M. (1992) 'Social influence and the influence of the "Social" in computer-mediated communication', in M. Lea (ed.), *Contexts of Computer-Mediated Communication*. Hemel Hempstead: Harvester Wheatsheaf.

Sproull, L. and Kiesler, S. (1986) 'Reducing social context cues: electronic mail in organizational communication', *Management Science*, 32: 1492–512.

Sproull, L. and Kiesler, S. (1991) *Connections: New Ways of Working in the Networked Organization*. Cambridge, MA: MIT Press.

Steinberg, S. (1996) 'Netheads vs bellheads', *Wired*, 4 (10).

Steinfield, C. and Fulk, J. (1986) 'Task demands and managers' use of communication media: an information processing view'. Paper presented at the Academy of Management. Chicago.

Stone, A.R. (1991) 'Will the real body please stand up?', in M. Benedict (ed.), *Cyberspace: First Steps*. Cambridge: Cambridge University Press.

Strickland, L.H., Guild, P., Barefoot, J. and Patterson, S. (1975) *Teleconferencing and Leadership Emergence*. Carleton: Carleton University.

Suchman, L.A. (1987) *Plans and Situated Actions: the Problem of Human–Machine Communication*. Cambridge, NY: Simon and Schuster.

Sussman, G. (1997) *Communications Technology and Politics in the Information Age*. Thousand Oaks, CA: Sage.

Thomas, David (1996) 'Feedback and cybernetics: reimaging the body in the age of the cyborg', in M. Featherstone and R. Burrows (eds), *Cyberspace/Cyberbodies/ Cyberpunk: Cultures of Technological Embodiment*. London: Sage.

Tracey, Michael (1998) *The Decline and Fall of Public Broadcasting*. Oxford: Oxford University Press.

Turkle, Sherry (1984) *The Second Self: Computers and the Human Spirit*. London: Granada.

Turkle, Sherry (1995) *Life on the Screen: Identity in the Age of the Internet*. New York: Simon and Schuster.

Turkle, Sherry (1996a) 'Who am we?', *Wired*, January: 149–52, 194–9.

Turkle, Sherry (1996b) 'Parallel lives: working on identity in virtual space', in Debra Grodin and T. Lindlof (eds), *Constructing the Self in a Mediated World*. Thousand Oaks, CA: Sage.

Turoff, M. (1989) 'The anatomy of a computer application innovation: computer-mediated communications', *Technological Forecasting and Social Change*, 36: 107–22.

Turow, Joseph (1997) *Breaking up America: Advertisers and the New Media World*. Chicago: University of Chicago Press.

Ungerer, H. with Costello, N. (1988) *Telecommunications in Europe: Free Choice for the User in Europe's 1992 Market*. Brussels: Commission of the European Communities.

United Nations (1998) *Human Development Report 1998*. UN Development Programme. New York: Oxford University Press.

US Department of State (1997) *Countries' Reports on Human Rights Practices for 1997*.

Vallee, J. (1978) *Group Communication through Computers. Vol. 4: Social, Managerial and Economic Issues*. London: Institute for the Future, Report r-40.

Vallee, J. (1984) *The Network Revolution*. Harmondsworth: Penguin.

Vallee, J., Johansen, R. and Lipinski, H. (1975) Group communication through computers, Vol 111. Pragmatics and Dynamics. Institute for the Future, Report R-35.

Van Cuilenburg J. and Noomen, G. (1984) *Communicatiewetenschap*. Muiderberg: Coutinho.

van Dijk, Jan A.G.M. (1991, 1994, 1997) *De Netwerkmaatschappij: Sociale aspecten van nieuwe media*, 1st, 2nd, 3rd edns. Houten: Bohn Stafleu van Loghum.

van Dijk, Jan A.G.M. (1993a) 'Communication networks and modernization', *Communication Research*, 20 (3): 384–407.

van Dijk, Jan A.G.M. (1993b) 'The mental challenge of the new media', *Medienpsychologie*, 1: 20–45.

van Dijk, Jan A.G.M. (1996) 'Models of democracy behind the design and use of new media in politics', *The Public/Javnost*, III (1): 43–56.

van Dijk, Jan A.G.M. (1997a) 'The reality of virtual communities', *Trends in Communication*, 1: 39–63.

van Dijk, Jan A.G.M. (1997b) *Universal Service from the Perspective of Consumers and Citizens*. Report to the Information Society Forum. Brussels: European Commission/ISPO.

van Dijk, Jan A.G.M. (1998) *The European Model of the Information Society*. Report to the Information Society Forum, Brussel: European Commission/ISPO.

van Dijk, Jan A.G.M. (1999) 'The one-dimensional network society of Manuel Castells', *New Media and Society*, 1 (1): 127–38.

van Dijk, Jan A.G.M. (forthcoming) 'Models of democracy and concepts of communication', in K. Hacker and J. van Dijk (eds), *Digital Democracy: Issues of Theory and Practice*. London, New Delhi, Thousand Oaks, CA: Sage.

Van Rossum, H., Gardeniers, H. and Borking, J. (1995a) *Privacy-Enhancing Technologies: The Path to Anonymity*, Vol I. TNO Physics and Electronics Laboratory. Rijswijk: Registratiekamer.

Van Rossum, H., Gardeniers, H. and Borking, J. (1995b) *Privacy-Enhancing Technologies: The Path to Anonymity*, Vol II. TNO Physics and Electronics Laboratory. Rijswijk: Registratiekamer.

Van Tulder, R. and Junne, R. (1988) *European Multinationals in Core Technologies*. Chichester: Wiley.

Van Zoonen, L. (1989) 'Vrouwen en Interactieve Media', in H. Bouwman and N. Jankowski (eds), *Interactieve Media op Komst*. Amsterdam: Cramwinckel.

Van Zoonen, L. (1994) *Feminist Media Studies*. London: Sage.

Vartanova, P. (1998) 'New communication technologies and information flows in Russia'. Paper presented at Beyond Convergence: ITS-98 Conference, Stockholm, Sweden, 14–21 June. www.ITS98.org/conference.

Virilio, P. (1988) *La Machine de Vision*. Paris: Galilée/Trans: The Vision Machine. Bloomington: Indiana University Press, 1994.

Volpert, W. (1985, 1988) *Zauberlehrlinge, Die gefärliche Liebe zum Computer*. Weinheim/Basle (1985), Munich (1988): Deutshe Taschenbuch.

Walden, Ian (1997) 'Data protection issues across the Internet', *Electronic Intellectual Property Right (EIPR)*, 13: 50–5.

Walther, J. (1992) 'Interpersonal Effects in computer-mediated communication', *Communication Research*, 19 (1): 52–90.

Walther, J. (1995) 'Relational aspects of computer-mediated communication: experimental observations over time', *Organization Science*, 6: 186–203.

Walther, J. (1996) 'Computer-mediated communication: impersonal, interpersonal and hyperpersonal interaction', *Communication Research*, 23 (1): 1–43.

Wang, G. (1998) 'Regulating network communication in Asia: a different balancing act?'. Paper presented at Beyond Convergence: ITS-98 Conference, Stockholm, Sweden, 14–21 June. www.ITS98.org/conference.

Webber, M. (1963) 'Order in diversity: community without propinquity', in L. Wingo (ed.), *Cities and Space*. Baltimore, MD: Johns Hopkins University Press.

Weber, Max (1922) *Gesammelte Politische Schriften*. Tübingen: Mohr.

Webster, F. and Robbins, K. (1996) *Information Technology: a Luddite Analysis*. Norwood, NJ: Ablex.

Weingarten, R. and Fiehler, R. (eds) (1988) *Technisierte Kommunikation*. Opladen: Westdeutscher Verlag.

Wellmann, B. and Leighton, B. (1979) 'Networks, neighbours and communities. Approaches to the study of the community question', *Urban Affairs Quarterly*, March.

Westin, A.F. (1987) *Privacy and Freedom*. London: Bodley Head.

Weston, J.R., Kristen, C. and O'Connor, S. (1975) *Teleconferencing*. Ottawa: Social Policy and Programmes Branch, Department of Communications.

Whisler, T.L. (1970) *The Impact of Computers on Organizations*. New York.

Williams, F. (1982) *The Communications Revolution*. Beverly Hills, CA: Sage

Winston, Brian (1998) *Media Technology and Society: a History from the Telegraph to the Internet*. London: Routledge.

Wood, S. (1987) 'Deskilling, new technology and work organization', *Acta Sociologica*, 30 (1): 3–24.

Wood, W.C. and O'Hare, S. (1991) 'Paying for the video revolution: consumer spending on the mass media', *Journal of Communication*, 41 (1): 24–30.

Working Party on the Protection of Individuals with Regard to the Processing of Personal Data (1997) *Anonymity on the Internet*. European Commission, Directorate General XV, D/5022/97 final recommedation 3/97. Brussels: European Commission.

Wright, E.O. (1985) *Classes*. London: Verso.

Yang, Chung-chuan (1997) 'The impact of the Internet and the global information highway on telecommunications policy' (in Chinese), *Journalism Research*, 55: 16–39.

Zuboff, S. (1988) *In the Age of the Smart Machine: the Future of Work and Power*. New York: Basic Books.

Zuurmond, A. (1994) *De infocratie*. Contains a summary in English. The Hague: Phaedrus.

Zuurmond, A. (1996) 'Informatisering: technocratisering of democratisering?', *Beleid en Maatschappij*, 3: 134–44.

Zuurmond, A. (1998) 'From bureaucracy to infocracy: are democratic institutions lagging behind?', in I. Snellen and W. Van de Donk (eds), *Public Administration in the Information Age: a Handbook*. Amsterdam: IOS Press.

INDEX